About the editors

Mayke Kaag is a social anthropologist and a senior researcher at the African Studies Centre in Leiden, the Netherlands. Her research focuses mainly on African transnational relations, including land issues, engagements with the diaspora, and transnational Islamic NGOs, on which topics she has published widely. Within the African Studies Centre she is the convenor of a collaborative research group on 'Africa in the World – Rethinking Africa's Global Connections'.

Annelies Zoomers is professor of international development studies (IDS) at Utrecht University and chair of LANDac. After finishing her PhD in 1988, she worked for the Netherlands Economic Institute (Rotterdam) and the Royal Tropical Institute (Amsterdam) on long- and short-term consulting assignments for various organizations (e.g. the World Bank, IFAD, ILO, EU, DGIS) in various countries in Latin America, Africa and Asia. Between 1995 and 2007 she was associate professor at the Centre for Latin American Research and Documentation (Amsterdam) and was professor of international migration at the Radboud University (Nijmegen) between 2005 and 2009. She has published extensively on sustainable livelihoods; land policies and the impact of privatization; tourism; and international migration.

The editors would like to thank the African Studies Centre and the IS Academy of Land Governance for their assistance and support.

African
Studies
Centre

The global land grab: beyond the hype

edited by Mayke Kaag and Annelies Zoomers

Fernwood Publishing
HALIFAX | WINNIPEG

Zed Books
LONDON | NEW YORK

The Global Land Grab: Beyond the Hype was first published in 2014.

Published in Canada by Fernwood Publishing, 32 Oceanvista Lane, Black Point, Nova Scotia, BOJ 1B0 and 748 Broadway Avenue, Winnipeg, Manitoba, R3G 0X3

www.fernwoodpublishing.ca

Published in the rest of the world by Zed Books Ltd, 7 Cynthia Street, London N1 9JF, UK and Room 400, 175 Fifth Avenue, New York, NY 10010, USA

www.zedbooks.co.uk

Editorial copyright Mayke Kaag and Annelies Zoomers 2014
Copyright in this Collection © Zed Books, 2014

Fernwood Publishing Company Limited gratefully acknowledges the financial support of the Government of Canada through the Canada Book Fund and the Canada Council for the Arts, the Nova Scotia Department of Communities, Culture and Heritage, the Manitoba Department of Culture, Heritage and Tourism under the Manitoba Book Publishers Marketing Assistance Program and the Province of Manitoba, through the Book Publishing Tax Credit, for our publishing program.

Set in OurType Arnhem, Monotype Gill Sans Heavy by Ewan Smith, London
Index: ed.emery@thefreeuniversity.net
Cover design: www.roguefour.co.uk
Printed and bound by TJ International Ltd, Padstow, Cornwall.

Distributed in the USA exclusively by Palgrave Macmillan, a division of St Martin's Press, LLC, 175 Fifth Avenue, New York, NY 10010, USA

A catalogue record for this book is available from the British Library
Library of Congress Cataloging in Publication Data available

Library and Archives Canada Cataloguing in Publication
   The global land grab : beyond the hype / edited by Mayke Kaag and Annelies Zoomers.
Includes bibliographical references.
ISBN 978-1-55266-666-1 (pbk.)
   1. Land use--Developing countries--Case studies. 2. Eminent domain--Developing countries--Case studies. 3. Developing countries--Social conditions--Case studies. I. Kaag, Mayke, 1964-, editor of compilation II. Zoomers, E. B., editor of compilation
HD1131.G56 2014   333.73'13091724   C2013-908688-9

ISBN 978 1 78032 895 9 hb (Zed Books)
ISBN 978 1 78032 894 2 pb (Zed Books)
ISBN 978 1 55266 666 1 pb (Fernwood Publishing)

Contents

Figures, tables and boxes

Boxes

Introduction: the global land grab hype – and why it is important to move beyond

Mayke Kaag and Annelies Zoomers

Introduction: a twofold hype

The last few years have seen a huge number of publications, conferences and campaigns on 'land grabbing', referring to the large-scale acquisition of land most often in the global South. The term 'land grabbing' appears to be very mediagenic and is attracting journalists, civil society organizations and action NGOs, as well as concerned academics who have been working in local communities in the South for years and are now being confronted with this phenomenon against which locals seem defenceless. Multilateral organizations like the World Bank and the Food and Agriculture Organization (FAO) have also felt the need to express themselves on the issue. The attention is such that, without exaggeration, we can speak of a real 'hype'.

However much we welcome the attention to these current large-scale land acquisitions in the South, we feel that the hype is distracting and prevents a proper discussion and in-depth debate on the issues at stake. We propose therefore taking a step back in this volume and asking some basic questions: Does the 'global land grab' exist? If so, how has it materialized in different countries and what is actually new about it? And what, beyond the immediate visible dynamics and practices, is/are the real problem(s) and the root causes? We will explore these issues by way of selected country studies from Africa, Asia and Latin America. Such a comparative perspective will enable us to discover global variety and similarities and to indicate directions for further research on current land grab issues, thus helping to improve the quality of the public/academic debate and to develop practical solutions, beyond the hype.

Our contribution to the growing corpus of literature on 'land grabbing' aims to couple scholarly engagement with the phenomenon of large-scale land acquisitions in the global South and a critical view of the coverage of this phenomenon in the media, policy and academic circles. What we actually observe is a twofold 'hype': first of all, the rush towards land on a global scale since the early 2000s appears to be one hype, in view of the huge appetite of large investors for acquiring land and access to land. Secondly, the coverage in media, policy and academic circles appears to also be a hype. Since the publication of the much-cited report by GRAIN in 2008, an impressive number of policy reports, academic publications and special journal issues have appeared. Overall, the coverage of the phenomenon tends to fall into two categories: alarmist on the one hand (GRAIN 2008; Oakland Institute 2011; Oxfam International 2011), positive and hailing new opportunities for development (World Bank 2010) on the other hand. Increasingly, however, more nuanced and critical voices have appeared, with the *Journal of Peasant Studies* and the International Institute for Environment and Development (IIED) making important contributions to the debate. This more substantial analysis has yielded very valuable insights into the global drivers behind and global factors influencing the land rush, the categories of actors involved, and the historicity of the phenomenon (Cotula et al. 2009; Zoomers 2010; White et al. 2012). Some interesting, more locally oriented empirical work has also appeared, particularly focused on Africa (Hilhorst et al. 2011; Matondi et al. 2011). However, until now no systematic attempt has been made to analyse land grabbing at country level in a comparative/global perspective permitting an analysis of land grab practices in a broader array of historical and geographical processes, including the role of national policies and political realities. In addition, not much effort has been made to extend the focus beyond Africa. This study aims to fill this gap by both providing in-depth country studies from Africa, Asia and Latin America and developing a comparative perspective on land grab practices and dynamics and underlying processes, in order to gain more insight into differences and similarities on the ground and into possible translocal connections. The book's argument is that in order to understand current land grabbing practices and to design solutions, we definitely need to go beyond the hype and scrutinize forms, actors and rhetorics in a structured way. In addition, it is also important to take a closer look at the phenomenon of 'hype', as we think that by a better understanding of hype dynamics, we can find a clue to several aspects of the way in which the current wave of land grabbing is unfolding. Finally, we also aim to go 'beyond the hype' from a temporal perspective by asking what remains after the hype has gone – that is, when the most opportunistic investors (hype followers) have left. The cases of Indonesia and Tanzania in this volume provide some indication, showing that among other things there is a lack of clarity about rights on the abandoned land. The end of the hype will not automatically end the problem. We may assume that large-scale land acquisitions will continue, albeit at a slower pace. We can also assume that the media attention at some point in time will fade, but that there will still be need of a close scrutiny of the processes by which these land deals are made and what happens afterwards – that is, what they bring in terms of profit and problems, and for whom.

The current global land rush: what do we know?

Following the food crisis (2003–08), and stimulated by the growing demand for bio-energy, states and private investors began to purchase or lease millions of hectares of fertile land in Madagascar, Ethiopia, Mozambique, Senegal, Tanzania, Zambia, Ghana and a number of post-conflict countries such as Liberia, Sudan and DRC. Whereas the primary focus has been on Africa, land investments have also been made in large parts of Asia and Latin America.

How much land has been 'grabbed' globally over the last decade since the start of the 'rush' remains unclear, however, owing to the lack of reliable statistics, different definitions of large-scale land acquisitions among different sources, and the fact that land transfers are often invisible (Zoomers 2013) and/or concluded in secrecy. The World Bank (2010) counted 389 deals involving 47 million hectares in 2009. At the same time, other sources mentioned larger figures. The Global Land Project (Friis and Reenberg 2010) cites a minimum of approximately ten million hectares in each of Mozambique, DRC and Congo; and in twenty-seven African countries screened, it noted 177 deals covering between 51 and 63 million hectares. Oxfam Novib and the International Land Coalition have identified more than 1,200 land deals (real investments and intentions) since 2000, with a total coverage of 80 million hectares, mainly used for the production of food (37 per cent) or biofuels (35 per cent) (Oxfam International 2011).

According to the updated version of the Land Matrix (July 2013), providing an overview of land deals concluded since 2000, the total area amounts to more than 33 million hectares (775 deals). In addition, there is an area of 11,895 hectares (165 deals) where negotiations are currently taking place.[1]

Despite these different figures illustrating that in reality no one knows exactly how much land is involved or how many people are affected, it can be taken for granted that the area involved is huge, not only in Africa, but also in Asia and Latin America (Zoomers 2010). Several million hectares at least are covered by biofuels, sugar or soybeans in Brazil, Argentina, Paraguay and Bolivia, and by oil palm in Indonesia, with the area expanding rapidly.

There are, however, many reasons to refrain from such an area-oriented analysis focusing on 'messy hectares' (Edelman 2013: 485). Edelman argues that the 'fetishization of the hectare' as the most important defining characteristic of land grabbing '... is fraught with conceptual problems and leads researchers and activists to ignore other, arguably more significant, issues of scale, such as the capital applied to the land, the control of supply chains, and the labour relations grounded or brought into being on those hectares' (ibid.: 488).

We very much agree that such an area-focused analysis may lead analysts and policy-makers to downplay other issues and dynamics, and that 'more data' often means 'false information' and the creation of virtual realities (ibid.: 497).

A focus on the processes at stake may be more fruitful and makes clear, for instance, that the current land rush is contributing to land use change. Large-scale land acquisition has gone hand in hand with the rapid expansion of large-scale monocropping, often on the better agricultural land. Moreover, acquisition generally involves the more fertile soils in areas with sufficient rainfall or good irrigation potential, where there is better access to markets (Cotula et al. 2009). Losing this land for local food production has obviously disproportionate impacts on food security and livelihoods. It is increasingly recognized that, while some land may be underutilized, very little land is vacant or unused. Many of the affected areas are not empty, but occupied or used by various groups that utilize the land for various purposes such as grazing animals, gathering fuelwood and contributing to local livelihoods and food security.

In addition, large-scale land acquisition is also taking place at the expense of forest areas and is increasingly affecting ecologically fragile land. In Indonesia, for example, oil palm first went hand in hand with deforestation, but is nowadays taking place at the expense of peat lands. On the one hand, this is less productive; on the other, it increases ecological vulnerability (Susanti and Burgers 2011).

It should also be emphasized that current large-scale land acquisitions are not only related to the rush for agricultural land but may, for instance, also be induced by conservation objectives ('green grabbing': see Fairhead et al. 2012) and the rush for minerals and oil (Hall 2011).

According to the World Bank (2010), investors are deliberately targeting areas where government is weak. Much of the land involved is therefore located in post-conflict areas, where some of the populations are displaced and where ownership and/or governance relations are often rather unclear (Mabikke 2011).

While in the beginning of the land grab debate the attention was very much on Asian powers like China and the Gulf States as the main culprits in land grabbing, over time the picture has become more nuanced and more diverse. In addition to governments of countries such as China, South Korea and Qatar, there is a wide variety of other countries and investors.[2] Many firms from the USA and the EU, as well as from Argentina, Brazil, South Africa and Mauritius, are currently looking for arable land for food and/or biofuel/energy production beyond their borders. Field research makes increasingly clear, however, that not only foreign but also domestic investors are playing an important role (Hilhorst et al. 2011; Cotula 2013). These may act independently or in joint ventures with international companies. Whether local, transnational or local–international, land grabbers normally profit from close ties with the national and/or local governments of the target countries.

Because of the various constellations described in the foregoing, large-scale land acquisition is not necessarily always about enormous tracts of land or mega-projects in the hands of foreign actors but may also take the form of a conglomerate of smaller acquisitions involving various actors. What is clear from the available literature, however, is that most often local groups are not

4

or are poorly informed about land deals and do not participate in decision-making. In addition, they often do not receive compensation, or not to the degree promised beforehand.

Much of the analysis so far has focused on the global level, attempting to come to grips with the global processes behind the land grab perceived as a global phenomenon. Authors such as Fairhead et al. (2012) and Zoomers (2013) have clearly positioned the current wave of large-scale land acquisitions in the neoliberalist environment globally built up during the 1980s and 1990s.

The foregoing indicates that there exists a reasonable amount of knowledge about the contours of the so-called global land grab. What we feel is still largely lacking, nevertheless, is a more thorough investigation of its dynamics over time, as well as its manifestations on the ground in the various country contexts and localities where land grabbing takes place. We think it is important to further unpack the global land grab, both as a hype and as a reality, in order to better understand its problems and to better design solutions.

Understanding the current global land rush as a hype cycle[3]

While the current wave of large-scale land acquisitions began in the early 2000s, the hype became visible with the GRAIN report in 2008, which set in motion a hype among policy analysts, activists and researchers who began to cover, research and contest the 'land grab' in many ways. It appears that this coverage has not only stimulated further attention in the media but has also itself spurred large-scale land acquisitions, as companies drew the conclusion that something was 'going on' and became concerned that they would 'miss the boat'. This raises the question: how does a hype 'work'? What does a hype do? How does it evolve?

It is quite remarkable that in the social sciences in general, and development studies in particular, only scant attention has been paid to the phenomenon of 'hype'. Most of the theorizing has been conducted on 'media hypes' in the field of communication and media studies and on 'consumer/product hypes' in business studies.

Popular understandings of the term mainly underscore that there is a sudden and large amount of attention paid to a phenomenon in the media, but that in the end it appears to be 'just a hype' – reflecting that there is disappointment because what the media told us was so was 'not real' or not the whole truth. Expectations were raised but not met. In media studies, the ways in which a hype is created and the role of the media in this are central. In business studies, Gartner's theory of a hype cycle has made large inroads. According to Gartner (Fenn and Raskino 2008), hypes evolve in phases which are marked by overenthusiasm, dashed expectations and in the end a balance of opinion/realistic judgement, meaning that an innovation has become accepted and making progress and productive investments has become possible.

It is clear that in the field of development also, hypes can be discerned, in the sense of buzzwords and concepts that become very popular in development circles in a short time, sometimes even spreading like wildfire. Some of these hypes contribute to 'development fashions' (e.g. micro credit, remittances or 'good governance'). Nooteboom and Rutten (2012) call these 'magic bullets', concepts that promise to be the one-for-all solution to development problems. They create considerable enthusiasm and expectations (and can raise a large amount of money), but when it appears that such a solution is not an easy fix, it is soon abandoned for another magic bullet, another promising solution. We know that development problems are complex and multidimensional. Complexity does not sell, however, while promises of solutions do. Interestingly, in addition to hyped solutions, we can also distinguish hyped problems – including migrants, Islam or desertification.

In view of the foregoing, it is particularly interesting to look at land grabbing as a hype, as it unites these different dimensions. On the one hand, large-scale land acquisitions have been heralded as a magic bullet for solving the energy and food crisis: a hyped solution. On the other hand, and given wider currency in the media, land grabbing has been presented as *the* problem of the current neoliberal, globalized, multipolar world (where we had, for instance, desertification and the greenhouse effect before). This raises the question of why certain phenomena taken up in the media make it into a hype while others do not. It seems that land grabbing and how it appeared in the media has been quite attractive, as it tells a simple story with culprits (Asian 'powers' such as China and the Gulf states) and victims (poor Africans), which certainly in the beginning helped the creation of the land grab hype.

One of the questions in the literature on hype concerns whether hypes are wilfully and purposely created through communication strategies, or whether they can also just evolve in a synergy of different processes, as an unintended outcome. This is also an interesting question in our case: has the global land grab been hyped on purpose? Or was it just a natural process evolving coincidentally as certain processes were conflated to create this hype? While the latter appears to be the case initially, it can also be observed that certain parties helped to create, sustain or further the hype – for instance, governments of African countries publicizing the land opportunities in their countries, and international NGOs seeing the land grab issue as a means to strengthen their position and to justify their existence in a context in which support for development organizations in the West is decreasing (Mawdsley 2012). It seems that in 2008 it was the soaring prices of agricultural commodities (Cotula et al. 2009), cheap money looking for stable investments (World Bank 2010), the global crisis, stagnation in global agriculture and a lack of investments (Kugelman and Levenstein 2009), and the groundbreaking report of GRAIN (2008) picked up by the right media (Guardian 2008), NGOs and activists looking for new advocacy and activist agendas – which brought parties to cooperate over, debate and engage in the issue. Its mobilizing power was huge, and it connected previously unrelated investors, financial institutions, critical NGOs, farmer groups, consumers and concerned scholars in one large project of collaboration (Tsing 2005). According to Tsing, collaboration is not a simple sharing of information, nor should it be assumed that collaborators share common goals. They may, however, each from their own perspective and following their own interest, together create something new, which is very much shaped by the frictions between the different views, interests, backgrounds and objectives of the participants (ibid.). This is also how the land grab hype came about.

Why is it important to discern something as a hype? Fenn and Raskino (2008: 21) warn us that 'adopting innovation without understanding the hype cycle can lead to inappropriate adoption decisions and a waste of time, money and opportunity'. In order words, and applied to our case, just following the 'land rush hype' without recognizing the hype character of the phenomenon may lead to inappropriate adoption decisions and failed investments. What the case studies show us is that there has indeed been a hype in terms of a big rush for land, but also that there has been disappointment as the large profits were not as easy to make as had been forecast, for various reasons: local legal, institutional and political complexities, changes in the global market, etc. Consequently, disappointment as a result of overly high expectations that had been raised through the hype has certainly influenced the course of large-scale land acquisitions in several localities. What the case studies clearly show is that many of the announced land deals have never materialized, or have never been consummated (the land has not been taken into production by the investor), or production was stopped after a short period of time. On the other hand, there may also be disappointment among those who see land grabbing as a major problem, as in many instances reliable data on the magnitude and the scale of the phenomenon are difficult to obtain. And – now that the phenomenon may be not that huge in quantitative terms, as had been 'promised' by the 'hypers' – will this therefore lead to the removal of the subject from activist and academic agendas? We would very much deplore that outcome.

What the foregoing indicates is that in analysing the current global land grab as a hype, we need to look at the construction of the hype, including *what* land grab narrative has been hyped and why; the interests, gains and disappointments of the different actors involved; the collaboration of otherwise unconnected actors in the land grab project and the conflation of various (hitherto unconnected) processes; the mobilizing power of the hype in terms of money, power and resources; the different phases of the hype, their

7

expressions and consequences. What subaltern voices/ideas have been silenced in the process; what nuances have been washed out? We will come back to these issues in the conclusion to this volume, harvesting from the richness of the case studies in the following chapters – because, as stated earlier in this Introduction, while it is important to understand the global land grab as a hype, it is equally important to go beyond it in order to be able to answer the questions raised in the foregoing: What elements of the global land rush have become silenced in the hype? What nuances have been omitted? What is really going on on the ground in the various country contexts? If we follow the positive scenario mentioned earlier, that after the hype positive changes and workable, realistic solutions will become feasible, we need realistic data and analyses upon which to base these solutions.

Manifestations on the ground: the case studies presented in this book

The case studies in this book have been organized geographically (i.e. by continent), but they could have been clustered otherwise as there are various similarities (and differences) that cross-cut this geographical order. We will come back to these similarities and differences in the Conclusion. Here, we want to just briefly introduce the different case studies to provide the reader with a guide to their richness and how they show some of the processes and some of the elements of the phenomenon of the 'global land grab'. We have opted for studies at country level in order to enable a thorough analysis of the role of national legal and policy contexts, including how these are influenced by political and economic dynamics, in shaping land grabbing. This choice may have as a corollary that processes taking place at a more local level, such as the effects of large-scale land acquisitions on the opportunities of women (Behrman et al. 2011; Chu 2011) and on local power relations (Kaag et al. 2011), remain relatively out of sight. It should be underlined, however, that these processes are also very important and should be taken up in further studies.

Beginning with Africa, case studies on Ethiopia, Tanzania and Kenya show that current land grabbing has deep historical roots, from the colonial era through to the structural adjustment policies in the 1980s that paved the way for private investments from abroad from the 1990s onwards. Legal and institutional weaknesses have been exploited by the powerful to the detriment of the less powerful, be they local communities or marginalized ethnic groups.

George Schoneveld and Maru Shete focus on Ethiopia, a country endowed with vast reserves of fertile agricultural land and water resources that has become one of the top five destinations for commercial agriculture investment in sub-Saharan Africa. In the period 2007–09, during the height of the food and energy price crises, more than 1.6 million hectares of land were allocated to large-scale commercial agricultural investments – equivalent to almost two-thirds of the land allocated for this purpose over the preceding two decades. The vast majority of these investments are located in just three of Ethiopia's nine regions, namely more peripheral lowland areas where agro-pastoralist livelihoods prevail. While the Ethiopian government formally contends that the introduction of modern farming in its marginalized periphery will contribute to upgrading agro-pastoral production systems, early evidence suggests that numerous conflicts have been triggered and are threatening to continue as a result of the highly centralized implementation of these agricultural modern-ization policies and the unwillingness of the Ethiopian state to accommodate contradictory interests. The evident lack of consideration by the government for local realities is not necessarily a product of poor monitoring and enforce-ment capacity, but rather of a focused government strategy to modernize 'backward' rural practices.

In their chapter, Jumanne Abdallah, Linda Engström, Kjell Havnevik and Lennart Salomonsson focus on biofuel investment in Tanzania. They argue that large-scale colonial agricultural projects and foreign settler farmers were less of a factor in Tanzania as compared with Kenya, Swaziland or Zambia. The Tanzanian post-independent government thus had a better opportunity than most other African governments to address land and rural matters. The *Ujamaa* policy centred on collective agriculture, however, did not yield the desired result. The chapter shows that, as in other countries, structural adjustment policies paved the way for neoliberal development and investment policies and, from the 1990s onwards, more active efforts by the government to attract investments from abroad. External investors who acquired large tracts of land for biofuel in Tanzania have predominantly been European actors, giving the lie to the widespread idea that non-Western actors particularly are involved in land grabbing practices in Africa. Based on fieldwork in three communities, the authors show that many requests for land are not met; that in cases where land has been obtained, investment projects are not implemented; and that if implemented, the projects often fail. Projects go bankrupt or investors turn to food crops after a brief period of time. There appears to be as much of a biofuel hype as a land grab hype. In general, the needs and rights of local populations are hardly taken into account in the whole investment process, and the authors make a plea for a better knowledge of local livelihoods and social practices in making arrangements with local communities.

Jacqueline Klopp and Odenda Lumumba in their engaging chapter on Kenya show that 'land grabbing' or the irregular and illegal allocation of public land in Kenya is a serious problem that has deep historical roots. Unaccountable land laws and management systems inherited from colonial times have allowed massive manipulation of land as a form of power. These historical institutional and power configurations have primarily benefited local elites, especially those embedded in patronage networks around the president. While most recent land grabbing in Kenya is domestic, the same institutional structure and network of actors who facilitate local land grabbing also mediate access to land by foreign investors, as in the well-known cases of Yala Swamp and the Tana River Delta. Hence, the authors argue that as far as Kenya is concerned, recent large-scale foreign acquisitions of land are really part of a continuous land grabbing practice since colonial times. The only aspects that are new are the increasing external pressures for access to agricultural land and new players such as Qatar. The chapter goes on to explore the magnitude of the impacts on inequality, food insecurity and social cohesion of this continuous land grabbing in Kenya, and argues that unless addressed there is a large risk of deepening social and political upheaval with devastating consequences for the entire East Africa region.

While the African case studies focus on the 'classic' form of land grabbing – that is, as it appears in the media, in the form of large-scale land acquisition for agricultural uses, often by non-nationals and to the detriment of smallholders – in Latin America instances of classic land grabbing may be fewer. However, there are processes of changing land control that share characteristics with the more classic forms of land grabbing in the sense of scaling-up of farm sizes, more powerful actors and uses supplanting smallholders and small-scale uses, and, often, a 'foreignization' of space (Zoomers 2010).

Lucia Goldfarb and Annelies Zoomers in their chapter focus on the expansion of soy cultivation in Argentina. This process began in the pampas in the 1970s and did not encounter many problems, even when in the 1990s the process speeded up, helped by neoliberal policies, as large tracts of under-utilized land were available and could easily be converted into new production units by a limited number of old and new large landowners and investors, who began to lease land. Things changed, however, with the expansion of GM soy cultivation into the Chaco region, where forests were cleared and local peasants and indigenous groups were bought out or were legally or illegally displaced; they lost their land and were excluded from the benefits of soy growing. The state has actively promoted further expansion but has largely remained inactive in countering the negative aspects related to it. It has thus not invested in rural development, or in better regulation of extractive activities (including soy monoculture), or in the protection of the rights of the local farmers.

Femke van Noorloos describes how, in Costa Rica, land is increasingly commercialized and transferred to non-local actors. Aided by North American retirees and younger Western migrants looking for a change of lifestyle, Costa Rica's Pacific coastal areas have become important spots for residential tourism. The chapter traces the dynamics of land acquisitions related to residential tourism in Guanacaste province. It argues that displacement and land concentration mainly took place during earlier land grabs in the nineteenth and early twentieth centuries. Residential tourism has fragmented landownership rather than contributed to concentration, and it causes a process of gentrification and foreignization, rather than a land grab as such. This foreignization is problematic, however, as is the speculative character of the land market. In the tourist industry, economic and environmental aspects are interwoven in complex ways.

The chapter on the Andes by Rutgerd Boelens, Antonio Gaybor and Jan Hendriks takes a somewhat different perspective by not focusing on land grabbing as such, but rather calling attention to water grabbing, a phenomenon that often accompanies land grabbing and has huge implications for large categories of users beyond the mere land grab site. It examines illustrative cases of water and water rights concentration processes in Peru and Ecuador. It also scrutinizes how the urgent international issue of land grabbing requires increasing precision and profound reflection: often, the national and transnational process of land and land rights accumulation in fact go hand in hand inseparably with water grabbing. The different uses of water for humans, food, industry and nature have an intrinsic territorial dimension. Greater consumption of water resources for particular uses involves a greater need for control over certain territories. Consequently, in most Latin American countries, growing demand and decreasing availability of water of sufficient quality lead to intensifying competition and conflict among different uses and users not only of those resources but also of land resources and territories. Globalization and a neoliberal policy climate tend to help certain powerful actors – local, national and often transnational – accumulate water resources and rights at the expense of the economically less powerful. New competitors, including mega-cities and mining, forestry and agribusiness companies, claim a large share of the surface and groundwater resources at the cost of individual smallholder families, rural communities and indigenous territories. Unequal, unfair water distribution and related pressures on land resources and territories, both legally condoned and through large-scale 'extralegal' appropriation practices, commonly have severe impacts in terms of poverty while posing profound threats to environmental sustainability and national food security.

Turning to Asia, chapters on Indonesia, Vietnam and Cambodia offer commentaries on the land grab narrative in other ways, by focusing on the role of smallholders in land grab practices and by highlighting land grabbing for urbanization and large infrastructural works (which evidently also take place in Africa and Latin America). The chapters show, however, that here also, as in the foregoing cases, legal and institutional arrangements (or the lack thereof) offer opportunities to the more powerful to push forward their interest to the detriment of others.

Ari Susanti and Suseno Budidarsono focus on oil palm expansion in Indonesia. In the growing global debate on transnational land deals for agriculture, investments in oil palm plantations play a significant role. A wide body of literature shows that these investments have caused widespread processes of land use change, often involving forest and agricultural land conversion. However, little research has been undertaken on understanding the underlying factors that are likely to enable these land use conversion processes. The chapter analyses some of the most crucial land governance issues related to oil palm expansion in Indonesia. The authors show that not only large-scale oil palm investments cause widespread land use change: increasingly, smallholders from all over Indonesia are involved in converting land into oil palm plantations. Besides the lucrative benefit from oil palm, the incompatible regulations related to land rights have become an important reason for this rapid expansion. This is aggravated by the absence of sound regional planning (such as in Riau province, where palm oil production has become an important economic activity), which allows the conversion of land into oil palm plantations relatively easily.

In Vietnam, the ongoing modernization and industrialization policy has accelerated the conversion of agricultural land into other uses. Although the policy has contributed significantly to Vietnam's graduation from poor to middle-income country status, it has also been criticized by many people and in the mass media, owing to the negative impacts on the livelihoods of affected farmers. Ty Pham Huu, Nguyen Quang Phuc and Guus van Westen analyse land conversion for urban and hydropower development and discuss to what extent these conversion processes for different purposes have different outcomes for the country as a whole, as well as for various stakeholder groups. They argue that, in the transformation from an essentially rural economy to an urban, industrial and service-oriented society, unless there is a firm political commitment to protect the weak, land conversion exerts intense pressures on the livelihoods of farmers and others who have no stake in the rising industries, and they conclude that it is not the changes which are necessarily harmful, but the way they play out.

In their chapter on Cambodia, Michelle McLinden Nuijen, Men Prachvuthy and Guus van Westen argue that the country is a prime target for transnational and large-scale land acquisitions in Asia, owing to the weakness of institutions in this post-conflict setting, combined with relatively abundant land resources and low population densities. According to some estimates, over a fifth of the national territory – most of the land that is not in permanent use – has now been signed away in concessions for a range of purposes, often with little regard for current users. The authors analyse the social and economic effects of economic land concessions awarded to large investors at the regional level of north-eastern Cambodia, with a specific focus on the position of minority groups, and they use the case study of a large-scale sugar project in Koh Kong province to detail the various translocal links that culminate in the land deal as well as the implications for the livelihood of local residents.

The chapter on Gulf countries' involvement in Indonesia and the Philippines, and the chapter on China, offer a somewhat different picture: in these chapters the 'land grabbers' appear in focus, showing the contextual dynamics of the relationships between investing countries from the Gulf and target countries, and the diversity of actors, interests and changes over time in overseas land investment by China.

Gerben Nooteboom and Laurens Bakker describe how, after the 2008 food crisis and the export restrictions imposed on some staple foods by food-exporting countries, there was a consensus that food security was most acute for Gulf states (GCCs). Not the price hikes, but export bans made GCCs – largely dependent on food imports – nervous, and GCCs were expected to become major investors in fertile land for food production. The national governments of Indonesia and the Philippines quickly offered a lifeline and angled for petro-dollar investments. Newspapers announced MOUs signed, local politicians proclaimed windfall profits, and scholars, NGOs and farmer groups began campaigning or protesting. Four years later, none of the deals announced has materialized. The GCC investment hype in South-East Asia turned out to be a temporary trend, with domestic and regional investors taking the lead in agribusiness development instead.

Extensive media, NGO and scholarly attention to China's global resource-extractive activities supposes a major role for China in current land grab practices. Peter Ho and Irna Hofman analyse what is actually taking place with regard to China's foreign agricultural land investments. They discern three phases in China's involvement in agriculture abroad and show that state-backed investments ('development outsourcing' by the Chinese state) occur simultaneously with the increasingly self-initiated investments of Chinese private companies, which unfold in a variety of forms on the ground. They also show that 'land grabbing' is a moving target, as China is not only concentrating on Africa, as is often suggested in the debates, but is, for instance, also progressively involved in large-scale land deals in Europe and Australia. These changes over time make it all the more important to look beyond the hype and its set narratives.

Africa

1 | Modernizing the periphery: citizenship and Ethiopia's new agricultural investment policies

George Schoneveld and Maru Shete

Introduction

As a country endowed with vast reserves of fertile agricultural land and water resources, Ethiopia has become one of the top five destinations for commercial agriculture investment in sub-Saharan Africa (Schoneveld 2011). In the period 2007–09, during the height of the food and energy price crises, more than 1.6 million hectares of land were allocated for large-scale commercial agricultural investments – equivalent to almost two-thirds of land allocated for this purpose over the preceding two decades. The vast majority of these investments are located in just three of Ethiopia's nine regions, namely Benshangul Gumuz, Gambella and Southern Nations, Nationalities and People's Region (SNNPR). These are all so-called 'lowlands', a low-altitude periphery that surrounds the highland plateau, which is the economic and political heartland of Ethiopia.

In contrast to the highlands, where more intensive, mixed forms of agricultural production prevail, lowland production systems typically involve agro-pastoralist livelihood systems, characterized by opportunistic flood-retreat agriculture and seasonal cattle migrations (Bishaw 2001; Tolera and Abebe 2007). Owing to the high spatial and temporal variability in rainfall distribution in the lowlands, these areas are particularly susceptible to drought and, therefore, food insecurity (Pantuliano and Wekesa 2008). Agricultural production is thus concentrated in the highlands, which, covering only 45 per cent of Ethiopia's land area, support more than 90 per cent of its population (Zeleke 2003).

This has created a distinctive geographical divide in Ethiopia: between an ethnically homogenous highland population comparatively well articulated to markets and the public administration, and a considerably more autonomous, albeit highly economically and politically marginalized, ethnically very diverse lowland population. Although the government made various attempts to promote highland-to-lowland migrations in the 1980s to reduce interregional disparities and alleviate pressure on highland resources, poor infrastructure and harsh natural conditions have long inhibited the effective incorporation of Ethiopia's periphery (World Bank 2004; Hammond 2008).

With the recent rush in demand for farmland, however, the Ethiopian government is ostensibly seeing new opportunities to capitalize on the 'under-utilized' land and water resources of these regions, while simultaneously addressing issues of productive and political integration and food insecurity. However, since existing systems of production and affiliated (ethnic) identities have largely been a product of non-interference and ecological adaptation, changes to the resource base and increasing subjection to central planning could potentially have profound implications for local livelihoods. As land in Ethiopia is owned exclusively by the state and much of the lowland population enjoys no formal claims to land, this minority population is particularly exposed to the threat of dispossession. Thus, whether these investments ultimately serve the interests of the local population depends on how well the government is able to incorporate these local realities into the project development process.

This chapter seeks to address some of these early issues associated with the introduction of large-scale commercial agriculture in the Ethiopian lowlands. It does this by tracing the process by which investments are established and the manner in which local interests are incorporated. In so doing, we shed light on some of the motives that underlie the government's renewed interest in its neglected periphery, and some of the obstacles to aligning local and national interests.

The following section will provide a brief summary of the geographical and temporal agricultural investment trends in Ethiopia. The chapter then proceeds to frame this topic by discussing the evolution of Ethiopia's agricultural development strategies and its underlying policy discourse. Following a brief overview of the study's methodological approach and the case studies, we discuss the project development process. The chapter concludes with a reflection on findings.

Background

Geographic and temporal investment trends Data on farmland investments in Ethiopia are not kept in a centralized manner. In order to gain insights into investment trends, we attempted to reconcile information from different government agencies responsible for maintaining records. The Federal Investment Authority and the Ministry of Agriculture and Rural Development (MoARD), along with different regional investment bureaus and environmental protection agencies, provided their data sets to the authors for this purpose.

On the basis of these data, it was observed that in the four main investment regions (SNNPR, Gambella, Benshangul Gumuz and Oromiya) nearly 1.69 million hectares of land were transferred to agricultural investors between 1992 and the end of 2010 (Table 1.1). With the exception of investment in Oromiya, most investment land is allocated in the lowlands. Although much of Afar and Somali are also lowlands, the government has not promoted these areas for investment owing to long-standing security issues (Agricultural Investment Support Directorate – AISD, personal communications 2012).

Multi-regional projects accounted for 560,020 hectares over this period, all being developed by foreign companies.[1] Investors from East and South Asian countries are the most prolific, accounting for 29.8 per cent of the area acquired by foreign investors; this is followed by the Middle East (26.1 per cent) and Europe (19.1 per cent). Strong diplomatic relations between Ethiopia and countries such as India, Saudi Arabia and Turkey have shown themselves to be important drivers of investment.

In certain regions, data on domestic investments were unavailable owing to poor maintenance of records (Table 1.1). The data show lower investment intensity in those regions, with only 225,260 hectares acquired for the purpose by foreign investors. Assuming that the ratio of domestic to foreign investments is similar in those regions, then the total area transferred in these regions would likely range from 312,861 to 500,578 hectares. This then would imply that between 1992 and 2010, between 2.55 and 2.71 million hectares of land across Ethiopia has been transferred to investors. This is equivalent to between 54.2 and 58.2 per cent of the total area suitable and available for agricultural production (derived from World Bank 2011).

Trends of licensed investment projects in four Ethiopian regions show a rapid rise in the number of agricultural investment projects in the period

TABLE 1.1 Area of farmland acquired by private investors by region, 1992–2010

Region	Total area (ha)	Land acquired by foreign investors (ha)	Proportion of FDI out of total (%)
Harari	n/a	0	n/a
Afar	n/a	1,000	n/a
Somali	n/a	3,000	n/a
Tigray	n/a	57,030	n/a
Amhara	n/a	164,230	n/a
SNNPR	288,383[1]	207,316	71.9
Benshangul Gumuz	539,811	243,350	45.1
Gambella	421,273	225,012	53.4
Oromiya	436,198	193,432	44.3
Multiregional	560,020	560,020	100
Total	2,245,685	1,654,390	63.6[2]

Notes: 1. This excludes 245,000 ha allocated in 2011 to the parastatal Sugar Corporation for sugar production; 2. Since data on domestic investors were unavailable for certain regions, this figure is incomplete and accounts only for regions where records are complete.

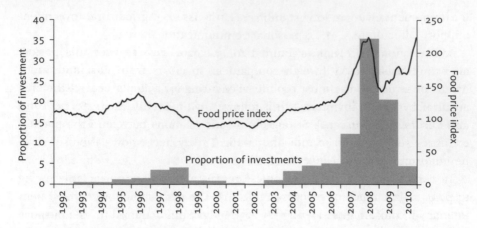

1.1 Food price index and proportion of investments, projects in Ethiopia, 1992–2010 (*source*: Authors' representation, based on MoARD and EIA data, unpublished)

2007–09, with a strong peak in 2008, when 69.1 per cent of all project licences for the period 1992–2010 were allocated. Arguably, high global food prices were a primary driver of land acquisitions over this period, as is evidenced by a statistically significant correlation between the FAO Food Price Index and investment intensity (Figure 1.1). Undoubtedly, the change in emphasis of Ethiopia's agricultural policies since 2005 also contributed significantly to rising investor interest, as detailed in the following section. The year 2010, however, appears to be an anomaly, when, despite high food prices, investment intensity was comparatively low. In all likelihood investments were deterred by unfavourable global financial conditions.

Strategies and policy discourse for large-scale commercial agriculture In the 2010 iteration of the five-year Growth and Transformation Plan (GTP), the Ethiopian government made the promotion of large-scale commercial agriculture one of its core strategic objectives (p. 8), thereby building on earlier commitments made under its predecessor, the 2005 Plan for Accelerated and Sustained Development to End Poverty (PASDEP). Although agricultural policies since the early 1990s have placed a strong emphasis on smallholder productivity and domestic linkages, owing to the limited successes of these strategies the government is increasingly focusing on more trade-oriented, large-scale commercial agriculture as the impetus for agricultural industrialization (Lavers 2012). This is premised on the assumption that such developments will contribute both to macroeconomic and rural development objectives. Macroeconomically, the government seeks to increase foreign exchange earnings, enhance food and energy security, generate fiscal revenues, and provide inputs for import substituting industries (FDRE 2007a, 2010a, 2010b). Locally, large commercial farms are assumed to contribute to poverty alleviation through technology transfers, off-farm employment, new market outlets for smallholders, opportunities for the uptake of high-value cash crops, and investments in social and physical infrastructure (FDRE 2010a; Kebede 2011; FDRE 2011a; Lavers 2012).

A survey conducted by Shete and Schoneveld (forthcoming) among forty-two district and regional government officials in Benshangul Gumuz, Gambella and Oromiya highlights similar sentiments among lower levels of government. Respondents exhibited particularly high expectations of the potential of commercial agriculture to contribute to technology transfers and local employment generation. The adoption of contract farming models is widely thought to contribute to the uptake of modern farming practice, which will elevate subsistence farmers into a commercial farming class, while the new employment opportunities are argued to bring about a shift from a subsistence to a cash economy.

To facilitate the government's policy shift, MoARD established a one-stop investment centre in 2010, the AISD. The AISD is responsible for all matters pertaining to agricultural investment, including land identification and allocation, investment promotion, monitoring and evaluation, management of spillovers, and the environmental and social impact assessment (ESIA) process. Formerly, these functions were handled by regional and district government, the Ethiopian Investment Agency (EIA) and the Environmental Protection Agency (EPA).

To streamline land allocations, the AISD Land Identification Group has established a land bank, which by late 2011 included 3.99 million hectares of land across five regions, equivalent to approximately 84 per cent of agro-ecologically suitable and potentially available land (FDRE 2011b; World Bank 2011). The government is particularly targeting areas with low densities and peripheral areas, popularly referred to by policy-makers as 'emergent' regions. This includes 1,317,268 hectares in Oromiya; 1,099,893 hectares in Gambella; 981,852 hectares in Benshangul Gumuz; 409,678 hectares in Afar; and 180,625 hectares in SNNPR (FDRE 2011b). The other four regions are still to be fully surveyed.

In addition to the promotion of private agriculture investment, the federal government has reinstated the government-owned Sugar Corporation, which is charged with increasing Ethiopia's sugar output sevenfold (Africa Report 2011). The largest Sugar Corporation project, at 245,000 hectares, is located in the South Omo Zone of SNNPR. The AISD has no direct involvement in these state-owned agricultural projects.

Methodology

Ten sites were selected for field research across three eco-regions: four in SNNPR, three in Gambella and three in Oromiya, and in such a way as

TABLE 1.2 Overview of the investment planning process

Phase	Description
1. Land identification and allocation	Mechanisms by which suitable and/or available land for particular types of uses is identified and allocated for investment. Concerned primarily with how competing land uses are accounted for (e.g. land of high conservation value, agricultural land and common pool resources) and prioritized.
2. Pre-implementation incorporation and accommodation of land users	Mechanisms through which land users are informed, consulted or given decision authority over land transfer and its terms. Such processes reduce the risk of project opposition and ensure project development is voluntary and in the interests of the local population.
3. Impact mitigation and community development	Once a project has commenced development, mechanisms to mitigate (potential) impacts and maximize (potential) benefits will ensure that a project optimally contributes to local socio-economic development. Monitoring of projects is especially important in this regard.
4. Dispute resolution	Mechanisms by which persons aggrieved are able to seek recourse are integral to ensuring that companies are held accountable for their activities. Adequate representation in cases of dispute is essential when those persons lack the (legal) capacity to claim their rights.

to adequately capture ecological and socio-economic variations. SNNPR and Gambella were of particular interest owing to their lowland location and the comparatively high density of agricultural investments. Although our focus was on assessing processes in the lowlands, we included the three highland sites in Oromiya in order to capture variations in the project development process between the lowlands and highlands.

In assessing the manner in which local social, economic and environmental considerations are incorporated into the investment planning process, four key sequential phases of the process were analysed, namely (1) land identification and allocation, (2) pre-implementation incorporation and accommodation of land users, (3) impact mitigation and community development, and (4) dispute resolution (see Table 1.2 for a description of each phase).

We engaged three main stakeholder groups (the government, the private sector and local land users) to identify how these groups interact during this process to address potential risks and opportunities. A total of forty-three semi-structured interviews were held with government representatives from different levels of government (federal, regional and district level). These interviews covered sectoral agencies responsible for investment promotion, land administration and environmental protection and various administrative institutions. Since a number of investors were unwilling to engage researchers on this topic, representatives were interviewed from only six out of the ten investments.

At each project, at least three focus group discussions were held with local land users: two with households from communities neighbouring the plantations and one with local plantation workers. The focus group discussions followed a predefined format for establishing the characteristics of local livelihood systems, the nature and magnitude of impacts, processes of collective action, and personal perceptions.

Overview of case studies

In Oromiya, recent investments have tended to focus on comparatively sparsely populated agro-pastoral areas of the Bale and Hararghe zones, former state-owned farms and flood plains (FDRE 2011b). One of the case studies, Serofta Modern Farming, is located in an area of the Arsi Zone that since the 1970s has been dominated by six large state-owned wheat farms (see Table 1.3 for an overview of case studies). Under a recent government initiative to privatize these farms, the government of Djibouti acquired two of the farms for the production of wheat for Djibouti consumption. The other two case studies, investments from Pakistan's Al-Habasha (HSM) and India's Karuturi, are both located within major river basins, which owing to their clay-rich soils and extensive waterlogging are generally not used by the local population for permanent cultivation. These areas are sparsely vegetated and swampy. As in much of Oromiya, a large proportion of the population in these three sites are sedentary subsistence farmers, many of whom possess land certificates for permanently cultivated land. In the mid-2000s, almost 95 per cent of rural households in Oromiya received land certificates that provide lifelong usufruct rights (though not the right to sell or mortgage land) (Crewett and Korf 2008).

The three case studies in Gambella are spread across five of Gambella's thirteen districts. Gambella's largest investment project, developed by Karuturi, stretches for approximately eighty kilometres along the southern banks of the Baro river, the district's largest waterway. The grassland areas towards the west of the Karuturi concession are dominated by various agro-pastoralist Nuer groups, while the forest lands towards the east of the concession are dominated by the comparatively sedentary ethnic group of the Anuak. The two other projects, the Ethiopian-owned Basen Agriculture and Saudi Star, owned

23

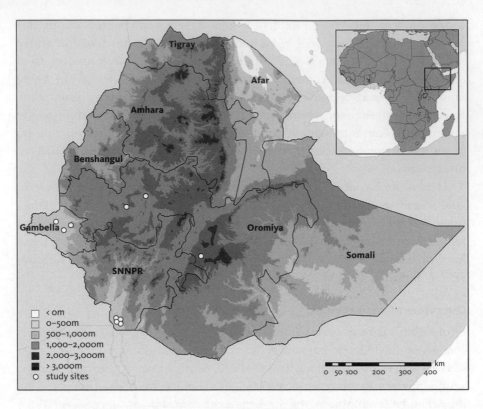

1.2 Topographical map of Ethiopia (*source*: Authors' representation)

by the Saudi Midroc Group, are located south-east of the Karuturi concession within Gambella's high tropical forest, in proximity to the Alwero Dam, which was constructed with Soviet support in the 1980s.

The case studies in SNNPR focused on the arid, sparsely vegetated lowland areas of the South Omo Zone. Of the 125,831 hectares of land allocated in the South Omo Zone to private agricultural investors, 82.9 per cent is located in the districts of Dassanech and Ngangatom, dominated by two agro-pastoralist ethnic groups that are its namesake. With the exception of the Italian renewable energy company Fri-el Green, all private investors in the study area were cultivating cotton. Expansion plans by the Sugar Corporation have also targeted South Omo, with road and canal development activities having to date focused on the Dassanech, Ngangatom and Selamago districts. The Omo river, which empties into Lake Turkana, is the primary source of water for most districts in South Omo. Agricultural investments, many of which require irrigation owing to the region's high rainfall variability, are therefore all concentrated around its riverbanks, as are most seasonal subsistence farming activities. Unlike in Oromiya, there have been no land certification initiatives in lowland SNNPR and Gambella.

TABLE 1.3 Overview of case study investments

Region	Company name	Date of land acquisition	Origin	Area acquired (in ha)	Area developed (in ha)	Lease payment (in ETB/ha)[1]	Employment (low–high season)[2]	Contract duration (years)	Type of commodity
Oromiya (highlands)	Karuturi Oromiya	2008	India	11,700	2,379	135	300–600	30	Maize
	Al-Hatasha Sugar Mills (HSM)	2007	Pakistan	28,000 (+15,000 conditional)	3,081	20	600–2,400	45	Sugar cane
	Serofta Modern Farming	2008	Djibouti	4,883	4,829	958.2	500–700	45	Wheat, potato
	Saudi Star	2009, re-signed in 2010	Saudi Arabia/ Ethiopia	10,000	9,394	30	400–600	50	Rice
Gambella (lowlands)	Basen Agriculture	2005	Ethiopia	10,000	4,212	30	800–1600	Unknown	Cotton, mango
	Karuturi Gambella	2008, re-signed in 2010	India	100,000 (+200,000 conditional)	9,217	20	700–1,100	50	Maize, sugar cane, oil palm
SNNPR (lowlands)	Fri-el Green	2006	Italy	30,000	500[3]	49	150–250	25	Oil palm
	Sugar Corporation	2011	Ethiopia	Estimated at 110,000 – 150,000[4]	735	Unknown	n/a	Unknown	Sugar cane
	Lucci Agriculture	2010	Diaspora	4,003	420[3]	158	70–110	25	Cotton
	Tsegaye Demoz	2010	Ethiopia	1,000	330[3]	158	90–150	25	Cotton

1. On 1 May 2012, 1 US$ was equivalent to 17.6 Ethiopian birr (ETB); 2. Data based on MoARD monitoring reports from November 2011 and on company interviews; 3. These figures are based on MoARD monitoring reports from November 2011. All other figures are based on remote sensing analysis (January 2012); 4. Data could not be validated by government sources. The estimated area planned for development in these districts is based on the road networks constructed between June and December 2011 (derived from field measurements and Aster L1A imagery).

Findings

Land identification and allocation The AISD Land Identification Group claims that land is allocated only when it is free from human settlement, forest and wildlife. It asserts that in addition to remote sensing analyses, it consults various local and regional government agencies to determine the potential nature of land use conflicts. However, in practice the criteria are rarely met. For example, in the densely forested Gambella region, the majority of the area allocated comprises high tropical forests. Moreover, all three concessions are located within the Gambella National Park, which was established in 1974, though it has never been officially gazetted. The western parts of the Karuturi concession are the destination of the second-largest mammal migration in Africa, which takes place annually between South Sudan and the Baro river. Moreover, the Duma Swamp, a wetland of particular importance to fish and wildlife, is located within the Karuturi concession and downstream from the Alwero Dam, which is the primary source of water for the Saudi Star concession. Similarly, the HSM concession covers large parts of the Didessa Wildlife Sanctuary, a birdlife habitat, and the area under development by the Sugar Corporation comprises much of the Murelle Controlled Hunting Area, an area frequented by large mammals.

While environmental considerations clearly do not figure prominently in land identification efforts, more heed tends to be given to socio-economic factors. Land is generally allocated away from human settlements. In SNNPR, for example, a distance of at least five hundred metres is maintained from the densely populated riverbanks; and in Gambella, the most populous districts, Lare and Jikawo, are not actively targeted for agricultural investment. Despite this, some of the projects do comprise densely settled land. For this reason the leasehold certificates for Karuturi Oromiya and Basen have been withheld; their land has to date not been formally demarcated, and boundaries are currently based on the site plans from their leasehold contracts. The AISD claims that mistakes were made in the initial allocation and new boundaries will be drawn to prevent displacement. In the case of the Sugar Corporation and HSM, however, owing to the national strategic importance of these projects, the government claims that some degree of displacement is warranted. It is anticipated that the two projects will require the displacement of an estimated 1,400 and 1,700 households, respectively.

Despite efforts to minimize direct displacement, at none of the sites can it be said that at the time of allocation they were free from human activity. At nine of the ten projects, the land was used as pasture and for shifting cultivation and/ or flood-retreat agriculture. In Gambella, forested areas were also actively used by local communities for the harvesting of non-timber forest products (NTFP). Permanently cultivated land, on the other hand, is often spared, with only two of the ten concessions comprising only small areas of permanent farmland.

26

The overlap of land allocated for investment with ecologically and socially significant landscapes would in theory be identified through the environmental and social impact assessment (ESIA) process. Land, for example, cannot be developed without the prior approval of the ESIA by the EPA (Proclamation 299/2002). However, in all cases activities on the land commenced before submission of the ESIA or, in some cases, even before the allocation of the leasehold certificate. For example, Saudi Star started developing its land in mid-2009, while the leasehold certificate was allocated only in December 2010 and the ESIA document submitted in May 2011 – in an ideal situation, the chronological sequence would be the reverse.[2] Thus, while the ESIA process is meant to serve as an instrument that identifies the potential socio-economic and environmental impacts to *inform* land allocations, by being conducted after the land is allocated and developed it has become a mere technicality.

With the AISD now managing the entire ESIA process while simultaneously being responsible for investment promotion and land allocation, significant conflicts of interest arise. This is also apparent from the opacity of the ESIA. For example, none of the regional and district governments interviewed, even agencies directly accountable to MoARD and the EPA, provided input to the ESIA process or were provided with copies of the final ESIA report. In Gambella, for example, the Land Administration and Environmental Protection Agency, responsible for land use planning in the region, sought access to copies of the ESIA reports for use in updating the 1999 Gambella Land Use Plan and performing environmental audits, but it was refused a copy by the AISD. Similar requests by the Ethiopian Wildlife and Conservation Agency (EWCA) and various district governments were also unsuccessful. Although ESIA laws require that such documents be made public, the AISD argued that it would be inappropriate to share such documents since they contain 'sensitive corporate information'. In practice, it appears rather that the AISD is seeking to limit both internal and external opposition to investment projects.

In September 2011, the AISD continued to further centralize investment-related activities by completely removing any right to allocate investment land from the regional governments in Afar, Benshangul Gumuz, Gambella and Somali. According to the AISD, these regional governments were not sufficiently capable of managing investments as a result of poor coordination in land allocations, rampant corruption and limited monitoring and enforcement capacity. This means that the regional governments in the lowlands no longer have any influence over how large parts of their land are utilized. Although the AISD claims to consult district and regional governments in the land identification process, in SNNPR and Gambella local government agencies had no knowledge of the location of land in the Land Bank, raising very real questions as to the actual participation of lower-tier government in this process.

Pre-implementation incorporation and accommodation of land users While the government is planning to allocate land certificates in the lowlands in the context of the so-called 'villagization' programme, at the time of research none of the sampled lowland communities had formal user claims over their land.[3] Consequently, the Ethiopian law does not offer these communities any protection against expropriation or provide for any mechanisms to elicit community consent or provide compensation.[4] From the seven sampled lowland concessions, there were no forms of consultation or compensation at six of the concessions – this includes a forty-five-household community within the Saudi Star concession and a seventy-household community within the Tsegaye Demoz concession, both of which had already resettled at the time of research. In all cases, awareness of commercial development came only when land development activities commenced.

The Sugar Corporation was the only lowland project in the study where community consultations were observed. In 2010, the district government registered community assets; the communities were told that this was for the purpose of resettlement for sugar development. Later, the district government initiated a sensitization campaign to inform communities of the nature and implications of the project. They were informed they would receive compensation and be resettled in the to-be-refurbished 'Korea Camp', the former housing estate of the North Korean cotton project, in the main town of Omorate. Community engagements were, however, more promotional than they were consultative, with emphasis largely on the benefits communities could expect to derive from project development, such as plantation employment and outgrower schemes.

In the highland sites, local populations were more directly incorporated into the pre-implementation phase than in most of the lowland sites. At HSM and Karuturi Oromiya, for example, most surrounding communities were informed by local government of development plans prior to project commencement, although – much as in the case of the Sugar Corporation – engagements reportedly had a largely promotional objective. At Karuturi Oromiya, for example, communities were promised well-remunerated employment, new roads, access to electricity, and boreholes; at HSM, new clinics and schools and opportunities to become sugar outgrowers were promised. This served to quell early resistance to the projects by creating high community expectations of future development.

Although resettlements were planned for both projects, consultations to that effect were not conducted, with most communities appearing uninformed of any such plans. At Karuturi Oromiya, three communities consisting of more than 1,500 households were initially slated for resettlement; however, according to the district government, when the costs of doing so became apparent these plans were shelved. While this has prevented loss of permanent, certified farmland on the elevated periphery of the concession, human activities on the flood plain, consisting largely of shifting cultivation and grazing, will be displaced by plantation development without any form of compensation. The land on the plains was not certified owing to the environmental significance of black soil and swampy areas.

While the district government inventoried all properties within the HSM concession in mid-2011, communities suspected, though were not informed of, its purpose. In contrast to the situation at Karuturi Oromiya, most of the affected communities did not possess land certificates for their permanent farmland. Since much of the population was settled in the area by the government in 2006, a year after land certificates were allocated in Oromiya, no such certificates were allocated. Nevertheless, monetary compensation and replacement farmland will be provided to all of the 438 households residing within the concession area.[5] Since the government is constructing a dam over the Didessa river in support of the project, its more direct involvement in the project has, arguably, prompted it to develop a more comprehensive resettlement and rehabilitation package, in similar vein to the Sugar Corporation. Also, the socio-economic footprint of the project is comparatively large, particularly considering that an additional 1,275 households are to be resettled from the 8,500-hectare reservoir area (FDRE 2007b).

Impact mitigation and community development With regard to impact mitigation, investors are primarily required to adhere to the stipulations of their land rental contracts, the Agricultural Investment and Land Lease Directive, and other pertinent legislation, such as the Labour Proclamation (No. 377/2003), the Water Resource Management Regulations (No. 115/2005), and the Environmental Pollution Control Proclamation (No. 300/2002). The directive on which the contracts are based requires investors to 'plant trees that are good for soil conservation', 'ensure that proper technologies are used in order to prevent soil erosion', 'protect religious, community-owned and wetland areas' and 'responsibly use chemicals' (Article 13). However, without further elaboration or quantification of these requirements, these provisions leave significant latitude for interpretation.

For example, what is meant by 'community-owned' is not detailed in the directive, but in practice refers only to certified land. By early 2012, eight out of the ten projects had already displaced community farmlands – none of these lands was subject to a land certificate. In the lowlands, farmlands targeted for conversion were typically the 'wet-season plots'. Owing to the annual flooding of major rivers in the lowlands (in these cases the Baro and the Omo), communities across these regions tend to cultivate away from the riverbanks as the rainy season approaches (wet-season plots) and cultivate the riverbanks when the rainy season passes (dry-season plots) – thereby providing two harvests per year. Since most concessions in the lowlands are located in the vicinity of the riverbanks, but with a 500-metre buffer, only the dry-season plots are typically spared. Similar conflicts were observed with community pastureland, which in one case in Gambella resulted in an intertribal conflict when a community was forced to migrate outside its territory in search of new pasture. Important grazing grounds in SNNPR have not been converted to date; nevertheless, given the confinement within yet-to-be-developed concession areas, similar conflicts over territory can be anticipated.

Environmental regulations also appear to be rarely adhered to. For example, Basen was the only company observed to be replanting trees. As is apparent from the neglect of ESIA-related proclamations and the widespread allocation of ecologically sensitive areas, lip-service is generally paid to most laws if these interfere with development. The EPA, which is in theory responsible for monitoring most of these environmental impacts, acknowledges its limited monitoring capacity to enforce such regulations and has not been involved in monitoring any of the ten concessions.

With the EPA lacking also the actual authority to perform audits, in practice the only investment monitoring activities are coordinated by the AISD. Land allocated through the AISD is typically monitored twice yearly, involving a team that consists of AISD representatives and officials from district, zonal and regional government (predominantly from the investment agencies). Investments are appraised on the basis of seven criteria: conformance to the land rental contract, labour conditions, labour quantity, use of machinery, contribution to community development, infrastructure development, and conservation practices. On the basis of the monitoring reports for South Omo and Gambella, the monitoring teams appear to be highly cognizant of the adverse impacts of agricultural investment. For example, the AISD acknowledged the existence of settlements within some of the concessions and that for the majority of projects labour conditions, environmental practices and contributions to local development are poor.

With regard to community development, Saudi Star was the only company to have contributed to community development, having gifted 250 beehives to local communities and built a community centre. While most government institutions contend that technology transfers and smallholder integration are important investment spillovers, such processes were not observed at any of the sites – with no government involvement in promoting spillover observed to date. In certain cases, company yields were found to be lower than those of nearby communities; and in others, communities were not familiar with the crop cultivated. Furthermore, most neighbouring communities exhibited little interest in working on the plantations owing to low wages, which in some cases were as low as US$0.60 per day. On average, 89 per cent of workers employed on the ten plantations have no contract and are casually employed as day wage labourers, which typically provides between three and four months of full-time employment per year. In the lowlands, the vast majority of local employment beneficiaries were found to be 'idle labour', such as children and young adults. At one of the plantations in Gambella, employees estimated that more than 400 of the 700 day wage labourers were children in the age range eight to fourteen.[6] With day wage labour considered to be a supplementary, rather than alternative, livelihood activity, households are unwilling to sacrifice the labour of those involved in cattle rearing and farming (for which the labour-intensive months coincide with those for plantation work).

Despite these issues, companies are reprehended only for failure to develop at the pace specified in their land rental contracts, not for other failings. For example, four of the ten projects received official warnings that failure to develop would lead to the termination of their leasehold certificates, which for Fri-el Green led to the loss of half their concession area in late 2011. In Gambella, the government revoked the leases of twenty-five other companies in 2011 for not sufficiently developing the land. The investor-centric approach of these monitoring missions is also evidenced by the excessive emphasis in the monitoring reports on providing investors with more institutional support to expedite development, without suggesting any actions to manage the negative implications of such developments. In relation to labour conditions and technology transfers, the federal government argued that intervention would not be required since over time the market would correct any imbalances.

While the EIA and the associated Environmental Management Plan (EMP) could in theory serve as important instruments to formulate context-specific impact mitigation strategies, considering the lack of pre-implementation community engagement it is questionable whether community concerns are appropriately accounted for in project planning and design. Moreover, with no reference made to the EMPs in the biannual monitoring missions, it is unlikely that these serve as actual performance benchmarks. Although the AISD has adopted the 'Social and Environmental Codes of Practice' for agricultural investment (FDRE 2011c), as these codes of practice are voluntary it is unlikely that profound shifts in corporate responsibility can be anticipated.[7]

In justifying the absence of direct remediating measures, regional and federal government generally argued that concomitant rural interventions would address some of the early costs associated with land use competition. For example, the villagization programme is over time expected to sedentarize agro-pastoralists and promote more land-intensive livelihood activities that are spatially confined and controlled through individualized landholdings, as opposed to communal rangelands. It is, therefore, claimed that the current conflicts between agricultural investment and pastoralism and flood-retreat agriculture will be resolved over time.

In SNNPR, the government is also in the process of implementing a series of projects to further facilitate this shift. For example, since 2009 it has been promoting the uptake of more productive cattle species to minimize herd size and of irrigated farming to phase out flood-retreat agriculture. However, agropastoralists expressed little interest in moderating cattle numbers owing to the social function and status of maintaining large herds. While communities did actively farm the irrigated plots, surveyed households indicated that they were unwilling to abandon their wet-season farming plots since these were considered less labour-demanding and did not entail the risk of crop failure in cases when irrigation pumps were out of service because of fuel shortages, as has been known to happen in the past.

Dispute resolution Given landscape transformations and the limited preparedness of affected communities to adopt new systems of production or plantation employment, community discontent over opportunity costs associated with the loss of access to traditional livelihood resources could be observed at most of the case study sites. This discontent was in many cases found to be exacerbated by the limited effort by companies to develop amiable community relations. This is evident not only in the complete absence of formal community engagement mechanisms, but also in the frequency of company–community conflicts, which in many cases are comparatively petty and preventable. To many, such conflicts symbolize company disregard for local communities and have become important sources of distrust. While most conflicts resulted primarily in a deterioration of company–community relations, in three of the ten cases expatriate staff had violent run-ins with local communities, which in two cases resulted in fatalities. This is largely a result of the limited opportunities to settle disputes amicably – not just with companies, but also with the government.

At four projects, for example, affected communities indicated that when they approached the companies to discuss their concerns, they were referred to the government. Since companies, in the absence of any contractual relations with communities, are accountable solely to the government, and the government, through the leasehold contract, is obliged to ensure that 'land is free of impediment', companies appear to have no far-reaching obligation or incentive to accommodate the needs of communities.

As a result, twenty-one out of twenty-five sampled communities sought out the government to mediate conflicts. It is typically the *Kebele* chairman that then acts as the representative in such matters, the *Kebele* being the smallest administrative unit in Ethiopia, equivalent to a municipality, and the *Kebele* chairman being the elected administrative representative. Within the case study sites, local sentiments towards the *Kebele* chairman differed greatly. In the highlands, he was generally perceived to be an effective and embedded representative of the community, while in the lowlands, notably in SNNPR, he was viewed as a political appointee, aligned more with the government than his constituency. His intervention was in most cases aimed at preventing further loss of farmland and pasture and encouraging companies to fulfil their developmental promises. However, there was no evidence of such interventions yielding any tangible results. At a number of the lowland projects it was claimed that the district and regional government often responded to complaints by reprimanding communities for 'agitating the public' and for being 'anti-development'.

Most communities tended to surrender to this lack of support, with a significant show of deference to government authority. Since few concrete benefits have to date accrued with lower-level government, at many concessions the concerns of relevant district administrations, despite differences in long-term expectations, are typically in line with those of the communities (see also Shete and Schoneveld forthcoming).[8] Although these concerns are communicated to the AISD, with district government having limited authority over both allocation and implementation, their capacity to influence corporate practice and government investment strategies is in practice negligible.

The only observed case where the court system was consulted was when a group of contract workers at HSM filed a class action lawsuit against the company for arbitrary dismissal. However, since non-certified land and casual labour have no legal protection, the issue of community 'legal capacity to claim' is of limited relevance to Ethiopian concession allocations. Moreover, with the passing of the Societies and Charities Proclamation No. 621/2009, foreign NGOs and those receiving more than 10 per cent of their funding from foreign sources are not permitted to perform human rights and conflict-related work (Article 14 (2j-n), 14(5)). Therefore, considering the limited capacity of NGOs and local institutions to adequately represent community concerns and the limited legal grounds for contestation, in practice project-affected communities have few opportunities for seeking recourse.

Discussion and conclusion

The ten case studies offered insights into how well local socio-economic and environmental considerations are being incorporated into the investment planning process and the manner in which this shapes the relationship between large-scale commercial farming and traditional forms of production. While the Ethiopian government formally contends that the introduction of modern farming in its marginalized periphery will contribute to upgrading agro-pastoral production systems, early evidence suggests that numerous conflicts have and are threatening to arise as a result of the highly centralized implementation of Ethiopia's agricultural modernization policies and the unwillingness of the state to accommodate contradictory interests.

This research has shown that while procedures and protocols are in place to identify potential land use conflicts, allocation decisions in practice illustrate clear biases against particular land use systems. With the government evidently avoiding areas that are under intensive, sedentary forms of production, ecologically significant landscapes and areas dominated by land-extensive livelihood systems (e.g. pastoralism, hunting and gathering, and shifting/opportunistic cultivation) are disproportionately targeted for conversion. While financial motives (e.g. avoiding compensation payments to holders of land certificates) partially underlie this phenomenon, biases reflect more importantly government's dismay over what is regularly referred to as the 'backward', 'uncivilized' and 'inhospitable' periphery. This is reflected not only by the allocation decisions, but also by high levels of awareness of land use conflicts, the absence of consultation, participation or impact mitigation mechanisms, and the refusal to engage communities in post-implementation dialogue. Thus, the evident lack of consideration by the government for these local realities is not necessarily a product of poor monitoring and enforcement capacity, but rather of a focused government strategy to modernize 'backward' rural practices.

Within various tiers of government it is generally accepted that resistance to expropriation and 'modern' forms of production is inevitable, and, as one senior official in SNNPR put it, that 'only by demonstrating the value of modern farming methods will they abandon their cattle and learn to become civilized'. Moreover, it is often argued that new employment opportunities in particular will enable recipients to invest in more productive cattle and agricultural inputs, thereby promoting intensification. Hence, a combination of push factors, from losing access to essential livelihood resources, and pull factors, from new livelihood options through villagization, employment and intensification programmes, are meant to sedentarize peripheral communities and bring these into the domain of the state.

However, findings show a widespread resistance to taking on plantation employment and a reluctance to abandon traditional livelihood activities, particularly among the agro-pastoralists. This can in part be attributed to the deeply ingrained social identities that are derived from these activities, but also to the perceived risks associated with increasing dependence on insecure income from casual employment and government resource supplies and with sacrificing important safety net activities. Early evidence already suggests that land fragmentation and loss of access to vital livelihood are increasing the vulnerability of affected households to shocks; for example, by loss of wet-season farmlands, pasture and non-timber forest products – all of which are important for consumption-smoothing strategies. As a result, many households will over time be forced to abandon these activities and submit to the development plans of the state.

While it is too premature and beyond the scope of this research to evaluate the long-term implications of this shift in economic terms and in relation to human development indicators, the issue at hand transcends social empiricism. Fundamentally, the lack of consideration for local realities suggests a growing disconnect between a developmental state in pursuit of agricultural modernization and normative human and citizenship rights. Despite decentralization reforms and advances in ethnic political representation under the current regime, the recent recentralization of the investment process is increasingly undermining the capacity of sub-national institutions to respond to the needs of the population, thereby undermining principles of ethnic federalism enshrined in Ethiopia's Constitution, notably their right to self-determination. With this compounded by increasingly prostrate civil society organizations, rural communities have no real means to ensure that their development needs are accounted for, or to contest the appropriation of the commons. In its current form there is therefore little compatibility between government modernization initiatives and 'traditional' livelihood systems. This calls into question both the virtue of government's human development rhetoric in relation to large-scale commercial agriculture and the focus of most research on the topic on quantifiable indicators, rather than on issues of agency and choice, in contextualizing trade-offs.

2 | Large-scale land acquisitions in Tanzania: a critical analysis of practices and dynamics

Jumanne Abdallah, Linda Engström,
Kjell Havnevik and Lennart Salomonsson

Introduction

This chapter presents the current status of agrofuel investments in Tanzania and uses empirical data from three cases of large-scale investments for agrofuel production in the Rufiji, Bagamoyo and Meru districts to provide snapshots of what is happening on the ground. The chapter also describes and analyses the history and trends in large-scale agricultural investments in Tanzania and key land acquisition processes, as well as the role of the state and other actors.

As in other agrarian developing countries, agriculture investments and modernization in Tanzania have been triggered by the increasing global demand for food and energy, as well as by greener global needs, and by a perceived win-win paradigm implying that these investments will bring benefits to all actors involved. The policy initiatives can historically be traced to the colonial era, when large-scale land alienation began to take place (Coulson 2013). An often referred to and ill-fated example is the Groundnut Scheme in the late 1940s (Iliffe 1979). Today, environmental protection interventions, through the expansion of protected areas, REDD[1] and other climate change initiatives, and the national *Kilimo Kwanza* ('Agriculture First') strategy implementing agricultural development corridors, are accelerating serious conflicts over land for many rural people. Concerned scholars and national and international NGOs have begun to argue against such large-scale investment plans owing to the emergence and escalation of problems and the evidence of risks connected to them. Investments have been growing in terms of scale, geographic spread, players involved and types of impact (Kaarhus et al. 2010).

Fieldwork was carried out in 2009, 2012 and 2013. Focus group discussions, in-depth interviews and the collection of secondary records were our main research methods. We interviewed investors, central government authorities (ministries of water, energy and minerals), a regional secretariat, and relevant officers at three district authorities. In addition, we carried out several focus group discussions within sample villages and with farmers' groups in the Meru, Bagamoyo and Rufiji districts.

Background to Tanzanian agriculture development and foreign investment

Tanzania inherited an agricultural economy relying on cash crops for export, introduced by the German and British colonial states. In the first year of independence, 1962, the government attempted to modernize agriculture through highly mechanized community development initiatives and by raising agricultural productivity, in line with World Bank advice (World Bank 1961). Later, in the mid-1960s, the Tanzanian state introduced a 'progressive farmer' approach, which aimed at supporting innovative smallholder production. Agricultural exports increased during the 1960s, but inequality, state expansion and surplus appropriation threatened to undermine President Nyerere's philosophy of social equality and self-reliance (Nyerere 1962, 1966; Mbelle et al. 2002; Havnevik and Isinika 2010). This development triggered the Arusha Declaration of February 1967, which aimed at resettlement of the rural population into villages, with the objective of increasing agricultural productivity and providing education, water and health services for all – the so-called *Ujamaa* Strategy. These interventions led to the physical resettlement of about two-thirds of the rural Tanzanian population. Increasingly, and in particular between 1973 and 1976, force was employed by the government to move rural people into villages (Boesen et al. 1977). Adverse weather conditions and their negative consequences for agricultural production from 1973 onwards were important underlying causes of the economic stagnation of Tanzania during the second half of the 1970s. Tanzania had by the late 1970s entered an economic, social, and political crisis, fuelled by expansion and economic mismanagement in the parastatal sector, the war with Uganda and global economic stagnation (Havnevik 1993).

During the 1970s, development assistance was increasingly directed to the industrial sector, while support of agriculture declined (Skarstein and Wangwe 1986). In addition, the state's agricultural price and marketing policies involved heavy taxation on agricultural smallholders (Ellis 1983). Overvaluation of the Tanzanian currency also added to agricultural taxation. Given the undermining of the production conditions of smallholder agriculture, the agricultural surplus declined and smallholders became more involved in economic diversification in order to increase incomes and avoid the state (Maliyamkono and Bagachwa 1990; Havnevik 1993).

In efforts to resolve the crisis, the Tanzanian government came into strong disagreement with the IMF concerning how the economy should be managed, which led to a breakdown in Tanzania–IMF relations in the period 1979–85. This contributed to decreasing levels of foreign assistance to the country, exacerbating the crisis further. Gradually, however, the relationship with the international financial institutions improved, and in August 1986 Tanzania signed economic stabilization agreements and reform programmes with the

IMF and the World Bank respectively. These took shape in a three-year Economic Recovery Programme (ERP), which aimed to reduce the role of the state in the economy and to remove subsidies for agricultural inputs and transport as well as consumer subsidies. In general, the pathway to be pursued by Tanzania was part of the new economic liberalization strategy of 'getting the prices right' and creating more space for the private sector (World Bank 1981, 1989). There was no longer any possibility of Tanzania pursuing a development strategy with a social profile. Hence, the then president, Nyerere, decided to leave the presidency in 1985, while he remained as chairman of the single-party CCM (Chama Cha Mapindugi – Party of the Revolution) until 1991.

The policy reforms that sought to revamp the agricultural sector through economic liberalization and to increase the efficiency of the economy by reducing the role of the Tanzanian state therein did not work as expected. The reform era of President Ali Hassan Mwinyi (1985–95) saw increasing corruption in the economy, and the relationships between Tanzania and the international financial institutions and donors deteriorated.

One of the first initiatives of President Benjamin Mkapa, who came into office in 1995, was to initiate a presidential commission investigating corruption, led by former prime minister Warioba. Initiatives were also taken to mend the relationships with the donor community through the establishment of an economic commission, led by the Canadian economist Jeremy Helleiner, which looked into how the fiscal discipline of the government and government–donor relations could be improved.

During the era of President Mkapa (1995–2005) fiscal discipline was restored and sectors beyond agriculture took on an important role in the economy and the export sector. In particular the mining sector, including mining of gold and gemstones, and the tourist sector grew rapidly. Gradually the role of agriculture in total Tanzanian exports declined. The new dynamic sectors, however, were to a large extent owned and controlled by foreign interests and companies, albeit in alignment with domestic financial and political interests (Bryceson and Jönsson 2010).

In 1997, the Tanzanian government began to prepare the ground for increasing foreign investments. The Tanzania Investment Act of 1997 was one of the first steps in this direction. The Act established the Tanzania Investment Centre (TIC), with the main objective of 'coordinating, encouraging, promoting and facilitating investment in Tanzania and advising the Government on investment policy and related matters'. To guarantee the TIC as a 'one-stop agency' for investors, all government departments, agencies and other public authorities were instructed to fully cooperate with the new agency. One important service to be provided by the TIC, which was to grow during the first part of the 2000s, was to facilitate acquisition of land for foreign investors in Tanzania with a time frame of only thirty days.[2] The TIC was mandated to provide a

Certificate of Incentive, which is a basic document for land processing and land allocation to investors. Formal procedures for the land application are provided in the Land and Village Acts.

The next Tanzanian president, Jakaya Kikwete, who entered office in 2005, placed strong emphasis on improving the investment climate for domestic and foreign investors. His government requested all Tanzanian regional authorities to establish local investment promotion offices and create regional business councils in order to enhance the conditions for external investors.

The strong promotion of foreign investments in large-scale agricultural cultivation was further concretized in the *Kilimo Kwanza* (Agriculture First) Initiative launched in 2009. Also linked to this development is the plan by the Tanzanian government to establish an Export Processing Zone on the coast immediately south of Bagamoyo town.

Tanzania had earlier signed multilateral and bilateral agreements on protecting and promoting foreign investments in the country when it became a member of the Multilateral Investment Guarantee Agency (MIGA) in 1992. MIGA, a member of the World Bank Group, has a mandate to promote foreign direct investments (FDI) in developing countries to help support economic growth, reduce poverty, and improve people's livelihoods. For example, MIGA provides political risk insurance guarantees against nationalization. In 1992 Tanzania also became a signatory to the International Centre for Settlement of Investment Disputes (ICSID), whose primary purpose is to provide facilities for conciliation and arbitration of international investment disputes.

Kilimo Kwanza is a departure from previous agricultural strategies, which had emphasized smallholder agriculture, although increasingly in a market context, in the direction of large-scale agricultural activities, by actively mobilizing domestic and foreign investors. Agriculture First is a national strategy aimed at accelerating agricultural and rural transformation. The initiative comprises a set of pillars that address the agricultural sector's challenges and take advantage of perceived potentials that exist to modernize and commercialize agriculture. The Tanzania National Business Council was involved in the design of *Kilimo Kwanza* and strongly encourages private sector involvement in agriculture. In addition, it promotes the identification of priority areas for agro-based production in order to meet the growing domestic/external market demands and the need for employment creation in Tanzania, and it focuses on the need for legal and institutional change in order to provide the ground for foreign investors in large-scale agricultural ventures. It also emphasizes the need to amend the Village Land Act of 1999 to facilitate investors' access to village land for agricultural investments, and to make land available to the TIC. A plan, long awaiting fruition, is for the TIC to establish a Land Bank, which could make land easily available to investors. Land would be provided to the Land Bank by identifying and recording unused (or 'idle') village land for agricultural investments. The perceptions of 'idle' land to be made available for investments vary between government agencies and villagers, however, and constitute an important cause of increasing conflicts over land.

Land laws and land acquisition processes

Reserved and village land In Tanzania, land is divided into three categories: *reserved* (about 30 per cent), *village* (about two-thirds of the land) and *general* land (about 2 per cent). Reserved land denotes forest reserves, game control and conservation areas, game reserves, etc., and is mainly regulated under the Land Act of 1999. Village land is under the management of approximately 12,000 villages in Tanzania and is regulated under the Village Land Act of 1999, which states that for village land allocation of more than 250 hectares, the relevant minister shall consider recommendations made by the Village Assembly through the Village Council, before giving his/her approval or refusal.

Since most of Tanzanian land is under village management, investors need access to village land for their investments. The land acquisition process on the ground in Tanzania is complex. Land within village boundaries is managed by village authorities on behalf of the government and the Commissioner of Land. According to the Tanzanian land laws of 1999, foreign investors can access village land only after it has been transferred into general land status. This has to be approved by the Commissioner for Land on behalf of the president. Once it has been transferred, it will not revert to village land again.

Under the Land Act of 1999, a foreign investor may occupy land through 1) obtaining derivative rights from the TIC; 2) the granting of right of occupancy by the Commissioner for Land; or 3) subleases from the private sector, licences from the government, or purchase from other holders of granted right of occupancy. Rights of occupancy and derivative rights can be granted for short- and long-term periods. Long-term rights of occupancy and derivative rights and leases range from periods of five to ninety-nine years and are renewable, but not beyond ninety-nine years.

Acknowledging the danger of large-scale alienation of village land, one suggestion put forward in the 2012 draft biofuel policy is to limit the maximum area allocated to investors to 20,000 hectares (MEM 2012).

The investors' application for right of occupancy should declare all rights and interests in land in Tanzania of the applicants at the time. After consent of the local authority or other bodies where the law requires such, the application should be directed to the Commissioner for Land and be accompanied by a Certificate of Incentives granted by the TIC.

According to existing laws, a village land use plan (VLUP) is required before investments begin. The Village Land Act[3] requires that private disposition on village land should observe 'any land use plan prepared or in the process of being prepared by or for the village'.

There is, however, no clear process prescribed in the laws in cases where an investor fails to develop the acquired land according to the investment plans. The number of cases where investments are not being implemented is high, leaving uncertainty as to who has legal rights to the land concerned.

Proper village land use planning is based on village land surveys. Access to accurate data on land size and location would make it possible to estimate land rent. In Tanzania, land rents are collected annually and administered through the Ministry of Lands, Housing and Human Settlements Development. The level of land rents is set by the central government, with 80 per cent of the proceeds going to the central government and 20 per cent to the local government. Under the terms of the property tax, rural land is essentially not taxed. In fact, for unsurveyed rural land (i.e. land which has not been surveyed for village land use plans), there is not even a requirement to pay land rent. This could be an incentive for investors to bypass village land use planning. If investment in rural areas takes place without proper land surveys and land use plans, a large portion of potential rural rents cannot be collected by the central government. Land is not taxed under property ratings of the local government, since land is public and belongs to the state. The complications related to land rents and village land use plans are compounded by a cumbersome process of obtaining environmental permits (ORGUT Consulting AB 2008). This could be one of the reasons for land rents in Tanzania being very low compared with market values: currently land rent is only US$0.3 per hectare per year.

General and idle land Section 2 of the Land Act defines general land as 'all public land which is not reserved land or village land and includes unoccupied or unused village land', while the Village Land Act does not include the phrase 'and includes unoccupied or unused village land'. The definition in the Land Act, we will argue, could be an important loophole for the Tanzanian state agencies at various levels to spearhead the transfer of 'idle or unused land' to the category of general land, from which it can be made accessible to large-scale agro-investors.

In all village group discussions connected with this research, the villagers dismissed the existence of idle land. They argued instead that land is not only used for farming, but also for other uses such as livestock grazing and the collection of non-timber forest products. They also showed us how they have set aside land for future generations.

Also included in the category of general land is land in urban and peri-urban areas, and land which belonged to state agricultural and livestock projects that became privatized during the 1980s and 1990s or has become non-operational for various reasons. Such land has to some extent been taken into use by livestock herders or through the establishment of rural settlements.

The Land Bank The Tanzania Investment Centre is mandated to establish a Land Bank in order to make land available to investors. Personal communication with a representative of the TIC in November 2008 revealed that the TIC lacked funds to finance the compensation to villages that would be required for the transfer of village land to the Land Bank. International donors were at the time also reluctant to provide assistance to the TIC to develop and administer a Land Bank, for fear that the process would lead to alienation of smallholders with weak land rights.

Instead, an ad hoc process of identifying land for foreign investors that is not specified in laws or regulations has emerged. Foreign investors are simply recommended by the TIC to identify and visit villages where land might be available for large-scale agro-production and investments. Such visits should, according to the advice of the TIC, begin with calling on the District Land Officer, who would guide investors to villages and their authorities for a discussion about possible leases of village land and what could be offered by the investor as compensation (Havnevik and Haaland 2011). This process necessarily leads to informal land discussions and negotiations that may lead to land acquisition processes. However, the cultural context of investors and villagers is usually profoundly different, which results in confusion as to what is actually agreed upon. The asymmetry in information and knowledge about laws and regulations connected with land and investments between villagers and investors usually casts villagers into the weaker role. This has become evident through reported cases of lack of understanding about what the lease of land involves and about the possibility of villages effectively gaining the compensation promised in discussions and negotiations.

Slow land use planning Village land use plans are mandatory before a village can provide land to external investors, as provided by the Land Use Planning Act of 2007. Land use plans are implemented at the national level by the Land Use Planning Commission (NLUPC). The establishment of the commission in 1984 was considered necessary after a realization that the policy, legal and institutional set-ups had not been effective enough. This was related in particular to the coordination of various land use activities and programmes undertaken by different sectorial organizations in the government, the private and the NGO sectors. The NLUPC assignment primarily includes preparation and implementation of the National Land Use Framework Plan. However, the NLUPC's capacity to develop village land use plans is weak. Currently only 10 per cent of the total of some 12,000 villages have had land use plans developed since the exercise started in 1984. It took twenty-four years before the village land use plan process was supported by law, but resources, more than laws, seem to be critical for speeding up the process.

Developments in the land policy and land acquisition processes

In fact, the Tanzanian land ownership and use systems were facing enormous problems at the end of the 1980s, when economic liberalization emerged in Tanzania. Rural people then began to reclaim the land they had possessed prior to villagization. In this process it was revealed that the villagization process itself had taken place without sufficient constitutional and legal backing. In order to avoid utter confusion and chaos in the national land management system, the state established the Presidential Commission of Inquiry into Land Matters under the leadership of Professor Issa Shivji. A major conclusion of the commission was that significant problems related to land ownership, use and management were connected to the state ownership of land. The commission subsequently proposed diversifying the vesting of the radical title of land in village land administered by the Village Assembly and general land administered by the Commissioner of Land (United Republic of Tanzania 1994a and National Land Policy, draft of March 1995).

The recommendations of the commission were backed by a detailed investigation of land disputes across the country. The commission in fact submitted some twenty-six volumes of the record of evidence from twenty regions with the report. Some of this material is included in the second volume of the report of the commission, which also included a summary of 1,200 letters of complaint regarding land issues that were received by the commission. Although the second volume of the report was printed, it was given only very restricted distribution in Tanzania by the Ministry of Lands, Housing and Urban Development (United Republic of Tanzania 1994b).

The manoeuvring of the Tanzanian agencies in the process leading up to the National Land Policy in 1995 reaffirmed that the radical title to land should remain with the president (Sundet 1997). The Presidential Land Commission, also, was able to make legal proposals that held back the land reclamation process that had begun in the late 1980s (Havnevik 1995). The laws regulating land ownership, management and use were subsequently confirmed in the Land and Village Land Acts of 1999. These Acts, however, did not become operational until May 2003. Directly thereafter, pressures began for the amendment of the Acts. The most recent pressures to amend the Land Laws are moving in the direction of the Land Laws creating better and easier access to Tanzanian village land for foreign investors (communication with Swedish embassy, 2011).

The Land Laws of 1999 had developed from a decade-long process of investigation and negotiation. Before they had come into force and entered the process of implementation, demands for them to be changed occurred. For villagers and rural smallholders, given limited information and education, this continuously changing legal framework is difficult to grasp. This also makes it difficult for village institutions and rural landholders to know their land rights. The large number of rules and institutions at the local level also leaves 'land rights negotiable' (Pedersen 2012: 279).

Do large-scale land acquisitions exist?

What's on paper – what's on the ground? A recent paper by Locher and Sulle (2013) states that the flaws in existing data create 'an unnecessarily blurred picture of the land deal situation in Tanzania and thus an inadequate basis for related political decisions ... and a misleading starting point for new research projects' (p. 2), and identifies several types of flaw in the documentation and reproduction of data. The issue of methodology and transparency of land deal data is not restricted to Tanzania, and has been described in various articles in a special issue of *Journal of Peasant Studies* (Scoones et al. 2013). It points to a 'profound uncertainty' about what is being counted, and the authors call for a 'second phase of land grab research which abandons the aim of deriving total numbers of hectares in favor of more specific, grounded and transparent methods' (p. 469). Our field research in 2012 was informed by the same concern of getting a better insight into what is actually happening on the ground.

In Tanzania, the changing legal frameworks regarding land ownership and management have created lack of clarity about the role of various institutions and the overall processes of land acquisitions and leases. This situation has also affected the accessibility of information from Tanzanian authorities on large-scale investments. Our visits to state agencies and district and village authorities have given the impression that no one has a full overview of the laws and regulations and how land is being allocated. Our research shows a striking gap between the number of investors requesting land and the number of investors that are currently operational. Our information and data were collected through field visits in the Rufiji and Bagamoyo districts in the Coast Region and the Meru district in Arusha Region. In addition, we collected information from literature listing investors who have required or acquired land in Tanzania (Kamanga 2008; TNRF 2008; ActionAid 2009; FAO 2009b; Sulle and Nelson 2009; Diaz-Chavez et al. 2010; Kaarhus et al. 2010; WRM 2010; FAO 2011b; Mousseau and Mittal 2011; Anseeuw et al. 2012; Massay and George 2013).

During our field visits in March 2012, our research could confirm only one operational large-scale agrofuel investment (Diligent Ltd in Arusha Region) and two investors with advanced plans (Agro EcoEnergy Ltd in the Bagamoyo district and Felisa Ltd in Kigoma Region); however, this latter company may focus mainly on sugar production. Felisa has since then shifted to food crops such as rice and sunflower, even though the oil palm plantations that had been planted are still there. Diligent Ltd went into voluntary liquidation in the autumn of 2012. Agro EcoEnergy had, by October 2013, still not reached financial closure. The company was still awaiting the decision on a large-scale loan guarantee application to the International Swedish Development Cooperation Agency, Sida.

We identified thirty-two investors who have requested more than two thousand hectares of land for agrofuel production in Tanzania during the last decade. The vast majority of them were foreign, and European companies predominated. In total, approximately 1.1 million hectares of land have been requested. Of the thirty-two investors, only nine actually did acquire land, of a total area of around 200,000 hectares. These figures are much lower when compared with the most cited information on land requests and allocations: more than four million hectares requested and 640,000 hectares allocated (Sulle and Nelson 2009).

We found that at least six of those nine investors to whom land had been allocated had started cultivation, and, at a certain moment, three of these six switched from agrofuel to food crops. Three of the six that started production have gone bankrupt. One of them – Sun Biofuels Ltd – was sold to a Mauritius-based investor in 2012 (Bergius 2012), but the new owner has not yet started production (Sosovele, personal communication, March 2013). One investor who was allocated land is now renting it to the villagers who used to manage the land for themselves (anonymous, Institute for Resource Assessment, personal communication). Two investors – Diligent Ltd and Prokon Ltd – based their business on out-grower models of production only. They have both gone bankrupt. However, according to Massay and George (2013), Diligent Ltd has been sold to a French company (Eco Carbon). Jatropha is the dominant crop for the companies that have gone bankrupt, and Nelson et al.

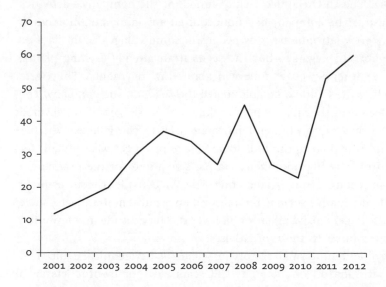

2.1 The number of new companies investing in agriculture, registered by the TIC annually, 2001–12 (*source*: TIC research and information division, 2013)

(2012) claim that the demand for land for jatropha cultivation has essentially evaporated during the last few years.

No in-depth analyses have been conducted on the reasons for these bankruptcies. Although they are to some extent context specific, several more general reasons have also been put forward, including loss of access to cheap credit and other forms of financing, due to the financial crisis, and the disappointing performance of jatropha (ibid.). Hultman et al. (2012) have compiled results from other studies on biofuel investments in Tanzania and state that the bankruptcies are related to poor planning and communication, the lack of a regulatory framework, and the pressure from NGOs not to allocate any more land to agrofuel investors before policies are in place.

The number of foreign and domestic agricultural companies registered by the TIC as investors in agriculture has increased from 2001 to 2012 (Figure 2.1). The stagnation in registration of investors from 2005 to 2007 depended on uncertainties related to the change of the presidency from Mkapa to Kikwete. The decline between 2008 and 2010 is probably explained by the global financial crisis. The increase in 2011 and 2012 is connected to food-related investments under *Kilimo Kwanza*. The TIC statistics include all investments with a Certificate of Incentive. Some of these have acquired land, while others have initiated the process of identifying land for investment.

Empirical evidence: Diligent Ltd The Dutch company Diligent Ltd operated a unique out-grower system with more than 100,000 farmers and was expanding rapidly towards central and west Tanzania when the liquidation of the company occurred in 2012. The CEO claimed lack of funds for the company's activities as the main reason. The company had not acquired any land; smallholders in the area already grew jatropha trees as hedges in some villages as far back as the 1960s. Diligent Ltd began to buy the seeds from already existing plants. Some women we interviewed complained about low payments. They were themselves peeling the fruits to be able to sell the seeds to the company. The seeds were collected in the villages by a middleman, a villager, who delivered the seeds to the factory and brought payment back to the village. Whether the right amount was paid to the individual village producer was difficult for Diligent to control. The high number of farmers required for the production made contract procedures complicated and costly. We consider this investment to have less risk of negative socio-economic and environmental impacts, since it was based on villagers' existing jatropha hedges. The attitude and ambition of the CEO were similar to those of NGOs.

The company had built a small factory in Arusha using technical equipment to extract the jatropha oil on site. The CEO claimed that by-products such as briquettes and billets were crucial for making the investment profitable. An American NGO supplied energy-saving stoves to villages and introduced briquettes and billets for cooking, but faced some difficulties of adoption among women. Awaiting a more stable domestic market, the oil was exported to the USA for processing and subsequent export to Europe.

In the absence of a Tanzanian biofuel policy, jatropha oil is regarded as an agricultural product in Tanzania. Therefore, payments of fuel levy and custom tax were not obligatory for Diligent Ltd. The company paid only local government tax, which should not exceed 5 per cent of the respective producer farm's gate price (a so-called cess). This is different from petroleum fuel taxes in Tanzania, in which excise and custom taxes are charged as one of the measures for increasing government revenue (Mkenda et al. 2011).

SEKAB/Agro EcoEnergy Tanzania Ltd Agro EcoEnergy Tanzania Ltd (hereafter Eco Energy) is a Swedish company with a concession of 22,000 hectares of land within the Razaba Ranch[4] in the Bagamoyo district. The company plans to grow sugar cane mainly for the domestic market. The Razaba Ranch land has been under state management for decades and no village was located on the land. However, according to the Environmental and Social Impact Analysis (ESIA) from 2008, the ranch is surrounded by three villages and four sub-villages, with a total population of 6,000 people (ORGUT Consulting AB 2008).

The Razaba Ranch land (approximately 28,000 hectares) was given by the Tanzanian government to the government of Zanzibar for cattle production in 1974. However, the cattle ranch was abandoned in 1994. In 2007, the government of Zanzibar agreed to allocate 22,000 hectares of the ranch area to SEKAB Tanzania Ltd, a satellite company of a Swedish company, SEKAB, owned by three Swedish municipalities, on a ninety-nine-year lease (ibid.). Eco Energy gained the right of occupancy to the land in May 2013 (personal communication with Eco Energy management, September 2013). The environmental permit for the project was obtained from the National Environmental Management Council (NEMC) in 2009. The land is planned for irrigated sugar cane production and processing of sugar, ethanol and power, mainly for the domestic market. Surplus ethanol will be distributed to Europe by SEKAB, according to a ten-year agreement (AfDB 2012).

Criticism emerged in Tanzania and Sweden related to the plans of SEKAB Tanzania Ltd, including the company's plans for investment in village land in the Rufiji district. There were also serious accusations regarding the ESIA process (Matondi et al. 2011; Sida Helpdesk 2009). SEKAB Sweden therefore decided to sell its Tanzanian and Mozambique satellite companies. SEKAB Tanzania Ltd was sold to Eco Development in Europe AB, which operates in Tanzania through EcoEnergy, basically under the same management as SEKAB Tanzania Ltd. The investment plan is essentially the same, although the current one comprises a slightly smaller area for sugar cane plantation and more forest plantation in order to supply the factory with wood chips.

When the cattle ranch, run by the government of Zanzibar, was abandoned in 1994, pastoralists moved in, and nearby villages began to use the area for cultivation, firewood collection, hunting and charcoal burning (ORGUT Consulting AB 2008). Some of these villagers now claim that they have rights to this land. While EcoEnergy management informed us that resettlement of these villagers takes place in accordance with International Finance Corporation Performance Standards on Resettlement, the narrative below shows how villagers are confused and claim to have been treated unfairly.

The sub-village we visited in March 2012 was inhabited by villagers who claim to have been resident on the territory of Razaba Ranch itself since the 1960s. Some of them were former workers on the cattle farm. They informed us of the following about their contacts with the district and EcoEnergy:

In October 2011, the Land Officer of the Bagamoyo district council notified the villagers about the intention to acquire land in the sub-village for the Eco-Energy investment. This was more than three years after the land acquisition process began at national level between the company and the government. The villagers were informed that those who were living in the sub-village would be compensated when leaving the land. The procedure for estimating compensation was conducted by the Bagamoyo district land valuer in October/November 2011. A special form was distributed to affected households to register types of immovable properties on their land. The forms were collected by a local government official, accompanied by company representatives. Two weeks later, a representative of EcoEnergy called a meeting with villagers whose properties were registered and informed them that the company intended to give them land inside the Razaba Ranch. However, the Tanzanian government refused and instead promised to provide the villagers with land in villages adjacent to the ranch.

Later, in another village meeting, the EcoEnergy resettlement officer announced that he had access to a satellite image that showed that only thirty-seven households existed in the sub-village. The villagers had not been shown the satellite image. A promise was therefore given to compensate only thirty-seven households and employ the rest of the villagers when EcoEnergy started activities within the ranch. Since the previous evaluation had included more than two hundred households, the villagers got upset and chased the company representative away. A group of villagers subsequently filed a court case against EcoEnergy for 'eviction' of community members from their land and demanded compensation of TZS10 billion[5] (US$6.45 million). The case proceedings were still taking place in July 2012. The villagers were still confused about which thirty-seven households will be compensated, and for how much. And they do not know what will happen to the other households in the sub-village.

According to Bagamoyo district officials, EcoEnergy has signed an agreement with the Tanzanian government that the government will be provided with 25 per cent equity in the company but with anticipation of dividends and capital gains to be paid after eighteen years. According to information obtained through interviews during our field visit, the Tanzanian government has entered a shareholding agreement with EcoEnergy by providing land as its share for equity piloting a new national 'Land for Equity' policy, and the company will offer working capital in the form of the money that was originally invested, along with additional investments required to be made thereafter. According to the Tanzanian minister of land, Dr Anna Tibaijuka, the government is now discussing how these shares could be distributed and benefit the people of Tanzania. One idea discussed was to sell them to the middle class (personal communication with Anna Tibaijuka, October 2012). According to an official of Sida, the original plan was that shares should also be offered at district and village levels (personal communication, October 2012). A Bagamoyo district representative complained during interviews (March 2012) that the district personnel were not involved in the formulation of the agreement between the investor and the government, and it was also claimed that the Bagamoyo district had not received a copy of the agreement.

Subsequent developments have involved the African Development Bank (AfDB), which is coordinating the financial contributions from development institutions to EcoEnergy's Bagamoyo investment. The AfDB has produced a number of reports over recent years, including an extended ESIA and a Resettlement Action Plan (RAP). EcoEnergy is now awaiting a decision from Sida regarding an application for a loan guarantee. Connected with this, Sida has conducted an environmental assessment based on the reports produced by the AfDB and a visit to the company in Tanzania (Sida Helpdesk 2012).

African Green Oil Ltd 'I can feel in my heart this land is still village land. But we are not using the land, because there is no statement from the investor that we can.' This statement reflects the story told by five male smallholder farmers in one of the Rufiji district villages where African Green Oil Ltd (AGO) invested in oil palm plantations in 2009. Only a year later the company disappeared. In this village a 200-hectare oil palm plantation was still standing in March 2012. Nobody in the village knew who had the right to the abandoned land.

AGO is run by a Norwegian investor based in London. AGO engaged smallholders in establishing smaller oil palm plantations in several villages in the Rufiji district during 2009. AGO initiated the investments without the completion of village land use plans and without any contracts signed by village authorities. The main reason for this was related to the procedures of the district officer responsible. He encourages villages to provide land to investors without a contract, in order for the investors to prove that they are serious about their investments. After having proved this seriousness by real work on the land, a formal contract should be arranged. Thus, the AGO invested without having a contractual right to access the land. According to Tanzanian law, the procedure should be the reverse.

The investor was accompanied by district officers when he arrived to negotiate with the village council. The village council accepted the request for land after the investor had listed a number of social services that he would provide if land were made available. AGO promised the village assembly that they would maintain the village water pump so that villagers could get access to domestic water. AGO also agreed to construct classrooms to improve the capacity of the village primary school, and to construct a dispensary in return for land being made available by the village for oil palm investment. However, when the investor received access to the land, he told villagers to show commitment first before the promised education, health and water services would be delivered. Villagers were also supposed to demonstrate to the investor that they were able to collect money and materials needed for development of the social infrastructure. The investor later refused to maintain the village water pump because it was very expensive.

AGO planted 200 hectares with oil palm on land previously used for collecting thatching grass, firewood and timber. The farmers told us about the working conditions during the clearing of land for planting oil palms. Villagers were organized in teams of ten, each team being assigned to uproot trees and pull out stems from one hectare per day. The land was later burnt to remove all vegetation. If the work was not finished in a day, the villagers were not paid the daily wage of TZS2,500 (c. US$1.5). Women especially needed more time for the tasks, and sometimes they earned only TZS2,500 for three days of work. This is not in accordance with the Tanzanian legislation on minimum wages and timing and payment of wages.[6] In 2010, AGO left the village, blaming scarcity of water. The villagers did not believe this: the palms the company left behind are growing and the fruit bunches will soon be ripe enough to harvest. But neither the villagers nor the relevant district officers were sure to whom the land and investment now belonged. The investor neither bought nor leased the land but used village meetings to acquire the land. Villagers have turned to the media to get national attention. They have also met with the TIC to ask questions and discuss their case. There, they learnt that AGO visited the TIC only once. The company then went to the Rufiji district upon the TIC's recommendation, but never came back with any report to the TIC.

Concluding remarks

Large-scale land acquisitions by external investors are not new to Tanzania or other places in Africa but date back to the colonial period. Alden Wily (2012: 1) calls the current wave of land acquisitions 'the continuing capture of ordinary people's rights and assets by capital-led and class-creating social transformation'. Many researchers describe the current land rush as larger in

scale and pace than before and state that the contemporary land struggles in
Africa are different from previous land sales because they seem to be at the
heart of a capitalist crisis of fuel, food and finance (Bush et al. 2011; Matondi
et al. 2011; Margulis et al. 2013).

Large-scale colonial agricultural projects and foreign settler farmers were of
more limited scale in Tanzania when compared with Kenya, Swaziland or Zambia.
The Tanzanian post-independent government thus had a better opportunity than
most other African governments to address land and rural matters. The Tanzanian government made use of this option when President Julius Nyerere, in the
late 1960s, implemented a major restructuring of the rural areas – the so-called
Ujamaa strategy. The process, however, was not anchored in the country's laws
and constitution. This led to major confusions and conflicts when economic
liberalization emerged in the late 1980s and weakened the power of the state.
The subsequent policy and legal processes reaffirmed the land management
role of Tanzanian villages, which should be based on village land certificates
and village households' land certificates, in which the name of the spouse also
had to be registered. However, according to the Land Laws of 1999, the radical
title to the land continued to rest with the president and was to be managed
on his/her behalf by the Commissioner of Land.

Village land use plans were to be followed and implemented by state agencies and ministries. These plans should guide village land use and should help
to identify possible use of village land by others, including investors. Nearly
two-thirds of Tanzanian land thus came under village management. Currently,
Tanzania has about 12,000 registered villages, but only about 1,000 of these
have village land certificates and village land use plans.

Our case studies comprise different organizational models: (1) where agrofuel is already being produced by villages (jatropha); (2) where village land is
converted from food to agrofuel (oil palm); and (3) where state land is leased
to a private company for sugar production (sugar cane plantation). In all cases
the investors are European: British, Swedish and Norwegian/British.

During the last decade there has been a growing interest on the part
of external investors in Tanzanian and African land for the production of
energy (agrofuel) and food for export. The Tanzanian state, in cooperation
with donors, had since the mid-1980s been focusing on structural adjustment,
debt and poverty reduction, and democratization. Only from the latter half of
the 1990s did the Tanzanian state begin preparations for an institutional and
legal framework for attracting foreign investments.

In parallel, the Tanzanian state shifted its strategic emphasis concerning
agricultural development from villages and smallholder farming to large-scale
farming. Gradually, many stakeholders came to acknowledge that the Tanzanian
village-based land management system posed obstructions to providing collateral for banks issuing agricultural credits and loans, as well as to freeing

land for foreign investors. Pressures to amend the Land Laws to accommodate these concerns consequently emerged even before the implementation of the Tanzanian laws had taken hold.

Overall, in our assessment, the historical and recent developments have pointed to a lack of clarity about Tanzanian land management, including a lack of clarity in procedures for identifying and freeing land for foreign investors. Our research confirms that the Tanzanian land management system and the institutions involved are facing major challenges in adhering to laws and regulations. A major problem is the limited implementation of village land demarcations and village land use plans, which should be in place before allocation of village land to external interests. These problems are related both to historical processes of land ownership and management and to the lack of capacity of the Tanzanian state to implement and enforce laws and regulations.

Our research shows that procedures for foreign investors to access land for investment have become ad hoc and that Tanzanian institutions do not have a full overview of what is going on in the sector, nor do state officials at various levels follow laws and regulations. Direct meetings and negotiations between investors and village authorities for identifying land for investors, which are encouraged by the TIC, often lead to high expectations, misunderstandings and conflicts which affect potential investment plans and their implementation.

Of the thirty-two investors that we identified who had requested large tracts of land (over two thousand hectares) for agrofuel production in Tanzania during the last decade, only ten investors actually acquired land, of a total area of approximately 200,000 hectares. This amounted to only about 20 per cent of the total land requested (1.1 million hectares). Our findings also show a large gap between the number of land allocations for investments (ten) and implementation of the investments. Hence, the overall tendency is for land requests not to be met and for implementation of investments based on land allocations to be very slow and/or unsuccessful. Our assessment is that this development is caused by a number of factors, including historical, institutional and efficiency problems, such as ineffective policy formulation processes, lack of financing and droughts, and governance problems, such as contradictory policies and inconsistent enforcement, also described, for example, by Hultman et al. (2012) and Nelson et al. (2012).

The detailed investigation of the case studies where implementation actually did begin made these problems more concrete. They related to conflicts over land and settlement rights (EcoEnergy), faulty procedures in land allocations (Rufiji district), lack of investor realization of promises (AGO), uncertainty as to who could manage abandoned village land (Rufiji district/AGO), and lack of profitability (Diligent Ltd). In addition to this global market conditions have changed. The EU recently decided to reduce its targets for future use of certain crop-based agrofuels (e.g. sugar cane), subsidies for ethanol are being reduced, ethanol has to be produced sustainably, and the discussions about indirect land use change, which are still unresolved, may have a negative impact on the future global market for agrofuels.

The large-scale investments that are operational are investments in food crops such as rice and sugar cane for sugar production. The vast majority of investments, if not all, are in former state-owned land. For example, several of these estates gained access to the land in connection with processes of privatization of state farms in 2006.[7]

Managing expectations among local communities seems to pose a major challenge for investors. The importance of allowing enough time to perform thorough studies about soil quality, weather patterns and current and future impacts of climate change is also clear. It is crucial that investors have an in-depth knowledge about local culture and values, and the question is to what extent these investments really can use the current livelihood strategies and needs as a basis to build upon. And if they cannot use them, is a win-win situation really likely to be the result when these widely different cultures, market systems and technologies meet?

3 | Kenya and the 'global land grab': a view from below

Jacqueline M. Klopp and Odenda Lumumba

Introduction

During the food crisis in 2007/08, 'global land grabbing' – the acquisition or long-term lease of land in Africa, Asia and Latin America by investors, usually foreign – emerged as a serious concern among smallholder farmers and advocates of food security. Kenya is one country that directly experienced this global land grab; a number of new large-scale foreign investments in land-based enterprises occurred around the 2007/08 crisis,[1] especially in the rich Tana River Delta. However, to Kenya this grabbing was not a fundamentally new phenomenon. In fact, land grabbing is both popularly perceived and academically theorized in Kenya as part of the way Kenyan politics has operated since the days of imperial conquest and colonization, and continuing up to the present.

The protectorate and subsequent colonial government of Kenya set up a system of land administration and governance that privileged access to land for colonial state projects and a narrow band of foreign citizens, companies and investors. In contrast, 'natives' became 'tenants of the crown' (Okoth-Ogendo 1991). In the post-colonial period, local elites consolidated their power and position through exploitation of unreformed laws and the existing administrative system and practices around land. This overall system continued to favour centralized and unaccountable control over land, allowing politically connected actors to accumulate and speculate in land, all the while continuing a history of marginalization and dispossession of the poorer groups in society. It is thus hardly surprising that severe inequality in land access and ownership afflicts the country and, in fact, is getting worse (World Bank 2008).

As a result of this history, land grabbing in Kenya is more broadly understood as the irregular and illegal allocation of a wide array of public land (Republic of Kenya 2002, 2004). Such public land could include anything from small public utility plots to large swathes of forest, as well as agricultural land, which is the primary focus of a growing group of international actors. This means land grabbing impacts not only farmers and pastoralists, agricultural production, food security and forests but also cities. Cities are where rural migrants take refuge and where foreign and local investors also have hotels and other real estate, and where both informal settlements and inequality are growing. In turn, as these growing urban areas sprawl, often via these same problematic land transactions, this feeds into pressures on valuable ecosystems and agricultural land (Mundia and Aniya 2006). Overall, this makes land grabbing at the local level a more complex phenomenon than is often portrayed in current global discourses, where the notion of a land grab tends to be a 'catch-all phrase to describe and analyze the current explosion of large-scale (trans) national commercial land transactions' (Borras et al. 2011: 210) – usually rural.

Out of this experience, networks of land reform advocates in Kenya focus not only on resisting land grabbing and improving the regulatory environment around land transactions, but also on a deeper transformation of unaccountable land laws and management systems – and on the practices and values that have grown up to normalize and legitimize these systems. This means that the common focus of attention in discussions of the 'global land grab' – large-scale foreign investment in agricultural land – is just a subset of the many kinds of 'grabbing' that are taking place, one of many fronts in the struggle against the manipulation of land rights by powerful politicians and state actors who – as in colonial times – are also the partners and brokers in deals with large-scale investors, if not 'investors' themselves.

For these reasons, this chapter aims to explain and examine the Kenyan experience with land grabbing and the light it can shed on the global land grab debates. We argue for a deeper historical understanding of the political economy and sociology of locally experienced land grabbing – and, very importantly, the movement that aims to transform the current dynamics around land and power. This local lens provides one way to better grasp the kinds of contextual and specific institutional changes required to combat manipulation of land rights by the powerful (indigenous or foreign) and move towards a more just and sustainable order with regard to land tenure and management.

To begin, we briefly show how key land governance institutions, born within conquest, have persisted into the post-colonial period and how they allow for massive manipulation of land – which primarily benefits local elites, especially those with privileged access to state institutions, particularly the Ministry of Lands and the President's Office. While most recent land grabbing in Kenya is domestic, the same institutional structure and network of actors who facilitate local land grabbing also mediate foreign investors' access to land. As a result, as in other parts of Africa, a number of opaque deals have been struck in Kenya for leasing land, exacerbating an already contentious and inequitable situation. However, we situate these large-scale foreign acquisitions of land within a continuous land grabbing practice in existence since colonial times. Without key reforms, increasing pressures stemming from growing demand for arable land, other land-based natural resources and energy are bound to make the existing situation worse.

We also show how resistance to land grabbing – a central part of Kenya's colonial history – re-emerged in force in the 1990s and has continued up to the present, culminating in a movement for reform. This struggle has led to a new policy and institutional and legal framework, including a National Land Policy (Republic of Kenya 2009), Chapter 5 in Kenya's new Constitution (Republic of Kenya 2010), and a set of new land laws aimed at dismantling the old institutions and developing stronger public oversight in land allocations and management. In theory, some of these reforms could dramatically alter general public accountability and decision-making around land allocation, control and use, including the way in which negotiations with external investors will be conducted. However, these changes, emerging out of a long and difficult internal struggle, might yet be subverted and reversed, precisely because the interests around the old system are so great. Finally, we argue that even though the global discourse on the global land grab differs from more localized understandings of land grabbing, this discourse has been helpful to local struggles. By drawing more global attention to the details of how land transactions are conducted and for whose benefit, the focus on the global land grab has helped foster more welcome scrutiny and generate broader support for the kinds of deep institutional reform that need to take place locally.

The origins of the system of land grabbing

The intimate connection between state power and the dynamics of land tenure is central to Kenya's history. Conquest of territory and land, spurred on by geopolitical manoeuvring, resulted in a British Protectorate (1895) and later a settler colony of Kenya (1920). Within this struggle a dualistic land tenure system was set up by the evolving colonial state. This system privileged settlers with individual leasehold (sometimes leases were for a unique 999 years in rural areas) or freehold rights to land. In contrast, using notions from feudal law, Africans were subjects of 'customary law' and as such effectively deemed 'tenants of the crown' (Okoth-Ogendo 1991). This meant that large tracts of fertile land were appropriated for settler or colonial government use, while the state tried to contain 'natives' in ethnically defined reserves. By reducing access to land, common resources and mobility, this reserve system helped generate pressures for Africans to search for labour in settler farms, plantations or the growing towns dotting the railway lines that brought in supplies and moved goods to the ports.

The colonial land tenure system thus entrenched inequality of rights between settlers and natives and gave opaque administrative structures linked to the most powerful office (the governor, later the president and his principal agent, the Commissioner of Lands) enormous discretionary power to blatantly manipulate land rights. This system also created enormous inequalities. By 1944, the amount of land alienated to Europeans, including multinational corporations, was estimated to be 3 million hectares, of which only 350,000 were actually in cultivation; the number of settlers was 2,000; the number of farms 2,700; and the 'amount of undeveloped land was so extensive that the government was considering the necessity of introducing a tax on undeveloped land' (Meek 1949: 79). To make this land productive, white settlers hired African labourers from reserves who were often allowed to farm some of the land. In this way these 'squatters' put labour into this land and understood this to mean they had legitimate rights over it (Kanogo 1987). In the 1950s, a series of crackdowns, including evictions of African labourer/farmers, precipitated the bloody struggle over land and freedom that would become known to the world as 'Mau Mau'.

As part of what was a vicious counter-insurgency strategy, the state initiated land reform in the native reserves, extending leasehold land rights to certain Africans. The Swynnerton Plan of 1954 involved a break from allowing private land for settlers and 'public' or 'trust' land for natives. It extended land registration, consolidation and leasehold land to the reserves; and with the broad discretionary powers of the state, it did so in a way that favoured collaboration and punished supporters of Mau Mau, some of whom were also put to work in the Mwea rice farm, a state-run agricultural scheme[2] (Clough 1998). The reforms were structured to effectively create allies among collaborating Africans for the existing legal and institutional framework around land. The plan noted that 'in future these able, energetic or rich Africans will be able to acquire more land and the bad or poor farmers less, creating a landed and landless class. This is the normal step in the evolution of a country' (Swynnerton 1954: 10). Ultimately, the violent upheavals of Mau Mau and the horrifying, brutal colonial response helped catalyse independence by 1963.

At independence, how to deal with the thorny questions around land became a central political issue. One political faction, led by Oginga Odinga and Bildad Kaggia, argued for the reappropriation of white farms to settle the landless. In contrast, another faction, led by Kenyatta and Mboya, argued for a gradual approach of buying out white farms. When Kenyatta won the first election and became prime minister (and then later president), this meant that both the gradualist view of land reform and the centralization of power won out (Kanyinga et al. 2008). Land reform in the post-colonial period largely consisted of buying out European farms with World Bank and British government loans and creating settlement schemes.

The aim of these schemes, including the famous One Million Acre Scheme, was to ease the pressures of former Mau Mau and other landless and also to build a multi-ethnic country, with people buying land in schemes if they could afford it or could access a political connection. Scholars throughout the 1970s and 1980s noted that the way these settlement schemes unfolded allowed for manipulation by politicians and administrators and the incorporation of scheme access into patronage networks (Harbeson 1971; Leys 1975; Hunt 1984; Leo 1984). In line with the Swynnerton Plan vision of the 'wealthy progressive farmer', grants of large farms were made to Kenyatta, his family and politicians associated with him, making them wealthy and often politically influential. Indeed, the Kenyatta family continues to have both large tracts of land and a large stake in Kenyan politics.[3]

The Kenyan experience of land grabbing

While the problems with settlement programmes are widely known and documented, less recognized is the extent to which the colonial land laws and administrative apparatus (including state-run agriculture through entities like the National Irrigation Board) also remained in place in the post-colonial period, facilitating irregular and illegal land accumulation or 'grabbing'. This institutional structure included centralized control by the President's Office and the president's principal agent, the Commissioner of Lands (located in the Ministry of Lands), over lands appropriated by the colonial state and managed by the governor during the colonial period.

Most land in post-colonial Kenya fell under the categories of government (former Crown lands) and trust land (from the 'native reserves'). Both categories of land were highly open to directives from the president via the Commissioner of Lands in the Ministry of Lands. The ministry, which has land offices in the districts, also manages the registries where records of land transfers are made. While some provisions for public input through auctions were originally required for land to be allocated to individuals or companies, this requirement was routinely ignored and eventually dropped altogether. As in other parts of Africa, 'customary' rights were eroded and common property poorly protected within this system (Wily 2011), which was in many ways designed precisely to legalize alienation of those lands.

What this means in practice is that the land-accumulating practices of the connected and powerful, now the African political elite with state ties, persist to this day. This involves exploiting the opaque bureaucratic administrative mechanisms of the Ministry of Lands and a legal framework designed to facilitate land acquisition for the few. In fact, the costs of following the land and planning laws are exorbitant and involve so many actors (who can demand bribes) that this leads to the ubiquity of informal processes whereby networks of politicians and bureaucrats in the Ministry of Lands act as gatekeepers (Musyoka 2004; Ayonga et al. 2010). Those who are in a position to benefit from these processes, both in terms of extracting payments and in terms of accessing land, are bureaucrats and politicians and their financers and supporters, as well as the many professionals among lawyers, surveyors and developers who assist them (Manji 2012). As in colonial times, manipulating access to land and preying on the dependency created by this system remained and remains a useful political tool (Klopp 2008; Onoma 2008). Evidence of this is the way that land grabbing tends to spike prior to elections (Klopp 2000; Republic of Kenya 2004; Onyango 2012).

From resistance to reform

While Kenya's history has been filled until recently with struggles around land, its management and distribution, democratic space did not exist for a national public dialogue on how to address the glaring problems of land maldistribution, misgovernance and mismanagement. The opening of political space through the often violent and difficult struggles for democratic change in the 1990s allowed for much more public exposure of what Kenyans called 'land grabbing' or the irregular and illegal accumulation of public lands by the politically connected. An emboldened and often courageous press began to report on irregular accumulation of key public lands such as forests, school compounds and High Court grounds by politicians and bureaucrats, and also chronicled the numerous public protests against this 'grabbing' (Klopp 2000).

In response to mounting public alarm and civil society activism, in November 1999 the government appointed a commission led by former attorney-general Charles Njonjo to look into the land law system. The resulting report revealed widespread public concern over the need to curb presidential powers over land, to harmonize and clarify the law, and overall to add more public oversight to land matters more generally (Republic of Kenya 2002). This concern also emerged within countrywide consultations on constitutional review at the time. Indeed, an overview report on Kenya's constitutional review process in 2001/02 identified land as a key issue of public concern and noted that 'the majority of those interviewed complained bitterly about a repeat of what happened during the colonial period. People in positions of authority are grabbing land left, right and centre' (Kituo cha Katiba 2002: 24).

In December 2002, an opposition coalition won a historic election. This resulted in the first transfer of power from the political party (the Kenya African National Union) which had been in power since independence and which had effectively colonized the state, to the National Rainbow Coalition (NARC), led by Mwai Kibaki. Mwai Kibaki was sworn in as the new president with promises to reform the Constitution. Widespread anger at land grabbing in the run-up to the election prompted the new president to appoint the Presidential Commission of Inquiry into the Illegal and/or Irregular Allocation of Public Land (Ndung'u Commission). Unsurprisingly, it faced many challenges in terms of adequate budget and also lack of cooperation by the lands' administration and provincial administration under the President's Office. Despite the fact that the commission included several permanent secretaries, including the one in charge of corruption in the President's Office, many officials colluded in forestalling investigations and public hearings on knotty land grab cases involving the former president and other public officials. Clearly, these officials had an interest in holding back crucial self-incriminating information. Nevertheless, the final report from the commission revealed an enormous loss of public lands (at least 246,965 hectares of trust and government lands) in irregular and outright illegal deals, often linked to politicians, bureaucrats and their briefcase companies registered for the purpose of acquiring land in an irregular way (Republic of Kenya 2004; Syagga and Mwenda 2010). The costs to the public purse are staggering to consider.[4]

In 2003, the NARC government, which included some reformers, moved forward slowly on a fledgling land policy reform process. Significantly, for the first time this process led by the Ministry of Lands engaged civil society organizations. Fourteen regional consultations and other stakeholder meetings took place to review and critique emerging issues and recommend their redress in a new draft land policy, which now included civil society feedback.[5] Key to the process was the Kenya Land Alliance (KLA), which emerged as a way to constructively engage in the complex land problems and struggles that had intensified in the 1990s. The KLA is 'a not-for-profit and non-partisan umbrella network of Civil Society Organisations and Individuals committed to effective advocacy for the reform of policies and laws governing land in Kenya',[6] and it involves a variety of civil society organizations, which made up the thematic teams that looked at specific categories of land problems, ranging from pastoralist to urban informal settlement issues. The KLA very capably led the effort, organizing meetings and pushing the government towards change.

One interesting element to the reform process was the shifting position of international donors. During the Cold War, land reform, associated with leftist politics, fell off the agenda. In the 1980s and 1990s, which were dominated by the 'Washington Consensus', the focus was on protecting private property rights within structural adjustment. With the end of the Cold War, the failure of structural adjustment programmes and deepening concerns about both poverty and growing inequality, land reform has since returned as a focus, bolstered by research suggesting the importance of equitable land distributions and policies for development (De Janvry and Sadoulet 2002; World Bank 2005). Yet land reform had never fallen off the agenda in Africa; rather, it was simply suppressed. With democratization, concerns around land inequalities and problematic land-use decisions leading to poverty, deforestation, urban sprawl and other issues became part of a public debate that international development actors could hardly ignore.

In Kenya we see this shift in global development discourse and its impact. After years of shying away from land issues as 'too sensitive', a number of key donors began to encourage the government-led land policy reform initiative by providing technical and financial support to both the government and the KLA. In 2004 the Kenya Development Partners Group on Land (DPGL)[7] came together to support the Ministry of Lands 'in the development of a land policy framework, which deals with historical injustices, informal settlement upgrading and urban land management'.[8] However, despite this rhetoric, most support has been for the more technical, ostensibly less political, goal of introducing a better Land Information Management System.

Current progress on land reform also accelerated in response to the violence emerging out of the highly contested election in December 2007.[9] The National Accord brokered by Kofi Annan and signed by the two warring sides, Mwai Kibaki (Party of National Unity) and Raila Odinga (Orange Democratic Movement), stipulated the need for constitutional change, including reform of land governance. Some progress has been made five years on. On 3 December 2009, Sessional Paper No. 3 of 2009 on National Land Policy was passed and became official policy. Many of the changes proposed in the Sessional Paper made it into Chapter 5 of the new Constitution on Land and Environment. In 2011 an Environment and Land Court Act was passed, and, as of November 2012, sixteen judges have been appointed to the court and more will be needed for deployment in more marginalized areas with major land problems.

Key land legislation has also been repealed and replaced by three Land Acts that passed and became law in 2012 (the Land Act, the National Land Commission Act, and the Land Registration Act). And yet another key piece of legislation, to manage 'community lands' (including former trust lands), is in the process of being formulated.

Overall, key elements of existing reform include establishing an independent National Land Commission, rewriting and harmonizing fragmented and overlapping land laws, digitizing and rendering land records transparent to the public, and creating instruments to provide disincentives to hoarding land (better records and taxation, land ceilings). While these reforms could foster new levels of transparency and accountability around land transactions, all of them are facing various levels of resistance in the implementation phase.

Take, for example, the establishment of an independent National Land Commission. According to the Constitution (Section 67, Chapter 5), this new body is to a) manage public land on behalf of the national and county governments; b) recommend a national land policy to the government; c) advise the national government on a comprehensive programme for the registration of title in land throughout Kenya; d) conduct research related to land and the use of natural resources; e) initiate investigations on its own initiative, or on a complaint, into historical land injustices and recommend appropriate redress; f) encourage the application of traditional dispute resolution mechanisms in land conflicts; g) assess tax on land and premiums on immovable property in any area designated by law; and h) monitor and have oversight responsibilities over land-use planning in the country. Public land is now defined (Section 62, Chapter 5) as including the former unalienated government land that was previously governed by the now repealed Government Lands Act. It was this Act which gave the president and his principal agent, the Commissioner of Lands, too many opaque powers of allocation. Thus, this reform is designed to give local people more say over public land through direct participation and indirect representation through democratic county assemblies, with the National Land Commission helping them administer land and set land policy. This is intended to help curb the abuses so clearly articulated in the Njonjo and Ndung'u commissions (Republic of Kenya 2002, 2004) and democratize decision-making over land use.

Despite the passage of the National Land Commission Act (2012), which stipulates that the president should appoint the commissioners seven days after receiving their names, the president delayed in appointing the commissioners vetted by parliament. It was only after two citizens (one from Turkana and the other from Mombasa), supported by the Economic and Social Rights Centre (Hakijamii) and the Kenya Land Alliance, took the president to court and he was deemed in violation of the law that he formally gazetted the commissioners. Fears further exist that the commission will be undermined by both lack of budget appropriations in the 2012/13 National Budget for its functioning and the attempt by the Ministry of Lands to have the commission hire ministry officials and have the new commission generally dependent on the ministry. Furthermore, the current law maintains the land registry within the ministry, and sorting through ministry records and rendering them open and transparent will be a serious struggle for the commission and civil society. Finally, the process of developing the new land laws, led by consultants, has been poorly organized, with inadequate discussion and participation by independent experts and the public (Manji forthcoming). This fact and the existence of errors and inconsistencies in language have given rise to pressures for review, which is currently taking place. Overall, then, the process of reform is only just beginning; but if the intent and spirit of the new legal and policy framework are followed, it will be more difficult to allocate large tracts of public or community land against the will and interest of local communities.

The 'global land grab' viewed from Kenya

At the same time as reform networks such as the KLA struggled to get new policy, legal and institutional frameworks into place to create more transparency, accountability and inclusion in decision-making about land, the spike in global food prices hit in 2007/08. Like other parts of the world, Kenya experienced a number of new large-scale investments in land-based enterprises. In Table 3.1 we have tried to summarize these investments, although – because of the poor transparency of some of these deals – it was not always easy to access up-to-date and accurate information (Makutsa 2010; Nunow 2013). What is shown in the table is derived from various media and policy sources and was cross-checked whenever possible.

From this summary, we can make a number of observations. First, a number of these investments preceded the 2007/08 crisis, the most prominent case being the ongoing and controversial Yala Swamp project of Dominion Farms Ltd. Begun in 2003, it aims to produce food, some ostensibly for local consumption.[10] This project reflects the fact that prior to the food crisis, Kenya had a long history of large-scale commercial farming and an official policy of encouraging foreign investment in such farms, dating from colonial times to the present (Smalley and Corbera 2012). Institutions that allow political access to trust land (now community land) facilitate this process by providing access to large tracts of land to companies via political brokers within the system. In the Yala Swamp case, politicians, including the then prime minister's brother and local councillors from Siaya and Bondo county councils, were the brokers (FIAN 2010; Makutsa 2010). Local councils, custodians of former 'trust lands', have been notorious for withholding information, failing to hold public consultations, and distorting decisions for private gain (KARA 2011). Makutsa, in her study for the Eastern Africa Farmers' Federation, noted that 'in most cases the local authorities do not present the proposals to the communities that will be affected', although they do sometimes hold meetings to introduce the investor (2010: 28).

Secondly, we observe that many proposed investments have stalled, becoming entangled in legal battles and facing resistance from below. If a project has begun at all, such as in the case of Bedford Biofuels, farming is occurring on only small portions of the entire land ostensibly allotted. Another obstacle for a number of companies, including Bedford Biofuels, is obtaining a licence from NEMA,[11] a process that can take many years. In the cases of Jatropha Kenya Ltd, which had already cut down precious Dakatcha forest to plant part of its crop in Malindi, a licence was denied. The environmental and social impact assessment process in Kenya is still flawed from the point of view of protection of local communities and their environment. Little emphasis is placed on the social impacts within the assessment process. Furthermore, the way environmental impact assessments are conducted by investors themselves can raise conflicts of interest that corrupt the process (Barczewski 2013). Nevertheless, the licensing process has slowed down a number of these projects, creating space for more public dialogue and mobilization.

It is worth noting that some projects have in fact been cancelled. One of the most prominent cases is the proposed project by the Emirate of Qatar to grow food for export in exchange for financing to build a port at Lamu, on the Kenyan coast.[12] Another is G4 Industries, which pulled out citing environmental concerns. Overall, one striking aspect is the extent and success of local resistance to these deals. This resistance emerges both from local

TABLE 3.1 Summary table of some recent large-scale land investments in Kenya

Investor	Investor country	Sector	Crop	Hectares	Location	Official start date and status
HG Consulting	Belgium	Food	Sugar cane	42,000	Homa Bay	Begun in 2007. Continuing
Bedford Biofuels	Canada	Energy	Jatropha (60,000 ha)	160,000 (perhaps acquiring an additional 200,000)	Tana River Delta	Begun in 2008. First crops planted 2011 (19,000 ha). Ended in 2013.
Biwako Bio-Laboratory	Japan	Energy	Jatropha	30,000	Kwale	Begun in 2007. Status unclear
Bioenergy International	Switzerland	Energy	Jatropha	93,000		
Green Power Holding AG	Switzerland	Energy	Jatropha	30,000		
Tiomin Kenya Ltd	Canada/ local subsidiary China	Mining	Titanium	20,000	Kwale	Begun in 2006 (mining licence acquired). Project stalled
Galole Horticulture Project	Kenya	Food	Maize	5,000	Tana River Delta	Status unclear
Xenerga & Eurofuel tech	Germany/ USA	Energy	Jatropha	100,000		Status unclear
Emirate of Qatar	Qatar	Food		40,000	Tana River Delta	Begun in 2008. Frozen and cancelled

Investor	Investor country	Sector	Crop	Hectares	Location	Official start date and status
G4 Industries	England	Energy	Oil seed	28,911	Tana River Delta	Begun in 2008. Cancelled 2011
Tana and Athi Rivers Development Authority (TARDA)- Mat International		Food	Sugar	120,000	Tana River Delta	Agreement signed in 2005. Ongoing
TARDA-Mumias Sugar Company	Kenya Govt/ Para-statal	Food	Sugar/rice	28,680 Possible additional 40,000 for food	Tana River Delta	Lease 1995; title 2008. NEMA grants conditional licence for 5,000 ha rice farm 2009. Court ruling upholds rights. Ongoing
Yala Swamp-Dominion Farm	USA	Food	Rice/fish	6,900	Nyanza	Begun in 2003. Ongoing
Jatropha Kenya Ltd/ Nuove Iniziative Industrali	Italy/ Kenyan subsidiary	Energy	Jatropha	50, 000	Malindi	Begun in 2009 NEMA denies licence for 10,000 ha pilot (2012)

actors who feel excluded from the negotiation process and access to resources, and from environmental organizations, local and foreign (Dixon 2013). Often these groups work in tandem to form a coalition, challenging the viability and raising questions about the likely impacts of these projects, using the media, protests and institutional mechanisms – such as public meetings, the environmental impact assessment and licensing process, and the High Court – to argue their case.

Another important observation is that a considerable number of investors are in fact government bodies, Kenyan companies or Kenyan individuals. In particular, the Tana and Athi River Development Authority (TARDA), a state corporation, has been involved in separate deals with Mumias Sugar Company, a public company, and Mat International, a private Kenyan company, to develop large-scale sugar cane plantations and create energy from the waste. Interestingly, in their study comparing the TARDA-Mumias Sugar and Bedford Biofuel deals, Smalley and Corbera found that the outside investor, Bedford, negotiated to formalize and recognize local land rights in a more collaborative way, while TARDA attempted to override local claims (2012: 1065).

Finally, a number of these investments are clearly linked to the push for biofuels and the new opportunities arising in this area. To the extent that critiques of jatropha as a biofuel gain force,[13] we can expect some of the pressure on farmland for this crop to possibly decline. However, the struggle to appropriate the last remaining commons in Kenya, such as in the Tana River Delta or Yala Swamp, will no doubt continue.[14]

Conclusions

The struggle to appropriate land for large-scale farming in Kenya against the claims of local people, including smallholder farmers and pastoralists, and without recognition of the environmental functions of many commons, has deep historical roots. Thus, even prior to the food crisis in 2007/08, Kenya was experiencing attempts by new foreign investors to access land for plantation farming, a practice which has continued uninterrupted from colonial times in many parts of the country. Current investment and agricultural policy and institutional frameworks around land are skewed in favour of opaque, top-down and politically negotiated deals, not only with foreign companies but also with Kenyan firms and public entities such as TARDA. Strikingly, official discourse still tends to favour 'progressive (i.e. wealthy, large-scale) farmers', much as the Swynnerton Plan did in 1954. This is to the disadvantage of smallholder farmers, who require more critical assistance to access land and improve productivity, but still provide the best bet for food security, environmental stewardship and equitable economic growth in the region (Rugasira 2013).

Nevertheless, large-scale deals to acquire or lease land have been confronted by substantial resistance, resistance that we expect to grow in the context of

Kenya's reform movement. We have shown that advocacy efforts in the last two decades have led to nascent, fundamental reforms, which, if successful, will help open up decision-making around land and rein in all forms of what Kenyans understand as land grabbing, including large-scale allocations of agricultural land. These reforms will also open up new venues such as the Environment and Land Court, county government and County Land Management Boards for local citizens and experts to have more say in how their land is managed and used and by whom. We have seen that movements against large-scale farming have already effectively used political spaces to mobilize, stall or halt a number of projects. With a more level legal and institutional environment, we can expect these public dialogues and mobilizations to gain strength.

Kenya has made impressive strides in terms of putting land governance and management on a more equitable, sustainable and ethical foundation; but relative to the need for change, the progress in implementing the new land governance system is slow. Members of the political class who have gained access to land by irregular and illegal means, their companies and foreign partners, and the banks, which have lent large sums of money based on land as collateral, will all try to undermine and stall changes to the status quo. Another roadblock to reform is the link between the political class and the landed and bureaucratic class that has benefited from facilitating these transactions. This is a strong and powerful constituency, which will resist land tenure reform and any measures, such as taxation, that hint at redistribution. Thus, it is hardly surprising that the Kenya Landowners Association has emerged as the National Land Policy's fiercest overt critic, determined to sabotage the new land policy and laws through legislative revision.

As the details of the land reform agenda are worked out through legislation and negotiation, there is a strong possibility that it can be undermined. For example, there are deliberate inconsistencies and typology errors in the new land laws that can either defeat or undermine the accountability and independence of the National Land Commission, and its yet-to-be-established devolved offices at county government level. Finally, implementation and institutionalization of legislation may also be subverted at the stage of providing guidelines, budget and staff for new institutions. Strong public awareness, pressure and input will be critical to avoid this.

Much will also depend on reformers within the state who are not aligned with these interests, and their supporters in civil society and among the wider public. Wider reforms will require resources, facilitation and careful implementation by the state. Since the current land tenure system and land distribution adversely affect large numbers of people, including businesses and developers locked out of land by the opaque dealings of the politically connected, a broad and populous coalition for reform is possible, utilizing democratic spaces.

In the end, the current large-scale land acquisitions in Kenya, exacerbated by global trends, including the search for biofuels and new investment opportunities by Wall Street, represent the last frontier of expansion for large-scale farming into the remaining rangelands, commons and areas where smallholder farmers have particularly poorly protected claims for historical reasons. Whether internal democratic and constitutional reform movements can finally enable a break from Kenya's long history of land injustice and dispossession and put the country on to a more equitable and sustainable trajectory remains to be seen. For now, to the extent that debates over the 'global land grab' help to raise critical questions about Africa's often weak and, in many cases, still-to-be-decolonized land governance systems, these debates play a constructive role. However, we need to get beyond the hype and move towards concrete, constructive support for local movements struggling with the complex and difficult task of transforming existing governance systems. These are the systems that enable the sidelining of large numbers of citizens and the allocation of shockingly large tracts of land to small numbers of state entities, companies and individuals for their often problematic and destructive projects.

Latin America

4 | The rapid expansion of genetically modified soy production into the Chaco region of Argentina

Lucia Goldfarb and Annelies Zoomers[1]

Introduction

There is no doubt that one of the most striking transformations that has taken place in Argentina over the last two decades is the enormous expansion in soybean cultivation and the speed with which rural life and landscape have changed. Some have already witnessed this process closely and since its inception, although few in the 1970s and 1980s imagined how extensively these beans could be planted. What nature and technology permitted at that time enabled capitalized farmers to dream of a pampean region covered with soy, but nobody imagined that soy would invade the margins of the roads, would reach the limits of the poorest suburbs of larger Argentine cities, would replace millions of hectares of native forests, and that the pampas landscape would extend to both the Chaco region and Patagonia and even into the Delta.

However, this massive and rapid process was relatively invisible to the general urban public, soybean monoculture being on the whole praised in the mainstream media while its consequences were not openly discussed. In this context, politics took a long time to adopt the idea that there could be a problem. Since the 1990s, successive governments may not have always promoted soy expansion directly, but all took a laissez-faire policy attitude. Concerned institutions have also proceeded through non-transparent decision processes in the application of promotional measures. Only with the outbreak of a conflict between the national government and the agricultural business associations (*Mesa de Enlace*) on export taxes in 2008 was the power of soya producers noticed and the relevance of the sector for the national economy broadly recognized – although this was only the beginning of a debate that most probably will continue for many years.

In the context of a global rush for agricultural land – the 'hype' that this book refers to – the expansion of the frontiers of soy fields in Argentina can be seen as one of the most impressive processes in terms of the number of hectares and resources involved and the abrupt change of land use and landscape, as well as the economic, environmental and social consequences. However, 'hype' may not be the most appropriate term in this context. Agriculturization, pampeanization and soya-ization processes have an older history in Argentina, which – in combination with liberalization and overall commoditization – led to the soy boom around the 2000s. Likewise, land concentration, vertical integration and the presence of foreign capital are not unique to the soy chain. In a context in which the national debate is still in its infancy, the context of the 'global hype' may offer a good opportunity to gauge the latest changes in the control of land from both historical and global perspectives.

In order to address the implications of increasing pressures on natural resources – and land in particular – paying attention to processes triggered by soy expansion in the country, especially outside the central pampas region, becomes very relevant. Roughly speaking, the soy boom has been explained by the rise in international prices in the context of a growing demand for feed and energy crops, by technological development – genetically modified (GM)[2] soy and associated technology packages – and by changing relationships based on tenure, access and control over land. Therefore, it becomes important to understand the institutional context in which these relationships have favoured both the expansion of the soy frontier and its links with the concentration of land and other natural resources (in fewer, often non-local, hands), and how these processes have turned extensive Argentine landscapes and livelihoods into commodities.

This chapter, based on fieldwork carried out in Argentina between 2011 and 2012, provides a critical analysis of the rapid expansion of soy and the implications for inclusive and sustainable development. In it, we look at the features of the current and earlier soy expansion, the actors involved and the consequences – especially for the Chaco region, the most recent frontier of expansion. More particularly, we focus on exploring why – in spite of huge transformations – the expansion of the soy frontier continued 'quickly' without much contestation and outside the realm of 'dominant' discourses on land grabbing. It is only relatively recently – since the hype – that more attention has been given to the negative environmental and social impacts. Given the speed of soy expansion, it is important to ask what the drivers are and how it is possible to control the negative consequences on the environment and local livelihoods.

The chapter will begin with a historical overview of how the soy frontier expanded, followed by an analysis of the drivers. In exploring the dynamics of the GM soy frontier expansion, we will draw a distinction between three dimensions: the technology frontier, the land control frontier and the frontier of expanding capital (determined by market and state). Assessing the rapid expansion of soy in terms of 'land grab', we show that describing the effects in terms of land tenure and/or displacement is only the tip of the iceberg: it is in fact a complex technology and capital-driven process with many direct and indirect effects, and with multiple implications for the core of development.

The expansion of the soy frontier: how did it happen?

There is no other region in the world which has devoted so much space to a single GM crop as South America. In 2009, the area covered with GM soy was around 40 million hectares (Domínguez and Sabatino 2010). In Argentina, being the world's largest exporter of soybean oil and soybean meal (supplying about 45 per cent of the world market), more than 50 per cent of the agricultural land is covered with this crop. After the USA and Brazil, Argentina is the third-largest soybean producer in the world, exporting soybeans mainly to China and the EU.

Industrial production of soy in Argentina began in the late 1970s in the 'nucleus zone' or 'pampas' region. The expansion of conventional soy initially took place as a way to give value to underutilized land, contributing to land use intensification (i.e. the shift from cattle ranching and dairy activities to capital-intensive agricultural activities), and for a long time it took place steadily (not yet 'booming'). A turning point in the expansion of soy was 1996, when Argentina legally approved GM soy production[3] while it was still forbidden in all the neighbouring countries.[4] By doing this, Argentina became an outlet for

4.1 South American Chaco region (*source*: Tomei and Upham 2011)

massive and rapid expansion across the region of 'illegal' transgenic soybeans, which today are also one of the main export crops of Brazil and Paraguay and increasing in weight in Bolivia and Uruguay, leading to the popular name of *'Repúblicas unidas de la soja'*.

After its introduction in 1996, GM soy was rapidly distributed not only within Argentina, but also over the continent. Large companies began to expand production by leasing land from small and medium producers. Expansion began in the core pampas region and is currently moving to the north of Argentina – even into and from Brazil, Paraguay, Uruguay and Bolivia in a trans-regional capital move (Borras et al. 2012) – among other things in order to reduce climate risks. Brazilian soy entrepreneurs – such as the so-called Brazilian king of soy, the Andre Maggi Group – are now purchasing land in Argentina, arguing that some costs are cheaper there. And soy growers in Paraguay, mostly Brazilian migrants or their descendants (the *brasiguayos*), are expanding their soy plantations into the Paraguayan Chaco region, since they perceive that the original production area in eastern Paraguay is reaching its limits.

At the same time, however, there are clear indications that the GM soy frontier is likely to move across the Atlantic Ocean towards Africa, where 'bridges' between countries such as Brazil and Mozambique are the starting points for connections that bring know-how, machinery and GM technologies, as well as increased interest in African land. Argentina's machinery producers and land speculators are not likely to lose this business opportunity either.

The technology frontier The speed of expansion of GM soy was enormous; between 1997 and 1999 the area expanded by 2 million hectares on average per year. Already in 2002 GM soybeans amounted to 99 per cent of total soy production. The attraction of using GM soy instead of conventional soy was not so much a question of yields (productivity of conventional varieties is sometimes higher), but rather the compatibility with no-tilling systems, the easy field operations, and the simplicity of weed management (Benbrook 2005, quoting G. Gobocopatel 2002). The new GM seeds facilitated pest control over large areas of land and made expansion in scale much more viable. Because of the introduction of GM soy, however, producers became highly dependent on herbicides and fertilizers. This resulted in a rapid increase in herbicide use, raising questions about the economic and environmental sustainability of this production system.

With the massive introduction of the technological package of GM soy, this production model began to expand in the direction of areas that until then had not yet been considered as suitable for agriculture. Examples are Argentina's north-east and the Chaco region, which are vulnerable both in environmental and social terms (Brailovsky and Fogelman 2004; Pengue 2009).

In the Chaco, in the last fifty years 2 million hectares of forest have been cut in the centre and south of the region for the cultivation of soy and cotton, leading to environmental degradation.

After introduction of the technological package of GM soy, expansion proceeded very quickly. The new way of organizing production through planting management pools, machinery and labour contractors and storage facilities allowed decreasing costs through the scaling of production, which in turn generated even more incentives for territorial expansion (González and Román 2009; USDA Foreign Agricultural Service 2010). Production is increasingly becoming large-scale and concentrated because medium and smaller producers were insufficiently able to make the required investments in technological innovation (such as new seeds, agro-chemicals, less crop rotation). By applying techno-fix solutions, large-scale enterprises have a better chance to 'correct' environmental and social costs, considered as externalities of the business model.

It can be concluded that the combination of technological innovation – no tillage plus genetically modified glyphosate-resistant soy – and a particular way to control land through new forms of administration (pool model), which will be further developed in the next section – changed the way in which land can be devoted to a single crop, cultivated in large production units and managed by few hands, with almost no human labour, and the scale of this. Interested actors, such as seed and agro-chemical multinationals, have actively promoted this model, with the paradigmatic case of Monsanto allowing Argentine farmers to produce and multiply GM soy without paying royalties and turning a blind eye to illegal circulation of the seed across the South American region over many years.[5]

Still, other regions outside the pampas are going to be opened for soy production through biotechnological innovation. For instance, the Obispo Colombres Experimental Station[6] is working on biotech soy development and improvement of farmers' practices in the north-west region of the country (Robin 2010). As a result, yields have improved in this region, while storage facilities and crushing facilities are also moving up north. This shows that technological innovation is a key factor in the advance of the agricultural frontier, allowing GM soy to be produced on various types of soils and in various climates.

The land frontier However, it was not just the combination, in a single package of technology, of the application of no-tillage techniques and glyphosate-resistant soy seeds developed by the multinational Monsanto which was responsible for the rapid expansion of the soy frontier. It was also the fact that, at the time the new technology appeared, large areas in the pampas devoted to cattle or underutilized hacienda land were made available for new and

4.2 Argentina: current soy-producing provinces

relatively quick occupation, while there was also extra-sector financial capital ready to be invested.

In Argentina, for a long time (including the period of Import Substitution Industrialization in the 1970s) there was a decreasing interest in farmland: large areas of latifundia (large landed estates, land reforms having never taken place) were increasingly abandoned, and especially in the 1990s people lost their interest in farming. Capital flowed to the industrial and other sectors, especially after 1991, when in the context of the Washington Consensus the interest in agricultural production declined. The National Grain Board (*Junta Nacional de Granos*) was closed, bringing an end to state support of the agricultural sector.

It was in this context of large availability of 'underutilized' lands that technological innovation took place, opening the possibility of turning land that was not naturally suitable in the past into land available for agriculture. Large-scale companies and investment funds took the initiative of organizing 'sowing pools', establishing and managing the use of the technological package. They were able to control large tracts of land and began to control the whole production chain, based on the previous dissemination of no-tillage technologies among producers. In the core area provinces such as Santa Fe, cradle of 'direct tillage', soy production advanced rapidly on the basis of land leases to achieve scale. It is the combination of this new form of organization (sowing pools), technological innovation (no tillage, GM seeds), and the availability of new areas through the development of new climate-resistant seeds which explains the rapid expansion of soy production in the pampas region and beyond. Thus, the expansion of agriculture, and particularly livestock and soy, is not necessarily linked to large properties in the cadastral sense, but to large production units. Between 1988 and 2002, the agricultural area increased by 15 per cent in the whole country and 50.3 per cent in the regions outside the pampas.

As a consequence of the rapid expansion, annual crops and cattle ranching in the pampas region were sidelined. By the end of the 1990s, high international soybean prices and 'saturation' of the core area led to shifts in the investment pattern, from the pampas region to the north-west of the country and into the Chaco forest, to acquire land for soy production, either through land use change, or through clearing of native forests (Slutzky 2010). According to Benbrook (2005), between the moment of legalization of GM soy in 1996 and 2004, 32 per cent of the expansion of soy plantations in Argentina took place on land previously used for other crops, 27 per cent on former pastures and hayfields, and 41 per cent took place at the cost of forests and savannahs by clearing.

Whereas in the pampean region soy expansion was realized without major transformations in property relationships, the situation was very different in the Chaco region. Here soy expansion went hand in hand with large-scale land transfers, favoured by still very low prices in comparison with the core region (Barsky and Fernández 2008) and the incorporation of new land into agriculture. In this region the cultivated area grew 48 per cent between 1988 and 2002, especially in the provinces of Santiago del Estero and Salta, where the agricultural area doubled between 1988 and 2008 (Slutzky 2010). In both provinces, this process took place at the cost of native forest lands (with carob and quebracho trees) and at the cost of small-scale subsistence farming and livestock breeding (by peasants and indigenous groups which often lacked legal land titles). Increasing land prices and commercial interest in these lands have put enormous pressures on 'possession' and 'indigenous territory' statuses, causing tensions with local land dwellers and often even open conflicts, as former land uses are being replaced by soy plantations or industrial livestock.

Soybean producers in the pampas, who already controlled the land in this area through ownership or management, made good money. Many of them decided to use their profits for the purchase or lease of additional land in the northern regions. It is therefore mainly the successful producers from the pampean provinces, such as Buenos Aires, Córdoba and Santa Fe, who are currently buying land in the northern provinces, such as Santiago de Estero, Salta and Chaco. Since land users in this area often do not possess legal land titles, expropriation is fairly easy. For investors, in terms of opportunity costs the purchase or occupation through fraudulent or legal eviction of relatively cheap land compensates for unstable yields and the cost of vegetation clearance, as well as for higher transport costs.

The combination of ownership and other forms of access to land, such as lease contracts, continued to increase nationally by 25 per cent in the period 1988–2002, and these mixed forms, typical of the pampas region, are also becoming more common in the Chaco region. The process has been described as the 'pampeanization of the Chaco', and allows production in larger units by new players who were already present in the nucleus region. 'Accidental contracts' in particular have been instrumental as a strategy to enlarge the production units for soybean, wheat, sunflower and livestock. At the beginning of the soy era, individual entrepreneurs could afford to invest in land in the Chaco provinces. But recently prices in the increasingly dynamic land market have risen so high that larger extra-provincial and extra-regional companies, investment pools and foreign investors have displaced local capital on the demand side. Even with rising land prices, pools are still able to afford investments in estates of 40,000–50,000 hectares. In many cases, these are only speculative investment funds, which acquire land for renting purposes. Those who lead this process are mainly producers from the pampean provinces, such as Buenos Aires, Córdoba and Santa Fe.

Besides the 'soya-ization' of the pampas, and the 'agriculturization' of the Chaco, which has brought soy into the forests and to the lands of indigenous groups and peasants, there is a third development taking place: the increase in cattle-raising as a result of displacement from the pampas to other regions. For example, in the province of Santiago del Estero, the dynamics of the land market set in train by the 'soy boom' by the end of the 1990s quickly left no 'empty' lands for agriculture for new investors. Financial operations with land during the soy boom (2000–07) were handled among private buyers and sellers, and large-scale soy plantations were relatively easily developed since these lands were the best in the province (mainly because of the availability of water); the lands were easily controlled and accessed through purchase and – if necessary – easily cleared, since forest protection and territorial planning legislation were not yet in place. However, once the way was paved by soy, cattle ranching activities also increased, mainly on remaining lands, which were considered 'marginal' (or not so suitable for soy production). In other words, soy expansion on the one hand led to the push of cattle farming outside the pampas region, but on the other hand it also helped to pull cattle-raising into the Chaco region (soy and cattle-raising expansion mutually influence each other). Santiago del Estero is one of the most affected provinces in terms of land use change as well as in terms of the arrival of investors from other provinces. Its cattle numbers increased 40 per cent between 1988 and 2002 (González and Román 2009).

In other words, the consolidation of the GM soy hegemony in the Argentine pampas region displaced traditional cattle ranching to the north. But GM soy also jumped into the Chaco forests, because of cheap land, lack of regulation and the underlying myth of 'empty lands' (GAIA et al. 2008; Borras et al. 2012), attracting new actors, such as real estate speculators, cattle growers and soy producers, including those of local, extra-regional and international origin – in many cases at the expense of the forest, peasant lands and *monte*.[7] In general, extra-regional investors have dominated the process of 'soya-ization' of the Chaco, with local connections especially in the field of technical support. Areas targeted for soy investments could be characterized in general as easily accessible through purchase, while land conversion was carried out through deforestation of vast areas, which were not necessarily empty but access to which was difficult to control by locals, even if they held rights to the land. The relationship with the local people was, in fact, less personalized on lands acquired for soy than on those targeted for cattle; generally, investments for soy cultivation were represented by managers, which has both advantages and disadvantages when it comes to conflicts with local communities and individuals.

The market frontier (versus the role of the state) The rapid expansion of the soy frontier cannot be explained without taking into account the role of the state and the appearance of new markets.

Looking at the role of the state, we see that the national government for a long time has pursued a purely market-driven development (laissez-faire), focusing on the need for economic recovery. Neoliberal policies shaped the rules of the game, and it is only recently (since 2003) that more attention has been given to social issues (such as democratization) and that there is some space for debate and critical reflection. The conflict between the soy sector and the government in 2008 over export taxes provided an opportunity for open discussion (which was not so visible before). At the same time, however, until now the national government has not made a serious and explicit effort to achieve more inclusive and/or sustainable development, while the industrial agriculture frontier continues to expand. In Argentina, in the beginning period, the soy boom (and income from export and/or taxes) was seen as the solution to paying external debt and dealing with the economic crisis (at that time, owing to the crisis, more than half of the population lived below the poverty line).

Taking a market perspective, GM soy expansion in South America is related to the growing demand for animal protein food in Europe – and more recently in China and other Asian countries – a demand which also requires large amounts of soy oil for food consumption. In addition, export markets for soy received a boost through the rapid increase of the biofuels market (mainly the result of EU targets for reducing its greenhouse gas emissions progressively up to 2050). This new demand is perceived by the governments of South American countries, as well as by actors in the production chain of soy, as an opportunity to diversify products and markets. In the Argentine case, the conditions for biodiesel production are already in place owing to the existence of a highly efficient integrated soy sector (Tomei and Upham 2011). Biodiesel can be produced from the same biomass that produces soybean oil and meal and is therefore highly dependent on industrialized agriculture, which is able to homogenize raw material for processing into various by-products (TNI et al. 2007). Argentina is thus in a good position to benefit from this demand in the EU. In addition, there is an increasing national demand. The Argentine government promoted the creation of a domestic market and encouraged the soy sector to diversify. Through Law 26.093 (2006) the government established biodiesel-to-diesel blending targets of 5 per cent for 2010 (7 per cent in 2011), with the expectation of increasing it to 10 per cent in the following years. Nowadays, around 15 per cent of the soybean crop in Argentina is used to produce biodiesel (USDA Foreign Agricultural Service 2011).

Most of the investments in the biodiesel industry come from the usual big players of the international soy sector (FOEI 2008), such as Glencore, Nidera, Dreyfus, Bunge and Cargill, in alliances with a powerful domestic soy processing sector and domestic investors. To encourage investments in the biodiesel industry, the national government imposed a differential export tax that favours the production of biofuels over soy oil and meal (which production continues to be dominated by Monsanto and Syngenta).

Additional demand for soy as biodiesel may be conducive to further expansion of the agricultural frontier, exacerbating social and environmental problems already evident in relation to past and current GM soy cultivation, as well as increasing commercial pressures on land in the Chaco region. However, recent central government measures and an increasing conflict with EU import markets have placed some question marks over, and brought conflict into, the biodiesel sector in Argentina. The recent announcement of Spain – the buyer of 70 per cent of Argentine biodiesel exports – forbidding biodiesel imports from outside the EU led Argentina to complain to the WTO. At the same time, the national government has raised the taxes for biodiesel exports to the level for other soy by-products, thereby changing the direction of its promotional policy. The effect seems to be exacerbated by the 15 per cent reduction in the biodiesel price on the domestic market, which has negative impacts for the medium and smaller non-integrated enterprises. Nevertheless, the EU has been denouncing Argentine dumping through tax exemptions and has claimed the existence of more efficient biofuels from rapeseed and palm oil. In consequence, owing to both national and international factors, there is uncertainty about the biodiesel sector's future.

Assessing the impact

Rapid soy expansion has helped the Argentine economy to recover from its severe economic crisis and is generating benefits for a limited group of people who are directly attached to the soy and biodiesel industry. The continuing expansion, however, is increasingly accompanied by tension and conflicts. In the Chaco region, in particular, people are forced to move; soy expansion is increasingly going hand in hand with legal disputes and violent eviction (especially in those cases where people have only informal titles). The National Campesino-Indigenous Movement (MNCI-Via Campesina) estimates that approximately 200,000 rural families have been forced away from their lands owing to the advance of soy. Provinces where this process has been most violent are Santiago del Estero and Córdoba, where heavy machinery owned by sowing pools and landowners went over peasants' houses and land parcels. In addition, REDAF[8] documented that by 2011 around 950,000 people – inhabitants of indigenous and campesino (peasant) territories – have been affected by land or environmental conflicts related to the expansion of the agricultural frontier, led by GM soy. Most of these conflicts had begun by 2000, when the GM soy model reached its boom point (Aranda 2011). Many of these groups were occupants and holders of possession rights, which, according to Argentine law, involve a form of tenure security. Possessors of these rights have been living on the land for more than twenty years and have realized a range of 'possession acts': working, caring for and improving the land.

In the soy frontier, land prices show a tendency to increase, and the pressures on local land markets therefore also increase, having negative consequences for the security of land access for local groups. Small-scale farmers and indigenous communities are affected, as are cattle and food producers, who are in many cases pushed away to new zones. The tensions lead to claims for the regularization of possession and indigenous rights. The problems arise because in the Argentine Chaco provinces a larger number of peasants do not hold titles to the land they occupy and work on. For instance, approximately 75 per cent of peasants in Santiago del Estero are in this situation. Different mechanisms of pressure on the indigenous and peasant population as well as mechanisms of enclosure occur. These include violent evictions, unequal legal disputes, the pollution of water, soil and crops, and the clearance of forests, which are sources of livelihoods for the communities in the region. The expansion of the frontier only speeds up this process, since the price of formerly 'unproductive' land rises, attracting not only new land users but also speculators.

The expansion of the soy frontier into ecologically vulnerable areas is also increasingly generating environmental problems. Biodiversity is highly affected through deforestation, but also by poisoning of water and soils with herbicides: the massive application of glyphosate, for instance, kills animals and microorganisms, but also contaminates food crops and affects people's health. Excessive use of pesticides and little crop rotation turn the soil sterile over the years. Several (mainly poor) communities in towns and cities in the main soy-producing provinces in Argentina have been affected by serious health problems caused by indiscriminate fumigation practices with herbicides in areas neighbouring the plantations and in poor urban settlements where pesticides are stored. In 2003, local NGOs reported an alarming incidence of child cancer, 50 per cent higher than the national average, which was attributed – among other factors – to illegal fumigation in neighbouring GM soy fields. This diagnosis motivated a group of women (Madres de Ituzaingó-Anexo) to organize themselves politically and publicly seek confrontation with local soy producers by initiating legal actions against fumigation with pesticides. This was a pioneer case in the country, which served as a precedent to many other localities, where illegal fumigations were prohibited and legal ones regulated.[9]

Thanks to the hype about land grabbing, more attention has been paid globally to the negative implications of large-scale land acquisition, albeit that land grabbing is still mainly associated with the purchase of large tracts of land by foreigners and/or foreign companies and states (China and the Gulf states, for example). In Argentina, before now, most of the discussion on land grabbing was focused on processes of 'foreignization of Patagonia', the purchase of land by American and European millionaires (Sánchez 2006), but nowadays increasing attention is also paid to soy expansion. There is increased room for discussion on the social and environmental costs of ongoing soy expansion, but this has not yet resulted in concrete policy measures. To the extent that the national government is directly involved in agricultural policies, the emphasis is now on implementing the national PEA2 (Federal and Participative Agro-food and Agribusiness Strategic Plan, 2010/2016), through which Argentina seeks to strike a privileged position as a global provider of food. The main goal is to expand the agricultural frontier by about six million hectares, giving priority to modern and large-scale farming and industrial agriculture. Moreover, some historically poor provinces, neglected by the state, have been recently targeted for the Historic Reparation Acts, which include a range of infrastructural projects, as in the case of the Figueroa Dam, built in 2011 (including also 30,000 hectares for agricultural and cattle production). Mention should also be made of the IIRSA[10] project aimed at constructing a new infrastructural network in South America, which will particularly affect the future of the South American Chaco region as a whole since it is aimed at constructing a large new infrastructure network on the continent.

In the current policies, with the exception of forest policy and the implied territorial planning, there is not much priority given to the protection of fragile ecosystems (such as the Chaco or the Delta region). In addition, there is no policy in support of peasant production systems and/or indigenous groups. There is therefore a considerable risk that frontier expansion will increasingly generate social and environmental costs.

Conclusions

In summary, the expansion of soy production in Argentina developed relatively 'ungoverned' and without subsidies, through private sector initiatives responding to market forces in a context of neoliberal policies. The expansion began in the 1970s in the pampas region, where land and agriculture had gradually been abandoned during the period of Import Substitution Industrialization policies and where expansion advanced at the expense of cattle-raising and diversified grain production. In the neoliberal period – when new production models (no tillage) and new technology became available (from 1996 onwards) – the expansion of soy took place more rapidly. This was possible because large tracts of underutilized land were available, and these could easily be converted into new production units by a limited number of old and new large landowners and investors who began to lease land. There was no major need for property change since flexible lease contracts provided the necessary scale. In other words, there was a process of capital concentration rather than of land concentration. This, together with no-tillage practices and machinery, the introduction of GM soy and an innovative way of managing and organizing production by sowing pools, constituted the basis for the soy boom.

The process was accompanied by crop change and the migration of cattle farming to the northern provinces, mainly to the Chaco region. There, direct investments in soy production were generally made by soy producers originating from the pampas region, since this group had succeeded in making good money from soy and decided to buy additional land in the Chaco. New land users found cheaper land, less regulation than in the pampas region, and small producers with precarious tenure situations. Investing in the Chaco involved additional costs because of the need to clear vegetation, the more expensive transport, irregular yields due to climate instability, and conflicts with holders of possession rights. However, cheap land and short-term benefits compensated for these costs.

The expansion of soy production did not lead to major changes in land-ownership relations in the pampas region, but this is not true for the northern area. In the Chaco region, forests were cleared and local peasants and indigenous groups were bought out or were legally or illegally displaced; they lost their land and were excluded from the benefits of soy growing. Nevertheless, the state largely remained inactive in the fields of rural development and the regulation of extractive activities, such as mining, forestry and soy monoculture. It acted only in the sense that it created incentives for the further expansion of these activities. Regulation for sustainability and the protection of the rights of local farmers have not been properly addressed. The main problems are the failure to protect the rights of weaker interest groups and the lack of a long-term vision regarding the extent to which the use of glyphosate and other pesticides – which cause land degradation, the contamination of other crops, water pollution, health problems, etc. – is compatible with the need to bring about sustainable development.

In less than twenty years, Argentina (and the Southern Cone) has been transformed into the soy provider of the rest of the world. Dramatic changes have taken place in the landscape and the livelihood options of the population: the 'soya-ization' of the land and deforestation are pushing people from their land, without providing employment and/or a basis for sustainable development.

Until now, little or no attention has been paid to the rapid expansion of soy in the global land grab debate, and also within Argentina there has not yet been an open debate about controversies and dilemmas. In trying to steer the process, it is important not to focus too much on the land dimension: the expansion of GM soy is being shaped by an interplay of new technology, models of land control and expanding capital. In order to control current processes, it is important to focus on the various drivers, while keeping an eye open for the indirect and extraterritorial consequences. GM soy expansion can only be explained as part of a larger process of land valuation, commoditization of natural resources, and capital's expanding needs. The socio-historical process of the introduction, promotion, adoption and expansion of GM soy in the core region of Argentina determined to some extent the way in which the second phase of expansion is taking place in the northern provinces, where the scale of the changes has been much greater. The expansion of soy production did not produce negative effects within the pampas region, but generated processes of undesired change in the Chaco. The increased demand for land in the Chaco is and will be accompanied by accumulation, privatization, enclosure and displacement, redirecting resources away from local communities and as commodities for distant consumers.

In Argentina, to the extent that attention is paid to land grabbing, most of the attention has been paid to the role of foreigners who purchased land in Patagonia (Sánchez 2006) and the increasing role of 'typical global grabbers' (such as China and the Gulf states). To the extent that efforts have been made to bring land grabbing under control, this has materialized in the 'foreignization law', placing restrictions on the area of land owned by foreigners and foreign companies. Until now, the expansion of soy has not been subject to debate, in spite of its many negative consequences. Until now, GM soy does not fall into the typical definition of land grabbing, and no attempts have been made to bring this sector under control (which will also be difficult owing to its transnational character).

The current hype about land grabbing – and the worldwide concern over the social and environmental consequences of large-scale land acquisitions – may help to foster critical discussion of the link between 'processes of soya-ization' and 'inclusive and sustainable development'. At the same time, however, it will be difficult to bring the soy frontier under control. While soy is relatively well established and accepted in the pampean core (nucleus) region, the consequences of this development are not regulated or controlled through state policies and have not been openly agreed upon by the major part of Argentine society. In the current situation, the 'pools' and biotech companies are in power. The question for policy-makers – and taking into account the mentioned impacts – is how to slow down further expansion in the frontiers as well as creating mechanisms to make involved actors more accountable.

5 | Transnational land investment in Costa Rica: tracing residential tourism and its implications for development

Femke van Noorloos[1]

Introduction

The current global land rush is not a new phenomenon: land grabs, the dispossession of rural communities and deepening commercialization in rural areas have existed since colonial times. The novelty of current developments lies in the speed of change, the large scale of the phenomenon worldwide, and the expectation that it will continue for a long time (Anseeuw et al. 2012; Cotula 2012). Nevertheless, given the current hype about large-scale land acquisitions, it is interesting to trace recent developments to earlier processes of land-based change and make comparisons. In this chapter I focus on the north-west coast of Costa Rica (the province of Guanacaste), an area where real estate development and tourism have created many land pressures in recent years. However, the area has been subject to land grabs ever since colonization and particularly since the late nineteenth century, when a small number of foreign and domestic investors were able to acquire huge amounts of land in Guanacaste, mainly for the cattle sector (Edelman 1998). The aim is thus to give a more dynamic view of 'land grab' processes by tracing current processes to historical developments and by showing the long-term effects of a land grab that took place long ago.

The global trend for large-scale land acquisitions causes much concern. According to many studies, its implications have been mostly negative: increased preoccupation with food security and rural people's livelihoods; the displacement, enclosure and exclusion of local populations; conflict; and pressure on resources (German et al. 2011; Oxfam 2011; Anseeuw et al. 2012; Global Witness 2012). In Latin America, the expulsion of people from their lands is lesser in scale than in other regions; however, changes in land property relations should be seen in a broader perspective, as there has been a process of increased land reconcentration and inequalities in access to land, as well as 'deagrarianization' (Borras et al. 2012; Peluso and Lund 2011).

The debate on large-scale land acquisitions and commercial pressures on land has mostly focused on two types of land acquisition, namely purchases directed to food supply (food crops, agribusiness, pasture land) and biofuel crops. However important the issue of land acquisition for food and biofuel crops may be, we need to view new commercial pressures on land in their entire width (Zoomers 2010). Particularly in Latin America, land acquisitions outside the realm of food and fuel have been important (Borras et al. 2012). For instance, large land acquisitions are taking place in the context of climate change mitigation and adaptation (e.g. related to Reducing Emissions from Deforestation and Forest Degradation policies); mining concessions cause pressures on land; and the establishment of large-scale tourism complexes and residential tourism resorts also adds to these pressures (Zoomers 2010). Speculation in itself (land and houses as a safe haven for investment) is also a driver of large-scale land acquisitions (Anseeuw et al. 2012).

Tourism has only recently started to receive some attention in the land grab debate, and researchers seem to differ on whether to include tourism-related land acquisitions. I argue that tourism resources (landscape, view, land, water) are among the key resources for capitalist development and drive current land acquisitions. Residential tourism in particular is based on land and speculation. Residential tourism has recently become more prominent in developing countries: it is the temporary or permanent mobility of relatively well-to-do citizens from mostly Western countries to a variety of tourist destinations, where they buy (or sometimes rent) property (Aledo 2008; Benson and O'Reilly 2009; McWatters 2009).[2] Most residential tourists are Europeans or North Americans who migrate to the South in search of a more relaxed lifestyle, a lower cost of living, better weather, etc. Both the number of residential tourists and the size of the related land investments have increased markedly during the past ten years in various countries in Latin America, Africa and Asia. Residential tourism is thus a relatively new type of commercial pressure on land, a pressure which is expected to increase in many developing countries in the future – for example, in Costa Rica, Nicaragua, Panama, Ecuador, Chile, Uruguay, Argentina, Brazil, South Africa, Mozambique, Thailand and Turkey.

Residential tourism is generating increased pressures on land and resources. It is triggering a process of foreignization of land, since land has become an important object of investment for many external actors. This naturally takes place on a smaller scale and in a more concentrated manner than in the case of agricultural investment; however, the scale of the capital involved is large (see Borras et al. 2012). As most of the land investment takes place on privately owned land and not in outright illegal ways, the term 'land grab' is not fitting; nevertheless, increased land acquisition and control by external actors does take place.

In this chapter I aim to provide a better understanding of residential tourism and its implications for equitable and sustainable development in Costa Rica, and I trace these developments to historical processes of land grab, thereby contributing to the debate on the dynamics and long-term effects of large-scale land acquisitions.

This chapter is based on research in one of the main and (until recently) fastest-growing residential tourism destinations in Latin America: the northwest coastal region of Costa Rica, Guanacaste Province (Figure 5.1). This area has been connected to the North American economy since the late nineteenth century, through large-scale land investments and beef export (Edelman 1998). It has also been a well-known destination for short-term tourism for some decades; but particularly since 2002 residential tourism and the real estate market have undergone rapid growth. Between 2008 and 2011, I visited the area three times for several types of data collection: interviews with various population groups, a survey among residential tourists, participant observation, and analysis of secondary data sources.[3]

Guanacaste's historical 'land grabs' and connections to North America

In pre-colonial times, Guanacaste hosted an important and flourishing Chorotega civilization. After the Spanish conquest, the indigenous population disappeared almost completely, and with this decimation of the population the area became marginalized for a long time (ibid.). In the late nineteenth century, Guanacaste became linked to the North American economy (Van Noorloos 2011a), when the province saw transnational land acquisitions for cattle farming and the introduction of private property rights (Edelman 1998).

From the late nineteenth century until the early twentieth century, the livestock industry in Guanacaste experienced rapid growth. The result was increased demand for land, which led to the strengthening of the private individual property rights of the livestock estates through judicial innovations (land titling) and other developments (fencing and forced removal of peasants) (ibid.). In northern and eastern Guanacaste, the state very regularly gave land in 'concession' to private parties, and these concessions in fact granted private property titles; in practice, land was often given away by the state at very low prices (ibid.). In the Nicoya Peninsula and research area, the Church's and Church brotherhoods' properties were privatized and sold during the nineteenth century; local peasants who had occupied the land were displaced in various cases, but many other peasants were able to obtain private property rights on these former Church properties through the concept of squatters' rights, which were included in Costa Rica's laws in 1885 and 1888 (ibid. 70–1). During the late nineteenth and early twentieth centuries, a small number of people were able to acquire enormous amounts of land in Guanacaste. Although the livestock industry was more extensive in the interior part of the province, the *hacendados* regularly invaded coastal areas (ibid.: 88). Already by that time there were connections to North America: since the 1880s, there had been trade in wood from Guanacaste to North America, and a few of the large livestock estates were owned by US citizens (ibid.). As such, a corridor between North America and Guanacaste was in place (Van Noorloos 2011a). This initial 'land grab' in Guanacaste was closely interrelated with the strengthening of private property rights and led to the displacement of local peasants.

In the 1950s, the North America–Guanacaste corridor was strengthened: Costa Rica began to export Guanacastean beef to the USA. From about the 1950s to the 1980s, the livestock sector grew larger and more successful. The sector was dominated by large landowners (Edelman 1998), and commercialization was led by large-scale companies, both foreign and domestic (Ramírez Cover 2008). Cattle farming was one of the main reasons for the massive deforestation of Guanacaste's forests in the early and mid twentieth century (Calvo-Alvarado et al. 2009). At the same time, agro-industrial rice and sugar cane production took place in the province, dominated by large companies owned by national elites and greatly aided by the government through subsidies, price interventions, irrigation investments, etc. (Programa Estado de la Nación 2000; Ramírez Cover 2008).

A new 'land grab' had thus started. In the 1960s and 1970s, US citizens invested large amounts of money in land in Guanacaste for the production of rice and cotton, often together with Costa Rican elites. The huge sums of money that these foreign investors were prepared to spend on land infected the local real estate market with a speculative spirit, causing many local smallholders to sell their land. On the other hand, the existence of many large absentee and often foreign landowners was one of the reasons why *precarismo* (squatting) by peasants was still quite common – and often successful – in Guanacaste from the 1950s to the 1980s (Edelman 1998).

In the 1980s, after having benefited from a flourishing cattle farming industry for several decades, the province's economy went into depression, and policymakers and inhabitants alike embraced tourism as an alternative development strategy for the marginalized area. The government was quick to recognize the country's potential for attracting tourism and foreign retirees: incentives included the 1964 *pensionado* law, which offered advantages to foreign retirees settling in Costa Rica, such as tax breaks for importing cars and household goods. In Guanacaste, foreign retirees were not so common, although international tourism began to grow in the 1970s. The government began investing in tourism infrastructure in the 1970s, as Guanacaste's coast had been identified as one of the main potential tourism attractions of Central America (Morales and Pratt 2010). In 1978, Costa Rica's first government-planned tourism resort was established in Guanacaste: the Papagayo Gulf Tourism Pole (*Polo Turístico Golfo de Papagayo* – PTGP) (Salas Roiz 2010). However, the effects of these investments were felt only later. Despite government measures, tourism development in Guanacaste stagnated in the 1980s, just as it did in other sectors. However, land speculation continued, and on the coast foreign investors began to buy large properties (Van Noorloos 2011a). Hence, the process of large-scale land acquisition, strengthening of private property rights, and North American investment continued, but this time speculation focused on the tourism and real estate sector.

Costa Rica underwent impressive tourism development in the 1990s, and Guanacaste particularly benefited from this boom. While some agricultural activities grew, in general the primary sector was stagnant in the area, and tourism became a very important alternative source of employment (Programa Estado de la Nación 2000; Fürst and Ruiz 2002; CEPAL 2007). The 1990s marked Guanacaste's transition towards a service economy. Investments in land throughout the coastal areas were now being developed into tourism projects and urbanizations; and in newly discovered areas, land speculation continued. A small number of 'pioneering' North Americans were already living in the area, but residential tourism was still small.

By the 2000s, tourism had become Costa Rica's second-largest source of foreign exchange earnings, after goods exports (Programa Estado de la Nación 2007). The 2 million visitors threshold was reached in 2008. Guanacaste plays an important role: hotel accommodation has increased greatly in the province, particularly luxury four- and five-star hotels. By 2002, the rapid coming together of an extended airport, increased international charter flights from North America, and a number of high-end hotels and gated communities triggered the residential tourism boom (Janoschka 2009; Morales and Pratt 2010). As a result, a few large residential projects were further developed, and a wide range of new real estate projects were launched. Guanacaste was on its way to becoming a large-scale residential tourism destination, when in 2008 the global economic crisis hit the area and led to the cancellation of many projects and to a large oversupply of property. In 2013, a slow recovery is taking place, and new projects have been announced.

In summary, Guanacaste has undergone a number of boom–bust cycles since the first 'land grab' in the late nineteenth century. Dependency on the North American market has deepened with each cycle. Most land was in private ownership – highly concentrated in a few hands – from early on, offering an easy base for real estate and tourism investors.

The current hype: residential tourism development in Guanacaste

The residential tourism sector in the research area (the coastal area between Papagayo and Pinilla) comprised eight large projects and 136 smaller ones, with a total of 7,587 entities (apartments, houses, plots) in 2011. However, during the period of 'hype' of residential tourism investment (2005–08), much higher numbers were mentioned; many of the projects that were announced have never actually materialized or have reduced their ambitions since the crisis. Indeed, an additional 11,900 entities were announced or planned, but never

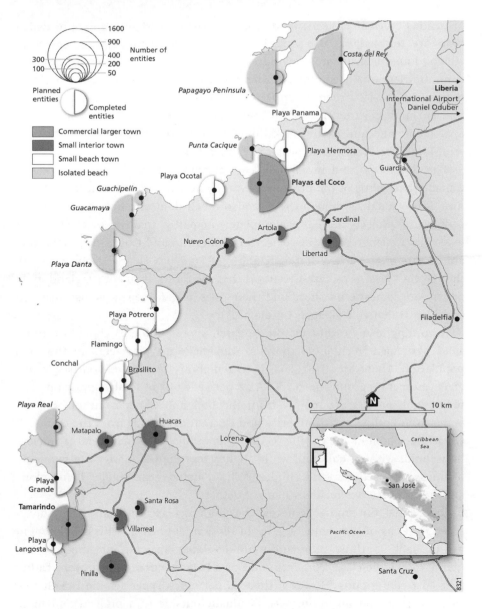

5.1 Planned/announced and completed residential tourism entities (plots, houses and apartments) per type of town, research area (2011) (*source*: Author's research)

completed (see Figure 5.1 for a visual depiction of planned and completed projects). Besides the media and researchers, particularly the developers and real estate agents themselves were responsible for these exaggerations of residential tourism growth figures. Despite these exaggerations, growth was clearly rapid between 2002 and 2008, and the landscape has changed profoundly as a result. The physical landscape of residential tourism in Guanacaste is made up of various types of projects: land plot subdivisions (urbanizations), in which plots are sold without the provision of many additional services; complete villa and apartment complexes; mixed projects; and all-inclusive luxury gated communities, which combine residential elements with large international hotels and services such as golf courses and marinas. As such, residential tourism and short-term tourism are often intertwined, also because most apartments and houses are rented out to short-term tourists for most of the year. Many projects in Guanacaste are gated communities.

The developers and investment capital mainly come from the USA and Canada (two-thirds of the projects are partly or completely financed by North American capital), although there is also much domestic investment: 40 per cent of the projects are either completely or partly financed by Costa Rican investors. Collaborations between North American and Costa Rican investors are common. As such, a 'foreignization' of land has clearly taken place, although the Costa Rica case illustrates that the recent focus of the 'land grab' debate on domestic investors and their roles as gatekeepers is also justified (see also Hilhorst et al. 2011; Cotula 2012).

According to my estimates, the research area is home to about two thousand permanent residential tourists, who make up 5 per cent of the total population. There are also 3,400–4,800 temporary residential tourists at any given moment, accounting for 8.6–12.2 per cent of the total population. The residential tourists are mainly from the USA and Canada, although some come from Europe, South America and Costa Rica (mostly from the country's Great Metropolitan Area – the 'GAM'). Almost half are members of nuclear households without children, while slightly less than a quarter are members of nuclear households with children. The remainder are singles living alone and friends or other relatives living together.

Residential tourism in Guanacaste has both increased in quantity and diversified in terms of the characteristics of residential tourists. This development will probably continue: more and more developers may tap into the potential market of middle-class segments and Costa Rican second-home buyers, rather than just elite groups. However, there is not much space left on the Guanacaste coast for buying property individually outside of a project, and more adventurous residential tourists are finding the area too overdeveloped for buying property. It is therefore expected that residential tourism will expand to the remaining empty beaches and towards the interior of the province. The number of apartment complexes on the coast is also expected to increase.

Externally led economic development

Since its first connections to the North American economy in the late nineteenth century, Guanacaste has undergone various boom and bust cycles; each bust deepened the province's dependency on the North American market. The residential tourism industry has created specific types of new dependencies.

A number of structural factors originating in 'the West' (in this case, the USA and Canada) are important for explaining the growth in, and potential for, retirement migration and for residential tourism more broadly (Van Noorloos 2011a): demographic factors,[4] increasing health costs and decreasing retirement pensions,[5] cheap interest rates and ease of acquiring mortgages in the USA (before the financial crisis), and the fact that current generations retiring in the near future have become used to international travel. General factors related to increased time–space compression are also of undeniable influence (ibid.), such as cheap and rapid travel, and improved and cheaper long-distance communication possibilities (MPI 2006; McWatters 2009). These structural factors are also interrelated with sociological changes in Western societies, where increasing numbers of people aim for a change of urban high-stress lifestyles ('the rat race') or aim to differentiate themselves from others by a different type of lifestyle (Aledo 2008; Benson and O'Reilly 2009). Related to this, the powerful ideas of a global real estate market and 'the world as a retirement destination' have been key to imagining the possibility of foreign real estate investment and residential tourism in Costa Rica (Van Noorloos 2011a).

Another important push towards residential tourism was caused by innovations in the tourism industry, which were brought into Costa Rica: investors and hotel chains, mainly from the USA and Spain, introduced combinations of short-term tourism and real estate/residential products (ibid.). Real estate and tourism have developed a profitable alliance in the wake of tourism's declining profitability (Deloitte-Exeltur 2005) and search for new ways of financing projects. In addition, another increasingly popular feature imported from the USA is timeshare arrangements and partial ownership; in these schemes, tourists own a vacation property for a specified period per year (fractional or interval ownership). Some authors analyse these influences more in terms of political economy and the expansion strategies of international hotel chains and tourism business from Spain and the USA, which have been heading to new areas – in the Spanish case, following the declining possibilities in the Balearic Islands and the wider region, and also using opportunities offered by political deregulation and free trade regimes (Cañada 2010). A number of Spanish, US and Canadian hotel chains have established themselves in Guanacaste, and they have played a role in putting Guanacaste on the map as a large-scale, high-end tourism destination.

In terms of economic effects, it seems logical that a formerly peripheral, isolated area will flourish economically as a result of the arrival of residential tourism. This was indeed the case in Guanacaste from about 2002 to 2008, when the region saw the rapid growth of both short-term and residential tourism.

Employment and business opportunities in tourism, construction, real estate and the related service sectors in almost all labour market segments increased strongly during this period (INEC 2000, 2011). At the same time, the number of people working in agriculture and cattle farming continued to decrease. Diverse economic activities developed around the construction and real estate sectors, and the traditional tourist sector and the related services continued to grow.

The growth of residential tourism has caused a chain of economic effects that are felt not only locally but also in distant areas. New employment and business opportunities often benefit other areas or people from elsewhere, both in and outside Costa Rica. Employment created by residential tourism is divided by place of origin: Nicaraguan migrants have low-paid jobs, such as domestic work, construction and security, whereas North Americans and domestic urban migrants often have highly skilled jobs in real estate, project development and management. Local Guanacastecans are in between: they are active in a variety of job types, but mainly in tourism and services (INEC household surveys and census 2011). In addition, many locally operating companies maintain strong linkages with external areas: real estate agencies in Guanacaste are often part of US chains, and the construction sector is dominated by large Costa Rican companies based in the GAM. Hence, there are various financial flows to and from distant areas, and development patterns are translocal rather than locally oriented (Van Noorloos 2011a).

Compared with land acquisitions in other sectors, residential tourism thus offers better opportunities for employment; even if employment and economic linkages are often translocal in character, this is not necessarily a problem. What is more problematic is that a greater focus on residential tourism – as compared with short-term tourism – can lead to the displacement of the small-scale tourism sector, a relative increase in low-paid and vulnerable employment, and greater inequalities between groups. Indeed, a comparison of short-term tourists' and residential tourists' expenditure patterns shows that residential tourism might be less beneficial for local people, small-scale businesses, etc., whereas it provides profitable opportunities for real estate development and related services. Furthermore, the impact of the post-2008 global economic crisis on Guanacaste has exposed the vulnerability of the sector: the growth of residential tourism has made the region increasingly dependent on the North American real estate market and credit opportunities. Hence, the crisis has hit hard, and economic opportunities in residential tourism and related sectors have declined sharply in Guanacaste since 2008; this is particularly true for construction and real estate. The fact that residential tourism and real estate development cause greater volatility is also shown by the poverty and unemployment statistics (INEC 1997–2011): poverty, unemployment and underemployment have increased at a much higher rate in Guanacaste than in other regions of Costa Rica since the crisis.

One of the reasons residential tourism growth can be problematic in the long term is its focus on the sale and transfer of land, rather than on the development of broader services. Land then becomes an object of investment and speculation, deeply interrelated with the financial sector. This often entails greater risks, vulnerability to shocks, volatility and inequality (Pike and Pollard 2010).

Access to land

We have seen that in Guanacaste most land has been in private ownership – and owned by a small group of people – since the late nineteenth century. Throughout the twentieth century, domestic and transnational land investment led to land concentration, high land prices and displacement of local populations. However, peasants had opportunities to acquire land (e.g. through squatting). The population number has been low since colonization, so displacement was not on a massive scale. This structure later offered an easy base for real estate and tourism investors to buy land.

The main problem with residential tourism is that it has boosted land prices up to extremely high levels. Indeed, residential tourism has caused spiralling land price inflation: in the research area, the prices of land and apartments/houses have increased on average, respectively, by 17.7 and 24.3 per cent per year (2000–11). The current average prices per square metre of US$188 (land) and US$2,717 (houses) have made land and housing inaccessible to most local and poor migrant groups. Since 2008, there have been slight decreases, though not enough to offer broad accessibility. Thus, many young people are unable to form their own nuclear families, or have moved towards the interior of the province, where land is still affordable. Others rent small apartments.

Nevertheless, residential tourism has not caused large-scale displacement. Some small-scale examples of displacement can be found in the coastal zone, where local people have been affected by land conflicts, de facto privatization and ambiguous land rights, mainly due to the inadequate implementation of regulations (Van Noorloos 2011b). Indeed, the socially and environmentally protective coastal regulations that have been put in place since the 1970s[6] have been under pressure from tourism development and have suffered from a lack of implementation and political will in recent years (ibid.). For example, there have been serious deficiencies in the land-use planning process, which has opened the door for tourism and real estate developers to elaborate such plans (CGR 2007; Román 2009). Also, the rules stipulated in the law to guarantee the use of coastal land for the public benefit are often not adhered to,[7] meaning that coastal strips of land have de facto been granted to foreign tourism companies, investors have acquired large areas of land by combining several concessions, and a real estate market for coastal land concessions has appeared (Fernández Morillo 2002; Salazar 2010). In addition, local populations that have historically occupied the coastal zone (e.g. in Ostional and Brasilito) have been claiming stronger types of land rights, such as concessions or private titles, which are often denied, thus making them vulnerable to displacement (Cabrera and Sánchez 2009; Matarrita 2009; Cañada 2011).

Land transfers do not always take place in a conflictual context: many Guanacastecans have sold their land voluntarily, though often under some form of pressure (Van Noorloos 2011b). The sale of land has been deeply intertwined with the change from a largely subsistence-based coastal economy based on agriculture and fishery towards a service economy based on tourism; and the lack of agrarian and subsistence-based options at a time when traditional state support for these activities has greatly declined (Edelman 2005) has prompted land sale in coastal areas (Van Noorloos 2011b). Squatting is now less common and less socially accepted, although laws are still quite protective in granting rights to squatters.

Taking a historical perspective has made it clear that displacement and land concentration have mainly taken place during earlier 'land grabs'. The present pressure on land is not causing massive displacement, because of the low population numbers, low agricultural use of land, fragmentation and spatial characteristics of investment. Residential tourism has fragmented landowner-ship rather than contributed to concentration, since tourism interests and real estate investors have acquired former cattle haciendas and subdivided them. Also, they have acquired land on isolated, often uninhabited beaches, because of the tourist quality of such areas. The land market in Guanacaste is highly fragmented: it consists of many segments with different price ranges and characteristics. As such, local populations are still living in the area alongside new richer groups.

Policy and community involvement

While the first 'land grabs' in Guanacaste took place in a context of state absence, the 1950s marked the entrance of a strong and social Costa Rican state and a state modernization project that extended far into the provinces. Not only did the central government establish large-scale projects in Guanacaste (e.g. large hydroelectric and irrigation projects), it also established many schools and health clinics (Programa Estado de la Nación 2000; Ramírez Cover 2008); hence, people benefited from relatively well-established institutions. Never-theless, the debt crisis of the late 1970s–1980s and the subsequent neoliberal policies marked the beginning of a new era. The sidelining of smallholder peasant production has characterized Guanacaste since the 1980s (Edelman 2005), and the lack of viable alternatives for smallholders plays a role in current land and economic conversion. At the same time, state policies focused on attracting FDI not only in large-scale, non-traditional agriculture but also in new tourism and services sectors.[8] In the 1990s and 2000s, whereas institutions were still relatively strong, it was increasingly difficult to counterbalance the forces of FDI-driven land conversion, environmental and social change, and neoliberal tendencies in Costa Rica's government, which had been set in pace in previous decades.

This contrast between Costa Rica's relatively strong and protective state institutions and laws (e.g. an exceptionally strong environmental legal framework) on the one hand, and the unregulated private-led development in Guanacaste's coast on the other, is one of the main paradoxes. Government implementation and control of environmental and spatial regulations have been largely deficient (Janoschka 2009; Barrantes-Reynolds 2010; CGR 2009, in Programa Estado de la Nación 2010). National institutions and particularly local governments largely lack the necessary human and financial capacities and internal coordination – and often also the political will. This has led to the chaotic and unplanned proliferation of residential tourism in Guanacaste, with a range of socio-environmental issues – for example, water exploitation and privatization, endangered conservation policies, and coastal zone privatization – and protests. Hence, strict national regulations and laws and elaborate checks and balances cannot always prevent damage in the face of rapid developments, important economic and political interests, and local government's traditional weakness.

With a central government that lacks a coherent policy, and with weak local governments and a private sector that cannot be expected to offer all the solutions, citizens and civil society have an important role to play in improving the implementation and control of regulations, and in achieving positive change. Indeed, communities and civil society are often assigned a key role in mitigating effects of large-scale land acquisitions, through participation in decision-making on land deals and compensation, protecting local land rights, and improving transparency (Global Witness 2012). Some successful protests in the interior of Guanacaste against the exploitation of local aquifers for tourism and residential projects on the coast have shown that local action can indeed be effective: they managed to slow down or halt residential tourism growth (see also Van Eeghen 2011). However, the power of communities and civil society to influence local affairs is still largely insufficient: central government and the private sector are increasingly recentralizing and privatizing the control of natural resources; the influence of NGOs and local groups is mainly *ex post* and not preventive; and the connection between these groups and local government is still weak. In addition, the fragmentation and diversity of the population make it difficult to achieve democratic participation in decision-making. Indeed, residential tourism has transformed Guanacaste into a transnational space (Torres and Momsen 2005), which hosts many groups that have different origins and different goals and interests, groups comprising local people, residential tourists and labour migrants (the latter mostly from Nicaragua and the GAM). The high level of fragmentation, mobility, temporariness and absenteeism in Guanacaste – combined with the presence of many migrants who do not envision a future in the area – circumscribes successful community organizing (Van Noorloos 2013).

Conclusion

This chapter has shown that the focus of the 'land grab' debate should not be limited to direct displacement but should also include long-term effects and broader processes of exclusion. The analysis of historical ongoing land acquisitions for different purposes in a specific area offers a unique opportunity to understand the long-term effects of 'land grabs' and the formation of 'corridors'.

The north-west coast of Costa Rica has been subject to land grabs ever since colonization, but particularly since the late nineteenth century, when a small number of foreign and domestic investors were able to acquire huge amounts of land, mainly for the cattle sector. Since its first connections to the North American economy in the late nineteenth century, Guanacaste has undergone various boom and bust cycles, and each bust deepened the province's dependency on the North American market, through beef export, investment in land for cattle farms, speculation, etc. Most land was in private ownership – highly concentrated in a few hands – from early on. Throughout the twentieth century, large-scale investment in land led to land concentration, high land prices and displacement of local populations. However, peasants had opportunities to acquire land – for example, through protective institutions for coastal land and squatting. The population number has been low since colonization, so displacement was not on a massive scale.

This structure later offered an easy base for real estate and tourism investors to buy land, thereby continuing externally led development and consolidating the North America–Guanacaste corridor (Van Noorloos 2011a). Since displacement and land concentration mainly took place during earlier 'land grabs', with the low population number the present pressure on land is not causing massive displacement. Residential tourism has fragmented landownership rather than contributed to concentration; it causes a process of gentrification and foreignization, rather than a land grab as such. Nevertheless, there are many problems: while residential tourism receives little attention in the land grab debate, this chapter has shown that it puts great pressure on local land markets. It endangers access to land for local and poor migrant groups, as land is increasingly becoming an object of speculation rather than production. These processes take place in a broader context: the sidelining of smallholder peasant production has characterized Guanacaste since the 1980s (Edelman 2005), and the lack of viable alternatives for smallholders plays a role in current land and economic conversion.

Compared with land acquisitions in other sectors, residential tourism offers better opportunities for employment; but, as in other sectors, much of the work is vulnerable, low in quality, and often performed by migrants; and real-estate-led development is vulnerable and volatile. The residential tourism industry has thus created new opportunities, but also specific types of new dependencies. Costa Rica's strict national regulations and laws and elaborate checks and balances often fail to prevent damage in the face of rapid developments, important economic and political interests, and local government's traditional weakness.

The case of residential tourism can teach us some important lessons for the debate on global land acquisitions. First, the overall development effects of land investments can be understood only by exploring the articulations between ecological, economic and social strands of sustainable development. For example, in the tourist industry, economic and environmental aspects are interwoven in complex ways. Secondly, the impact of residential tourism is not limited to the local or regional level: distant regions are also directly affected through flows of capital, goods, people, etc. By taking into account these translocal flows, corridors and effects, we can arrive at a broader understanding, which cannot be provided by static, bounded impact evaluations (Zoomers and Van Westen 2011). Thirdly, discussions on land issues often emphasize certain types of regulation and governance, such as voluntary regulations for responsible investment and strengthening national counterbalancing institutions. However, these measures may lack effectiveness if broader underlying developments are left untouched (Borras and Franco 2010b; Zoomers 2013). This research has also shown that while involving the local population in, for example, decision-making on land or compensation mechanisms is important, it is an extremely complex process.

Finally, a temporal and historical dimension should be integrated in evaluations of land investment and sustainable development (Seghezzo 2009): it is important to provide a dynamic perspective, whereas long-term effects are often not sufficiently taken into account. The case of Guanacaste shows that transnational land investment and external dependencies can be deeply rooted in a region's history. This makes current processes more difficult to regulate or counter, while at the same time these historical factors also influence the way in which current land acquisitions are affecting the region. In Guanacaste it is clear that 'land grabs' can set in progress a process of land-based capitalism and land concentration that is very difficult to counter at later stages: whereas economic activities have changed, external control over land is ongoing.

6 | Water grabbing in the Andean region: illustrative cases from Peru and Ecuador

Rutgerd Boelens, Antonio Gaybor
and Jan Hendriks[1]

Introduction

The world is experiencing a transnational trade boom in agricultural produce. Exports of fresh vegetables, fruits and flowers have doubled in the last decade. International trade in the biofuels sector is growing rapidly. Permissive governmental policies allowing expansion of water-intensive crops have led to accumulation of water and land rights by large agribusiness companies (Ploeg 2008; Peña 2011; Krishnan and George 2012). These expansion processes all compete for water and land with local communities, degenerate local ecosystems, jeopardize local food security, and profoundly alter existing modes of production and distribution of income (Boelens and Vos 2012).

Transnational companies are buying up land in countries in the South on a massive, unprecedented scale (Zoomers 2010; Borras et al. 2012). Analyses seldom relate this 'land grabbing' seriously and profoundly with 'water grabbing', even when the two are deeply interwoven (Gaybor 2011; Woodhouse 2012). As GRAIN puts it:

> Behind the current dispute for land, there is a worldwide struggle for control over water. Those who have been monopolizing extensive cropland areas in recent years, whether they live in Addis Ababa, Dubai or London, understand that the access to water they are obtaining, often free of charge and without any restrictions, may be worth more in the long term than the land itself. (Hobbelink and GRAIN 2013: 28)

With soaring prices for foods, biofuels and precious metals, water necessary for production acquires an increasingly important role and value on the international market, and accumulation of capital by transnational companies is closely linked with their need to control water resources (Arrayo and Boelens 2013; Kay and Franco 2012). As Mehta et al. put it, 'growing evidence suggests that in many cases land grabbing may be motivated by the desire to capture water resources' (2012: 194; see also Bebbington et al. 2010; Wester and Hoogesteger 2011; Woodhouse 2012). This chapter, therefore, argues for far more profound and explicit attention to, and analysis of, water concentration in the current land grabbing debate. Simultaneously, we will show how not all water grabbing is necessarily or proportionally related to the accumulation of areas of land.

Combined accumulation of land and water, through private companies' interests, in a neoliberal context of globalization, is a new expression of the way powerful regions assure their supply of foods and high-value products, by draining distant localities and economically less powerful peoples (Bueno de Mesquita 2011; Gaybor 2011). This hydro-colonialism transcends the classic North–South opposition. For example, GRAIN analyses the way India has emptied its aquifers during many decades of unsustainable irrigation. Now India plans to meet its demands by purchasing land and growing food abroad, where more water is available – 'the only way to feed India's growing population'. They also explain how 'Saudi Arabia does not lack land to grow food. What the Kingdom lacks is water and its companies are looking for it in such countries as Ethiopia' (GRAIN 2013: 28).

New expressions of land and water plundering pose a major threat to local population groups. In almost all large-scale land and water transactions, local families and communities that depend on these territories for their livelihoods and production systems are affected. This legal, extralegal or illegal looting – not only of their land but, above all, of their water sources – generally makes it impossible for them to continue living in their usual habitat.

This chapter will analyse the cases of Peru and Ecuador. We emphasize accumulation of water for agrarian purposes and the relationship with accumulation of land. At the same time, there is the need to acknowledge that the phenomenon of water seizure increasingly acquires much broader dimensions, above all in the sectors of mining, hydroelectricity and other energy, and human water supply sectors (e.g. Berge 2011; Perreault et al. 2011; Isch et al. 2012; Mehta et al. 2012; Chapter 8 on Vietnam, this volume). The characteristics of threats to local communities' security vary according to the usage sector. For example, the mining and hydrocarbon sector threatens local use by occupying and/or polluting rural communities, indigenous territories and watersheds (e.g. Budds and Hinojosa 2012; Sosa 2012). The hydropower sector often threatens local water security by drastically altering the continuity and timing of available water flows. As shown, for example, in cases analysed by Bauer (1997) in Chile and Roa and Duarte (2013) in Colombia, changing a river's flow regime seriously impacts the survival of fishing communities, while river water may be held back just when local farmers need water the most.

Although there has always been colonial and neocolonial pillage of water and land, it is ultimately acquiring new dimensions. Now the dimensions are global and driven by neoliberal laws and policies, by worldwide crises combining a series of transnational problems (e.g. climate change, energy crisis, food and financial crises).

Legal norms and national institutions involved in managing and controlling water resources are often reoriented as a function of these problems and interests. Increasing production and exportation of products – agricultural and other – requiring plenty of water and guaranteed water security has major implications for water governance. As in many other countries, Peru and Ecuador's changes in legal and institutional frameworks have been profound and with a strong impact.

The next section will present some overall conceptual considerations regarding the water grabbing process. The two following sections will analyse land and water grabbing in Peru and Ecuador. The final part presents brief reflections, discussion and conclusions. We find that, faced with these new, globalizing challenges, local groups of affected stakeholders need to apply multilevel strategies and involve larger scales, to pressure for their demands, mobilize support, participate in decision-making, and deal with new policies for accumulating and seizing land and water.

Accumulation of water in the hands of the few

Agro-industrial companies commonly strategize to maximize their investment's economic profitability by carefully identifying where they can find the cheapest, timeliest supply of inputs. They occupy those territories where they can get low-cost resources and then incorporate them into value chains, nationally and transnationally. For such a strategy, companies require a favourable investment climate, such as in Peru and Ecuador. One of the consequences of this strategy is the need to substantially reshape local correlations regarding access to and/or ownership of natural resources, in particular water and land. This normally profoundly restructures labour and livelihood relationships (Swyngedouw 2005; Achterhuis et al. 2010; Boelens and Vos 2012). Appropriation of land and water by large national and transnational companies involves re-allocation of water resources and property that used to belong to local families, communities and ecosystems, so it often generates contradictions and conflicts.

We can distinguish four interrelated levels of confrontation ('Echelons of Rights Analysis'; see also Boelens and Zwarteveen 2005; Boelens 2009), which together comprise the arena in which these water grabbing processes occur: the conflicts related to seizure of water and other resources per se; conflicts over determining the contents of rules and rights; conflicts over who has legitimate authority to manage and govern water; and conflicts among discourses that defend or challenge particular water political hierarchies and policies. These 'echelons' are directly related to and structure each other. An everyday illustration is documented by Cárdenas (2012) in a study for the Justicia Hídrica/Water Justice Alliance. He presents the example of Ica (see also www.justiciahidrica.org; Rendón 2009; Hepworth et al. 2010; Oré 2011), one of Peru's most important farming valleys:

In the Ica Valley, the climate, strategic location and fertile soils favour agricultural development even though this desert gets only 50 millimetres/year of rain. The aquifer contains almost one third of the country's underground water resource reserve. Currently, however, it is seriously over-extracted and the water table drops an average of 0.8 metres a year. Thousands of small and medium farmers are marginalized, since their wells and canals dry up and their pumps can no longer extract water. They cannot compete with the powerful water extraction technology of large agribusiness companies that have increasingly purchased land in the valley, with support from the government, which has made reforms favourable to agribusiness for export. A total of 0.1 per cent of users (the agro exporters) has accumulated 36 per cent of the water, whereas 71 per cent (small farmers) can access only 9 per cent of total water. Cárdenas quotes one stakeholder, who explains that, when official water rights are granted, the exact volume involved is often of little importance to the company, since this official access in practice means sufficient licence to steal more – official oversight of volumes actually extracted is minimal and almost impossible (see also Hepworth et al. 2010).

Companies access water not only by directly accumulating land and water sources. 'Transferring' water sources and infrastructure is equally important. For example, the Agrokasa company has only six wells on their plantation, but has purchased twenty-two wells from small farmers elsewhere, piping their water to its own land. Chapi has twenty wells, all located outside its property. These wells drain water that local villages used for their livelihoods (Cárdenas 2012).

At the first level of analysis, then, we see the struggle and conflict for *resources and access to resources*: who has access to water, to water infrastructure, to the materials and funding to use and administer water resources? Cárdenas illustrates, for instance, how in Ica ten companies extract over two-thirds of the zone's underground water reserve.

At a second level of abstraction, conflicts and agreements also arise, significantly, about the *contents of rules, rights and laws* determining water distribution and allocation. The case of Ica exemplifies how the rights and rules that used to protect small water users have now been amended to facilitate and protect investment of (international) capital and, consequently, accumulation of water use by large companies for export. Bans on extracting underground water are the most important legal instrument to prevent over-pumping, but in practice these laws are subtly adjusted or simply not enforced (see Wester and Hoogesteger 2011). In Ica, most new licences granted just before the official water ban have been for agro exporters. The question of which norms and principles should be considered legitimate is, therefore, an intrinsic part of struggles over water. At this level of dispute we also observe, for example, denial of customary water rights or their official reformulation under discriminatory criteria (Boelens 2009), as well as new rules enabling the deterritorialization of water rights, detaching them from local land, canals and wells. Similarly, as in Ica, there is decollectivization and individualization of water rights (Urteaga 2010), leading in practice to a buy-up of rights to land and wells, and thereby a de facto transfer of water rights.

A third way water rights are contested in water grabbing involves struggles about *legitimate authority*, the issue of who decides about water allocation and distribution, and who is entitled to take part in making the laws and rules about water management. In the arenas of water policy-making, above all when export chains' interests are at stake, decision-making is often exclusive. In Ica Valley, as explained by Hepworth et al. (2010), Oré (2011) and Cárdenas (2012), agro exporters use their economic and political power to influence decision-making by authorities, and get the licences and permits they need. The authority takes part in the conflict generated by water accumulation, not only by what it does, but also by what it does not do (e.g. not confronting illegal usurpation, not protecting priority uses). In the process of 'updating' water extraction rights, small users have been the ones who have lost rights, which the water authority has transferred to large farmers (Cárdenas 2012). Oré (2011) explains how indigenous water authorities in the valley lost their power of governance, first to hacienda plantations, then to the government with its technicians and bureaucrats, and finally to the large companies.

The fourth and last major area of dispute over water lies in the *discourses* used to address water problems and solutions. What languages and practices are accepted to frame and model water laws, and what are the preferred ways of conceptualizing water issues? How do the different regimes of representation characterize relationships among stakeholders, the social and technical setting, and access to and control over water? The transnational, neoliberal capitalist discourse defending and legitimizing water grabbing commonly asserts, for example, the need to modernize 'traditional and marginal practices and production systems' and to intervene in 'unproductive land' and transform 'under-used, wasted water resources', which makes it indispensable to tap the productive and water-use efficiency of large agro-industrial companies (Boelens and Vos 2012). Governments often create regimes of positive discrimination towards these transnational chains, granting them rights to large volumes of water in order to attract international investment and cutting-edge technology. Existing production systems and water rights are commonly denied.

In Peru, for example, as Urteaga (2010) explains, the neoliberal discourse has promoted legislation to change the alleged 'mismanagement and under-used potential of water' and to 'save water', facilitating transfer of water rights to more 'valuable' uses and rewarding 'more efficient users' who get an 'efficiency certificate': 'owners or operators who have a certificate of efficiency have preference in granting of new rights ...' (Water Law, Regulations, Article 72). Urteaga (ibid.) shows how such single-criterion instruments result in denial of social and ecological impacts and in accumulation of water by the few, since the agro exporters have the economic power to purchase cutting-edge technology – technology with which, ironically, they over-pump the aquifer unsustainably. Furthermore, the 'savings in water' are rewarded by new water rights which, as explained above, in practice means even more accumulation of water through illegal extraction and therefore depletion of the aquifer. This discourse means that small farmers are considered 'inefficient' and consequently excluded (Urteaga 2010; Cárdenas 2012).

The three basic ingredients that are defended and materialized in the neoliberal discourse and international modus operandi to amend national water administrations are decentralized decision-making, expansion of private property rights, and markets (Zwarteveen and Boelens 2011). Despite widespread proof of the major social problems that such prescriptions tend to create – among others, water grabbing – hegemonic policies reinforce this model rather than challenging it (see also Swyngedouw 2005). Privatization and commoditization of water supply services and water infrastructure that used to be common, public and non-tradable – and the corresponding legal and political reform – often become part of the process that Harvey (2003) has analysed as 'accumulation by dispossession'. This also shows how appropriation, expropriation or thievery of water are an integral part of the worldwide reorganization of capital happening through the contradictory processes of consolidation of economic power and social-institutional fragmentation of local stakeholders. The explosive growth of agro-exports and the consequent transnationalization of water fever are accompanied by a major change in how and at what political levels water is governed: from local organizations and national regulations towards investment and free trade treaties, and from local and national scales towards international scales.

Case analysis of Peru

Availability and use of water in Peru Peru would appear to have abundant, good-quality fresh water: the average availability in Peruvian territory is 77,534 cubic metres per inhabitant per year (Kuroiwa 2012). However, 97.7 per cent of this availability is located in the eastern watershed areas of the country (towards the Atlantic) while only 1.8 per cent of the water runs down the western slopes to the Pacific areas – the desert where over 65 per cent of Peru's population lives (ANA 2009). Here, water availability is of the order of 2000 cubic metres per inhabitant per year, close to 'water stress' as defined by Falkenmark.[2] Most of this water flows to the coast during the few months when precipitation is abundant in the highlands (December to March), which is an aggravating factor during the rest of the year when water is scarce.

According to data for 2000/01 (ANA 2009), 80 per cent of annual water consumption is for agricultural purposes, both on the Pacific and Atlantic sides (14 billion cubic metres/year and 2 billion cubic metres/year, respectively). Domestic use for human water supply is 12 to 14 per cent of total consumption, and the rest is absorbed by industrial and mining activities. Non-consumptive use of water, driving turbines in hydroelectric power plants, is of the order of 11 million cubic metres/year (MCM/year). These sectoral consumption figures can be assumed to have increased considerably over the last decade, in view of the country's economic growth.

According to the IV Agricultural Census of 2012, Peru has almost 2,300,000 farm units (i.e. an increase of 30 per cent – half a million farmers – since the former Agricultural Census of 1994), totalling a land area of nearly 7 million hectares of cropland. About 2.6 million hectares (36 per cent of total crop area) use irrigation and involve a total of over 800,000 irrigators (see Table 6.1):

TABLE 6.1 Farm units, irrigated areas and number of irrigators in Peru

Zone of the country	Farm units	Agricultural land area (ha)	Average farm size (ha/farm)	Area cultivated with irrigation (ha)	Number of irrigators
Coast	357,561	1,686,778	4.7	1,469,422	312,545
Highlands	1,444,530	3,296,008	2.3	989,482	464,914
Jungle	458,882	2,142,222	4.7	120,996	42,092
TOTAL	2,260,973	7,125,008	3.2	2,579,900	819,551

Sources: Columns 2, 3: IV Agricultural Census (2012); Columns 5 and 6: prepared by the authors on the basis of ANA records (January 2012)

As these data on the country's various zones show, it is absolutely clear that irrigation water is an indispensable resource to generate income and food security for a huge group of small and medium farmers. So, the over 300,000 irrigation users on the coast depend totally on the water either running off or transferred to the western slopes of the highlands, since there is practically no precipitation on the coastal plains. Without water, coastal land has no value at all for agricultural purposes.

Water use rights in Peru Both the General Water Law (1969–2009) and the current Water Resources Law (since 2009) stipulate that for grid home water supply and for production, users must have a water use right granted by the corresponding authority, in the form of a licence, permit or authorization.

Historically, water use rights' registration has been slow and faces many hurdles. As of 31 March 2004 (almost thirty-five years after the General Water Law was enacted) only 9,702 water use licences had been granted for agricultural use (Guerrero 2006). In February 2004, the government and some thirty agrarian federations signed the so-called 'Green Charter'. One of the fifty-three immediate measures agreed upon was to launch the 'Programme to Formalize Water Use Rights' (PROFODUA), to grant water licences en masse, free of charge, to agricultural users. As of 30 June 2009, that programme had delivered 367,467 licences, for a total of 451,825 farms,[3] corresponding to approximately 200,000 farmers.[4]

This formalization of water use rights for agricultural purposes by the state has been conducted almost exclusively for Peru's coastal areas. By contrast, although Peru's highlands have a greater number of farmers and more users of irrigation water, PROFODUA has reached only a couple of Andean valleys. It is precisely in the highlands that most of the (extremely) poor people live, those most vulnerable to climate adversities and in terms of social justice. The lower legal security regarding water rights affects most of the over 460,000 irrigator families in this part of the country (see Table 6.1). This generates uncertainty regarding access to and distribution of water among farmers who share irrigation systems, but above all in relation to new stakeholders and new water demands arising in certain zones.

This is why increasing use of public water supply and especially increasing demand by new (mega-)mining extraction projects in the highlands are perceived as threats. These concerns are often combined with the sense that water availability is waning because of climate change. Evidently, these perceptions by the rural population magnify the resistance they often demonstrate when new stakeholders demand (more) water in these zones.

Administrative procedures to apply for water use rights are quite complex and therefore costly. In practice, this procedure can be afforded individually only by farmers and companies that can pay for the effort. Currently, formalizing water use rights for small farmers has become viable almost only in the case of applying – collectively – for a 'block' water use licence and/or being a beneficiary of PROFODUA, in which case the procedure is considered free of charge. In view of the low institutional and budgetary dimension of the relevant entities, the situation prevails in which smaller water users are left almost defenceless, with few opportunities to formally ensure their water rights.

Accumulation of rights to and access to water in Peru Since approximately the middle of the twentieth century, the Peruvian state has made huge investments in water projects, particularly in the coastal areas and with the main purpose of increasing cropland area, as well as improving irrigation security in existing agricultural areas. Flagship projects have been implemented, such as *Colonización* San Lorenzo, the Chira-Piura Special Project, Tinajones, Jequetepeque, and the Majes Project. The water required for these irrigation schemes comes from major rivers flowing down from the western Andes. Constituting legal water reserves for these projects has led in several cases to disputes among interest groups and among departments of the country.

For several decades, water projects mainly benefited local farmers, satisfying the desire for local development, so the need to ensure legal water reserves was also motivated by this vision of development. However, since the 1990s there has been a fundamental change in these projects, targeting the economic agents who have the money to invest and produce for large-scale export (Burneo 2011). The new farmland is generally auctioned off under conditions that small and medium farmers cannot afford, so almost exclusively large companies continue buying up and amassing property under these 'Special Projects'. They are assured of irrigation water[5] and are also heavily subsidized by the government because the land is normally auctioned off at below the state's cost, while strong guarantees are granted to investors. This transfers huge amounts of Peruvian public funds to large agribusiness investors, leaving small and medium farmers with almost no benefits.

One of the first projects to introduce this model of concentrating land and water use rights with the few was the Chavimochic Special Project. Table 6.2 shows that eleven investors bought 86 per cent (37,780 hectares) of all the new farmland sold by the project. These purchases were accompanied by

TABLE 6.2 Largest buyers of lots in the Chavimochic Project, 1994–2006 period

Company	Gross area (ha)	Percentage of total area
Camposol SA	10,050	22.9
Compañía Minera San Simón SA	6,185	14.1
El Rocío SA	4,901	11.2
Empresa Agroindustrial Laredo	3,790	8.6
Rego Corporation	3,778	8.6
Green Peru SA	1,660	3.8
Danper Trujillo SA	1,640	3.7
Morava SAC	1,622	3.7
Sociedad Agrícola Virú SA	1,503	3.4
Ugás de la Torre Ugarte Manuel	1,347	3.1
Cefer Agrícola Chavimochic	1,304	3.0
Subtotal	37,780	86.1
TOTAL, project area (ha)	43,870	100.0

Source: Private Investment Promotion Department of the Chavimochic Special Project, quoted in Burneo (2011)

technical and legal assurance of access to water of the order of 400 MCM/ year for these companies.

The recent auctioning of new farmland by the Olmos Special Project confirms this pattern (see Table 6.3): fourteen companies bought a total of 28,000 hectares out of the 38,000 hectares put up for auction. This technically and legally assures them of water availability of nearly 300 MCM/year.

TABLE 6.3 Buyers of lots in the Olmos Project in auctions on 9 December 2011 and 12 April 2012

Companies allocated land	Gross area (ha)	Number of lots
Corporación Azucarera del Perú SA	11,100	11
GLORIA SA	4,500	8
Ingenieros Civiles y Contratistas Generales SA	1,000	2
Agroindustrias AIB SA	500	1
Pesquera Rosario SA	500	2
Anglo American Michiquillay SA	500	2
Empacadora Agroexport SA de CV	480	2
Danper Trujillo SAC	1,250	2
Chimú Agropecuaria SA	1,250	2
Agrícola Challapampa SAC	250	1
Parfen SA	4,000	4
Agrícola Pampa Baja SAC	1,370	2
Consorcio Corporación Mendoza del Solar SAC/ Ulexandes SAC	1,000	1
NIISA Corporación SA	300	1
Total area auctioned as of April 2012 (ha)	28,000	41
Total area of the whole project (ha)	38,000	51

Source: Prepared by the authors with data from the Olmos Tinajones Special Project (peot.regionlambayeque.gob.pe)

In the case of both the Chavimochic Project and the Olmos Project, almost all of the investors are consolidated Peruvian firms (including 'traditional' family holdings) or new emerging national companies. In this respect, the Peruvian case shows differences when compared with many other countries: despite the fact that the agro-food chains for which most of these firms produce have huge transnational dimensions, actual land grabbing is practised mainly by national companies with, moreover, intensive water grabbing based on relatively smaller surface areas.

Concentration of farmland and the resulting accumulation of water use rights do not happen only in the government's 'Special Project' auctions, but also in the buying up of farmland – new and existing – in zones alongside them, where these projects directly or indirectly provide water security. This is the case, for example, of two companies (Maple Etanol S.R.L. and Caña Brava) that produce biofuels, which have purchased nearly 20,000 hectares and obtained corresponding water use rights in the Chira River Valley, Piura.

Concentration of landownership and the consequent accumulation of water use rights for agricultural purposes even happen in valleys with less water security, turning the water scarcity scenario into a drama for most parties involved. The Ica valley is the epitome of this: in ten years the situation changed from sustainable extraction to over-pumping of the aquifers, of the order of 290 MCM/year (Revista Agraria 2012c), causing structural dropping of water tables and deterioration of the quality of pumped water.

In general terms, the new agro-export plantations and sugar-growing agro-industrial companies on Peru's coast total far more than 200,000 hectares: more than one quarter of the farmland in that part of the country (Revista Agraria 2011b). Of these companies, the Gloria Group already controls some 80,000 hectares, after its last purchases in the Olmos irrigation project; that is, it controls approximately 10 per cent of the agricultural land irrigated in Peru's coastal areas (Revista Agraria 2012a).

Buying land and obtaining the relevant water use rights for large agricultural companies and other investors generally involves top-quality farmland and a high degree of security for water availability, with both technical and legal guarantees. It is estimated that, in Peru's coastal areas, no more than thirty to fifty large owners – out of a total of approximately 312,000 registered irrigation users in that territory – have accrued usage rights totalling approximately 25 per cent of the water consumed for agricultural purposes, of the order of 4,000 MCM/year.

Case analysis of Ecuador

Availability and use of water in Ecuador Ecuador has abundant available water but a very heterogeneous regional and local spatial distribution pattern. Most water runs towards the Amazon region, and another major proportion runs towards the Pacific. Most of Ecuador's population lives in the highlands and in the coastal provinces. Unlike those of some countries in South America, such as Chile and Peru, Ecuador's coastal region is humid and tropical, with a smaller proportion of dry forest. Much of the water running to the Pacific forms large rivers.

According to information from the public water authority, 3,428 m³/s (cubic metres per second) has been granted on a concession basis, 80 per cent for hydropower, 15 per cent for irrigation, and the remaining 5 per cent for other uses. Regarding use for consumption, irrigation is the main sector, using nearly 80 per cent of the water for which usage rights have been granted (Table 6.4).

In 2000 Ecuador had 843,000 farms and an area under cultivation of 6.3

TABLE 6.4 Consumptive use of water according to rights

Use	Percentage of total
Agriculture	79
Industry	8
Water supply for domestic consumption	13

Source: SENAGUA (2010)

million hectares. The irrigated area is nearly 14 per cent of this total farmland (INEC 2002). In the first decade of this century, the irrigated area increased significantly, at an average rate of 2.8 per cent per year (ibid.; SENAGUA 2010), reaching about 20 per cent of the cultivated area in 2010, which is approximately 1.5 million hectares (MAGAP 2012). Now one out of every four farms has irrigation, and lately there has been major social investment in community, public and individual irrigation systems.

Water use rights in Ecuador Water use rights clearly embody power relationships (Boelens 2009). Ecuador's current Water Law, which has been in effect for forty years, establishes that water is a national domain for public use; and, therefore, all individuals or corporate bodies requiring water for productive uses such as agriculture must obtain a concession or right to use water. The law establishes that the right to use water has a definite time period, which the regulations define as ten years. This central issue is, however, repeatedly ignored. Concession is a fundamental mechanism for public water governance, establishing rights and obligations for beneficiaries. When allocating water, the state does not waive its power to apply penalties and even withdraw usage rights when the concession conditions are not met. However, in practice, the government generally does not apply this penalty; and when it tries to do so, it is precisely the major water-holding farms that do not want to abide by it.

Given the gargantuan irrigation water concentration with the few, particularly in certain provinces, the new Ecuadorean Constitution of 2008 orders the government to redistribute water rights concessions and do justice to small farmers – within a two-year time frame, beginning in October 2008.[6] However, the national water authority has failed to enforce this constitutional provision; on the contrary, a period was opened up to formalize water use, ignoring the law.

Concentration of water rights and access in Ecuador The magnitude of irrigation water concentration cannot be satisfactorily appreciated without taking into account two complementary forms of access, what Harvey (2003) terms strategies of dispossession. One is legalized, with rights allocated by the relevant authority; the other is against the law.

As for formalized concentration, the 1972 Water Law legalized part of the water use that had been illegal. By 2005, some 14,800 concessions for irrigation had been granted, accelerating in the next five years to 34,600 by 2010. During the neoliberal period of government in the 1990s, large agribusinesses in the highlands and in the coastal areas pressured to establish mechanisms to assure their concentration of ownership of land and irrigation water. They advocated privatizing water services and commoditizing water rights. Resistance by rural and diverse societal movements prevented enactment of the law that would have guaranteed these aspirations. However, an administrative resolution granted water rights for irrigation for an undetermined period beginning in January 1996, which perpetuates the concentration of water indefinitely.

The distribution of the area watered according to types of farms is profoundly unequal. One per cent of farms control 29 per cent of the country's irrigated areas, whereas 84 per cent of small farms with irrigation are cultivating only 26 per cent of the country's irrigated area (Gaybor 2011). The first group of farms averages 196 hectares each, and the latter average 2 hectares. This clearly reveals that concentration of land and water go together.

As in the case of Peru, in Ecuador the larger agricultural enterprises tend to be mainly national-based firms (including 'traditional' family holdings) or new emerging national companies – even though some of them (for example, in the banana sector) have large transnational dimensions. As already noted, a difference can be observed here with respect to many other countries, where water and land grabbing are mainly originated by transnational companies that have their bases abroad.

TABLE 6.5 Percentages of total and irrigated farmland in Ecuador, 2000[7]

Average area per farm (ha)	Distribution of irrigated area (%)	Distribution of farms with irrigation (%)	Area irrigated per farm (%)	Farms with irrigation (%)
2	26	84	21	32
13	23	12	10	18
42	22	3	9	13
196	29	1	27	25
8	100	100	14	28

Source: INEC (2002)

The agribusiness sector operates farms almost exclusively with irrigation, since irrigation is a determining factor to make high-profit production possible.

This explains why the 25 per cent of companies with over two hundred hectares have irrigation; those in this group that do not have this artificial water facility are mainly located in zones with acceptable levels of precipitation for their production processes. By contrast, a far smaller proportion of small and medium farms have irrigation, in the range of 13 to 32 per cent (Table 6.5).

An illustration of water concentration can be seen in several micro-watersheds that are part of the Lower Guayas River Basin. In selected stretches, covering a concession flow of 33 m³/s, only forty-three companies monopolize almost three-quarters of the water allocated by the government (SENAGUA 2010).

Whenever less surface water is available or readily accessible – because of distances, costs or conflicts between uses and users – more underground water is used for agriculture. In fact, from 2005 to 2010, underground water concessions rose by a yearly average of 10 per cent, while surface water concessions grew by a more modest 4 per cent (Gaybor 2011).

In addition to the rapid growth of formalized use of well water, groundwater use is much more territorially concentrated than surface water. For example, in three provinces of the Ecuadorean coast, where agribusinesses are dominant and small farmers still remain, use of underground water is more concentrated than anywhere else. Only twenty-three companies, out of a total of 130,000 existing farms, hold rights to 68 per cent of well water, granted by the state, with an average flow of 480 litres/second per company (CAMAREN 2010).

TABLE 6.6 Formalized concentration of well water

Province	Number of companies	Per cent of total flow
Los Ríos	7	74
Guayas	13	65
El Oro	3	81
TOTAL	23	68

Source: SENAGUA (2010)

For many years Ecuador has remained the world's foremost exporter of bananas. Unlike the situation two or three decades ago, all the banana production for export now depends on irrigation. This production is dominated by large agribusiness. The production process has major environmental impacts, such as pollution of surface and underground water and deterioration of related agro ecosystems. Another major crop that is very dependent on irrigation, grown in the Lower Guayas Basin, is industrial sugar cane, also dominated by capitalist companies (see also Nuijen et al. for Cambodia, Chapter 9, this volume).

Even though these business activities are highly profitable, nearly 70 per cent of national banana production is conducted using water illegally, and 30 per cent in the case of sugar cane (Gaybor 2008). These two types of commodities are grown on barely 5 per cent of Ecuador's total cropland, but in real terms they are using the equivalent of at least 50 per cent of water granted by the state, sufficient to cover an area of 1.1 million hectares with irrigation.

Evidently, concentration of water generates very unequal rural development. Business production is part of transnational chains and exports giant volumes of virtual water for the foreign market. Practically all of this is done under irrigation: bananas, flowers, broccoli, papaya, mango and pineapple, but also sugar cane fits in this group, both for table sugar and for biofuels to export (ibid.). There is a broad range of mechanisms that favour water concentration by the few by dispossession of common assets, excluding the great majority of the rural population from access to water. These mechanisms include distributing water rights as a function of the area planted, flat rates, sponsoring or consenting to dispossession, illegal distribution of water from sources, authorities enabling violation of norms, sectoral policies with a clear bias favouring capital. In fact, the means used for dispossession range from preparing the norms, to power groups applying and enforcing them, arbitrary 'stopping up' of rivers, massive, clandestine drilling of water wells, breach and violation of the law, and buying up land from small and medium farmers who have access or enable access to more water.

Discussion and conclusions

The hydrological cycle and many uses of water are intrinsically related to particular land uses and territorial occupations. Though the two are deeply entwined in many cases, the current land grabbing debate tends to omit explicit, sustained attention to the issue of water accumulation by the 'land grabbing' companies. For reasons of acquiring water (e.g. from distant places) and using water productively (e.g. food production), greater water consumption involves a greater need to gain control over certain territories, a control which includes both surface and groundwater resources. Therefore, the growing demand and decreasing availability of good-quality fresh water have not only intensified competition and conflict among different uses and users of water resources, but have also equally triggered a struggle over land properties and territories – and vice versa.

Since the 1990s, many Latin American countries have experienced a rapid process of water use rights accumulation for agricultural purposes by a small group of large agribusiness companies, agro exporters and other investors to ensure irrigation water availability on the land purchased. In Peru, for example, it is estimated that these companies consume approximately 25 per cent of the total volume used in irrigated agriculture. A considerable part of the land purchased by these companies is located in or near the areas of mega-projects promoted by the state, which (in their design phase, decades ago) were originally planned to improve water access for small and medium farmers. Now the companies have cropland with high legal and water security, far better than the water security of the majority of agricultural users. We also see that this often leads to a situation of leaving local communities and territories 'high and dry', exposed to social and ecological disasters.

The costs of investing in water infrastructure for these mega-projects have been substantially covered by governments, so there has been and continues to be a considerable subsidy (paid for by the taxpayers) for the companies awarded land in these zones.[8]

At the same time, the transnational characteristics of agribusiness chains express concentration of land and water in the phenomenon of exporting *virtual water* – the water required to produce and process commodities. Water extraction and agricultural (and mining) processing by large (trans)national companies result in a gigantic transfer of water resources, generally from poor, arid zones to economically powerful centres (Boelens and Vos 2012).

However, the problem lies not only in the *volumes* of water concentrated in just a few stakeholders. For example, in a non-agricultural transnational business such as the mining sector, the concentration or pollution of a small flow of water by a company can have drastic immediate effects, jeopardizing the survival of whole population groups who depend on this flow to provide their water for domestic consumption (e.g. Perreault et al. 2011; Budds and Hinojosa 2012; Sosa 2012).

The fluidity, fluctuation and 'invisibility' of surface and underground water are all factors that add great complexity to the efforts that have to be made to understand and counteract the process of water concentration and dispossession. Or, as Mehta et al. put it, '[t]he fluid properties of water interact with the "slippery" nature of the grabbing processes: unequal power relations; fuzziness between legality and illegality and formal and informal rights; unclear administrative boundaries and jurisdictions, and fragmented negotiation processes' (2012: 193).

Especially in non-agricultural water use sectors (e.g. drinking water pro-vision, hydropower generation and mining, which are not the direct topic of this chapter), water grabbing is not automatically and 'proportionally' related to acquiring vast areas of land. Furthermore, in its turn, although land accumulation is often related to water accumulation, this is not always a direct, proportional relationship in terms of volumes and area. The case of Ica is illustrative, where large agribusinesses often acquire wells outside their own property without purchasing the respective land.

A notorious problem is the fact that water use rights are not registered – and therefore not protected – for the vast majority of rural families in the Peruvian and Ecuadorean highlands. This is despite the fact that this region contains comparatively more irrigation users than other zones in these two countries. The lack of sufficient knowledge about, recognition of and protection for many farmers' water use rights (customary or formal), particularly in the highlands, is an important vulnerability factor affecting the water security of these social groups – especially considering the growing water demand of the new stakeholders appearing in these territories, with heavy asymmetries in terms of capacity and power to assure themselves of water resources.

Land and water grabbing are commonly presented as struggles over these material, productive resources. However, as we have analysed, many of the conflicts related to land and water grabbing go beyond the struggle over the resources and manifest themselves at four interconnected 'echelons' that shape land and water battles. In addition to the conflict over resources (water, land, labour, technologies, financial means), there is a simultaneous, deeply connected struggle over the contents of rules and rights related to land and water acquisition, allocation, use and preservation. Thirdly, there is the struggle over legitimate decision-making about land and water access and use, about who has authority to formulate and enforce the rules and rights, command land and water acquisition and management, and sanction the implementation of land and water user categories and their norms of conduct. Possessing 'legitimate authority' goes beyond the question of regulatory hierarchies to also involve the forces of the land and water world's epistemic communities, and the ways the land and water grabbing practices increasingly occur in settings where governance and authority are shifted from local customary and national government regulation to private international agreements, treaties and codes of conduct regarding land and water resource use. Fourthly, there is the conflict over discourses, over the composition and steering of power–knowledge–truth frameworks that legitimize and establish naturalized linkages among these echelons that defend particular configurations of resource distribution, rules and legitimate authority.

In the Andean countries, as in many other parts of the world, materializing social justice in water control almost necessarily requires collective bottom-up pressure. This requires not only local action but calls for connecting multiple scales of water action and governance – in response to water policies and the strategies of powerful adversaries. Threats to their territories and water resources require users' collectives to not only organize within their local institutions, but to resort to a variety of scales to defend their rights and pursue their development goals.

Expanding scales of water struggles is not only a strategic movement but also a direct consequence of the increasingly global nature of conflicts over water and the transnational background of the adversaries (Bebbington et al. 2010; Boelens et al. 2010). Local user groups' capacity to scale their alliance strategies is proving increasingly crucial in defending local water access and maintaining control over their rights and their future.

Asia

7 | Land governance and oil palm development: examples from Riau Province, Indonesia

Ari Susanti and Suseno Budidarsono

Introduction

In the growing global debate on transnational land deals for agriculture, investments in oil palm plantations play a significant role. A wide body of literature shows that these investments have caused widespread processes of land use change, often involving forest and agricultural land conversion. However, little research has been undertaken on understanding the underlying factors that are likely to enable these land use conversion processes. This chapter aims to analyse the most crucial land governance issues related to oil palm expansion in Indonesia. We show that not only large-scale oil palm investments cause widespread land use change; increasingly smallholders from all over Indonesia are involved in converting land into oil palm plantations. Besides the lucrative financial benefit from oil palm, the incompatible regulations related to land rights are the main reasons for this rapid expansion. This is aggravated by the absence of sound regional planning (such as in Riau Province, where palm oil production has become an important economic activity), which provides opportunities to convert lands into oil palm plantations relatively easily.

The land matrix report (Anseeuw et al. 2012) on transnational land deals for agriculture in the global South revealed that Indonesia is one of the targeted countries in Asia. Twenty-three land deals were identified, covering about 5.2 million hectares of land. Oil palm shares are by far the largest, up to 54 per cent of the land deals or covering around 2.8 million hectares. Other commodities involved in these deals are jatropha, corn, sugar cane, rubber and fruits. Foreign investments involved in these deals originate from Asian 'emerging' countries such as China, India, Malaysia and Singapore, from the Gulf states (Qatar), and from developed countries such as the USA, the UK and Australia. However, many investments in oil palm plantations come from domestic sources, including government-funded projects (ibid.).

Oil palm has become the most rapidly expanding tropical perennial crop in the last two decades, not only in Indonesia but also, for example, in Malaysia (Fitzherbert et al. 2008). This is mainly due to increasing global demand for palm oil for the food processing industry and biofuels. In the last fifty years in Indonesia, oil palm has expanded tremendously. While it occupied only 120,000 hectares in the 1960s, by 2010 approximately 8.4 million hectares were harvested, producing around 19.8 million metric tons of palm oil (Ministry of Agriculture 2012). Palm oil has become the largest export product after oil and natural gas and is widely perceived as an important commodity that serves national and regional incomes (Fischer 2010) as well as providing employment for the rural population (World Growth 2011). For these reasons the government of Indonesia plans to expand oil palm plantations further, up to approximately 20 million hectares by 2020, mainly in Sumatra, Kalimantan, Sulawesi and West Papua (Colchester et al. 2006).

It is alarming, however, that the land required to accommodate this expansion often becomes available through forest conversion and other agricultural land use conversion processes, including the conversion of rice fields (Burgers and Susanti 2011). Susanti and Burgers (forthcoming) show that these kinds of land use change processes are increasingly putting pressure on land. The process has been well documented in a number of studies related to oil palm expansion (IEA 2006; Edwards et al. 2010; FAO 2010a, 2011a; Koh and Ghazoul 2010). In many cases, these studies focus on the fact that oil palm expansion has triggered large-scale forest conversion. However, it is striking that little research has been undertaken on the underlying factors that enable such a rapid pace of forest conversion in a country where approximately 70 per cent of the land is under the control of and managed by the Indonesian Forestry Ministry (Ministry of Forestry 2011). The high rate of forest conversion into palm oil plantations should be rooted in developments which go beyond the control of the Ministry of Forestry, with its mandate in forest protection and sustainable use of forest resources and areas. Hence, a thorough understanding of land governance issues is a crucial factor in explaining this situation in Indonesia and is the main focus of this chapter.

The chapter is based on fieldwork, as well as on a review of existing literature, technical documents and regulations related to land administration issues, regulation and management. Statistical data from government sources both at national and regional level are added to provide a larger picture of the land debate. In order to understand how land governance issues impact the situation at field level, evidence is provided from our work in Riau Province.

Oil palm expansion in Indonesia

While oil palm (*Elaeis guineensis*) is originally from West Africa, it was first introduced to Indonesia in 1911 by the Dutch administration with the establishment of the first commercial plantation in the east coast of Sumatra.[1] Palm oil production grew rapidly, from 181 tons in 1919 to 190,627 tons of crude palm oil and 39,630 tons of kernel oil in 1937, owing particularly to the increasing uses of palm oil products for lubricants, soap production, candles and medicinal ointments, mostly for export. However, this development stopped during the Second World War. It took until the 1970s before the Indonesian government began to stimulate oil palm expansion again. Initially, this was done in the form of plantations coupled with transmigration programmes, aimed at stimulating development in the outer islands (Budidarsono et al. 2013). Through these programmes, oil palm emerged as one of Indonesia's most important crops. However, production really took off in the 1990s, with an average 10 per cent annual growth in oil palm plantations (Ministry of Agriculture 2012), partly as a result of a growing global demand for healthier fats and partly as a result of expanded Indonesian trade, economic liberalization and policy deregulation to attract investment (Basiron 2002). Recently, the demand has further increased since palm oil has come to be considered as a biofuel (Susanti and Burgers 2012).

The changing regulations: from large-scale monopoly to smallholders' involvement In the earlier stage of its development, oil palm was introduced and supported by government programmes in mainly large-scale plantation development schemes, and it had become a large estates' monopoly owing to the fact that its establishment requires substantial capital. More recently, smallholders' participation in palm oil production activities has been stimulated. A number of regulations related to palm oil production have enabled this. In 1977 the Nucleus Estate Smallholder (NES) programme was introduced by the Indonesian government funded by the government and also supported by the World Bank. Beginning in 1986, the nucleus companies had to take responsibility for financing the establishment of smallholder plantations through regular bank loan schemes (Jelsma et al. 2009). The nucleus companies (private and state-owned) were obliged to establish palm oil processing facilities as an integrated part of an oil palm estate.

Following the deregulation policies and liberalization of crude palm oil export in 1994, individual smallholder oil palm producers were no longer restricted by regulations that stipulated that they should be associated with nucleus companies. In 1995 Government Regulation No. 13/1995 allowed investors to establish processing facilities without managing oil palm plantations. With this regulation, many palm oil mills were established without being associated with specific oil palm plantations as their raw material suppliers. This created a new market for individual smallholders, who in the same year could also independently establish small-scale plantations (less than 25 hectares). Under the same regulation, individual small-scale producers could sell their produce to any palm oil processing mills. In addition, smallholders with a plantation size of less than 25 hectares are not required to apply for a plantation licence; only registration at the local estate crop agency is necessary (Ministerial Decree No. 357/KPTS/HK.350/5/2002 as by No. 26/Permentan/OT.140/2/2007). These further triggered the increase in the number of independent smallholders. And since then, middlemen acting as informal investors and buyers have been playing an increasingly crucial role in the rapid expansion of oil palm on smallholder land. The middlemen not only provide financial support for smallholders; they are also an important link between the palm oil mills and small-scale producers, as often the latter cannot deliver their products directly to the processing mill given transport constraints. Usually, a smallholder can receive funds from these middlemen to develop a small-scale plantation. In exchange, smallholders will sell to the middlemen in sharecropping deals, as a way to repay the loan.

To further accommodate this rapid expansion and the increasing importance of estate crops, Law No. 18/2004 on estate crops was enacted. Following the implementation of this law, the regulations on palm oil industry and plantation licensing were also revised. Ministerial Decree No. 357/Kpts/HK.350/5/2005 mandated oil palm processing mills to manage oil palm plantations in order to have a regular supply of their raw material. This obligation was strengthened by Ministerial Decree No. 26/Permentan/OT.140/2/2007, which stipulates that 20 per cent of the raw material of oil palm processing industries has to be produced from their own plantation.

The same regulation categorized oil palm plantations into smallholder (maximum 25 hectares) and large estates (maximum 100,000 hectares), with the exception of Papua, where the ceiling limit for the area is twice as large as in other locations. The limitation on area is not applicable to companies whose share is mainly held by a cooperative, by central and regional governments, or by communities which are in the process of going public. Foreigners or foreign legal entities which are willing to apply for these licences must collaborate with Indonesian citizens or legal Indonesian entities. This is in line with the Basic Agrarian Law (BAL), which stipulates that foreigners and foreign legal entities can have only secondary rights to lands, while Indonesian citizens and Indonesian legal entities can hold primary rights to lands. This helps to explain the high interest of domestic investors, including smallholders, in participating in land investments. So far, domestic investors are responsible for approximately 60 per cent of the total investment in oil palm plantations in Indonesia, strengthened by the fact that they can collaborate with foreign entities, which in many cases provide the required investment funds (Neraca.co.id 2012).

The oil palm boom All these supporting regulations contributed to Indonesia being the world's largest palm oil producer in 2006. Together with Malaysia, it controls around 85 per cent of the palm oil trade in the world (FAO 2010b). In 2010, Indonesia had around 8.4 million ha of oil palm being harvested, producing around 19.8 million metric tons of palm oil (Ministry of Agriculture 2012). In 2010, Indonesia exported around 16.9 million metric tons of crude palm oil, which was valued around 1.036 billion US$ (FAO 2010b). In the mar-

Box 7.1 The economics of Riau Province

Riau Province covers approximately 8.9 million hectares, of which 8.6 million hectares are state forest areas, including extensive and deep contiguous peat swamp forests (Badan Pusat Statistik Propinsi Riau 2011). These extensive forest areas are the focus of land use conversion into oil palm. In 2011, Riau Province had the largest area of plantation and contributed around 24 per cent to the national total area of oil palm plantation. The majority of oil palm plantations were cultivated by smallholders (53 per cent), and large estates cultivated around 47 per cent (Dinas Perkebunan Provinsi Riau 2011). There is an increasing number of new oil palm plantations being established on peatland areas. It is estimated that in the period 2000–05, around 60 per cent of new licences for oil palm plantations involved peatlands. Social conflicts are increasing, as plantation companies attempt to obtain village lands (Potter and Badcock 2001; Agriculture and Rural Development 2004). The options for small-scale production are also increasingly causing friction between local people and migrants (Susanti and Burgers 2012) who come to Riau to try to develop their own oil palm plantations. Local communities are increasingly losing their lands because they sell them to these migrants. As a consequence, local people often claim remaining forest areas as part of their ancestral lands. These newly claimed lands are also often sold to migrants, and these migrants then convert the lands into oil palm plantations. This process is iterative and the areas are increasingly situated in national park areas. In 2010, for example, WWF Indonesia estimated that 28,000 hectares of the 83,000 hectares in the Tesso Nilo National Park had been converted into small-scale oil palm plantations and settlements (WWF Indonesia 2010).

keting year 2012/13, the total production of palm oil was 28.5 million metric tons, with 20.1 million metric tons exported. The total domestic consumption was around 7.82 million metric tons, including 2.97 million metric tons for biofuels and the oleo-chemical industry (USDA Foreign Agriculture Service 2013). In the recently developed master plan for acceleration and expansion of Indonesian economic development (2011–25), palm oil has been selected as one of the key economic activities in so-called economic corridors. These oil palm corridors are to be developed mainly on Sumatra, Kalimantan and Papua-Maluku island. Sumatra island hosts the most oil palm plantations, particularly in North Sumatra and Riau Province (see Box 7.1). The investment required for this oil palm development is estimated at around 92 trillion Indonesian rupiahs (IDR) or around US$9.6 billion (Coordinating Ministry for Economic Affairs 2011).

The enormous boom in oil palm plantations, both large-scale and small-scale, has provided many positive contributions to national and regional development and employment. However, as the expansion can only be achieved when adequate land is available, the process has generated substantial land use change processes. It appears that oil palm expansion has created various problematic situations. Thus, it is estimated that 56 per cent of oil palm expansion from 1990 to 2005 in Indonesia replaced forest areas, and 44 per cent replaced croplands (Koh and Ghazoul 2010). The Ministry of Forestry reported that up to 2010, approximately 5 million hectares of state forestland had been released for agriculture or plantation purposes (Ministry of Forestry 2008c, 2011). Approximately one million hectares were peat swamp forests, which contributed significantly to national carbon emissions (Ministry of Forestry 2008b). Evidence from Riau Province shows that this kind of land-based development has indeed caused widespread forest conversion, and with smallholders joining the rush for the 'green gold', this will continue to increase (Box 7.1).

This development in favour of oil palm and at the expense of forested areas cannot be understood without knowing the institutional landscape (which exhibits the lack of a clear regulatory framework for land governance) and the weakening of the forestry sector. The emphasis placed by the Indonesian government on 'rapid economic growth' has rapidly undermined sustainable forest management and forest protection.

Land governance and natural resources management

The terrestrial area of Indonesia is 187.7 million hectares, which constitutes 37 per cent of the total country size (Ministry of Forestry 2011). According to the Constitution of 1945 (the root of Indonesia's land laws), this land is controlled by the state. This control over land was amended by the Basic Agrarian Law No. 5/1960 (BAL), which was adopted in 1960 in order to replace the Dutch colonial regime and provide a lawful security to Indonesian citizens, in particular with regard to agrarian rights (see Table 7.1). The 1960 law, complemented by another twelve laws, forty-eight regulations, twenty-two presidential decrees, four presidential instructions, 243 ministerial regulations, and 209 letters between ministers (BAKOSURTANAL 2012a), is Indonesia's most important law for organizing land tenure. According to the BAL, ownership rights can be assigned exclusively to Indonesian citizens and Indonesian legal entities. Foreign individuals and legal entities can acquire secondary rights such as rent or use of land, but only under limitations which are set by law (Sumardjan 1962). The BAL also set a limit on private ownership (Thorburn 2004) and recognized customary law (*hukum adat*) as the source of agrarian

TABLE 7.1 Land tenure forms as recognized by the Basic Agrarian Law No. 5/1960

	1	2	3	4	5	6	7
Transferable	√	√	√	with restriction	on agreement	elaborated by regulations	No
Duration	unlimited	35+25 years	30+20 years	on agreement	on agreement	elaborated by regulations	unlimited or on agreement
Can be mortgaged	√	√	√	No	No	No	No
State land		√	√	√	No	√	√
Non-state land	√		√	√	√	No	√
Indonesian citizens	√	√	√	√	√	√	No
Indonesian legal entities	√	√	√	√	√	√	√
Legal entities which are established according to Indonesian laws and based in Indonesia	No	√	√	√	√	No	√
Foreigners	No	No	No	√	√	No	No
Foreign legal entities which have representatives in Indonesia	No	No	No	√	√	No	√

1. Ownership right (Hak milik);
2. Right to manage land for commercial use (Hak Guna Usaha);
3. Right to construct and use buildings (Hak Guna Bangunan);
4. Right to use land and usufruct (Hak pakai);
5. Right to rent and use buildings (Hak sewa untuk bangunan);
6. Right to open land and to harvest forest products but not to own the land (Hak membuka tanah dan memungut hasil hutan);
7. Right to use land for religion and social purposes (Hak tanah untuk keperluan suci dan social).

law. This new agrarian system had inevitable economic implications particularly related to investment in lands and natural resources, although economic development was not the primary objective of the BAL (Sumardjan 1962).

In Indonesia, land administration is performed by different organizations, depending on the 'category of land'. The National Land Agency (BPN) is responsible for land administration of non-state land and land categorized as non-forest state land (together comprising about 30 per cent of the national

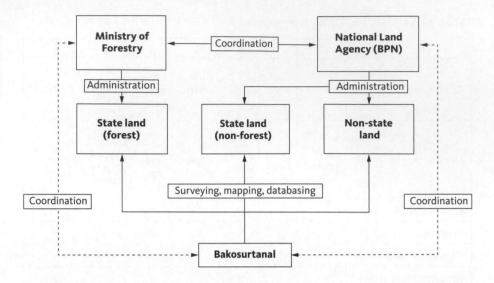

7.1 Land administration and responsible land agencies (*source*: Susanti, desk research)

territory) and maintains information about the ownership, value and use of land and its associated resources (UNECE 1996). Non-forest state land (i.e. any land with no land tenure form associated with it) is directly controlled by the Indonesian government, which has full authority to govern its designation, utilization, allocation and maintenance. Land associated with any land tenure form is categorized as non-state land (Djatmiko 2008).

At the same time, however, the Ministry of Forestry is responsible for land adm nistered as 'state forestland' (*kawasan hutan*) (as mandated by Forestry Law No. 5/1967 as by No. 41/1999). This state forestland is any particular area which is determined and/or designated by the government to be permanent forest (Ministry of Forestry 2011). To the extent that land needs to be surveyed or mapped, this is the responsibility of the National Coordinating Agency, called BAKOSURTANAL, which maintains the infrastructure for national spatial data (BAKOSURTANAL 2012b). In this case, no distinction is made between the different land categories (see Figure 7.1 for an overview of the current situation).

In addition to these complexities in land laws and land administration, there is an additional layer of policy institutions that makes the situation less transparent. Since the beginning of the New Order,[2] in order to facilitate investments and seek sources of capital other than oil and natural gas, the government issued a law on foreign and domestic investments and a basic forestry law in 1967 (Barr et al. 2006). The Basic Forestry Law No. 5/1967[3] aimed to unify the national forestry regulation system to maximize the utilization of forest resources and thereby serve national economic development. The law's main mandate is in forest protection and sustainable use of forest resources

TABLE 7.2 Forestland licensing recognized by P.50/2010, which was amended by P.26/2012

	IUPHHK-HA	IUPHHK-HTI	IUPHHK-RE
Location	Production forest	Production forest	Production forest with high conservation value
Type of forest	Natural forest	Plantation forest	Natural forest
Main activity	Harvesting, transporting, replanting, forest tending, guarding, product processing and marketing	Establishing plantation forest to provide industrial raw material	Maintaining ecosystem function; ecosystem rehabilitation through replanting, enrichment, thinning, maintaining flora and fauna diversity
Eligible applicants	Individual Indonesian citizen Cooperative Indonesian private company State-owned company Regional government-owned company	Cooperative Indonesian private company Indonesian private company with capital from (or partly from) foreign investment State-owned company Regional government-owned company	Individual Indonesian citizen Cooperative Indonesian private company State-owned company Regional government-owned company
Proposed to	Ministry of Forestry	Ministry of Forestry	Ministry of Forestry

IUPHHK-HA: Business licence for forest product utilization – Natural Forest
IUPHHK-HTI: Business licence for forest product utilization – Industrial Plantation Forest
IUPHHK-RE: Business licence for forest product utilization – Forest Ecosystem Restoration

Box 7.2 The roles of the forestry sector in Riau Province

The forestry sector has a long history in Riau Province. Natural forest has been harvested for commercial purposes, mostly for timber, since as early as the nineteenth century (Sumardjani 2005). In the early 1980s, the paper and pulp industry came into Riau Province, and large areas of natural forest areas were converted into industrial tree plantations. Natural forest concessionaries were increasingly replaced by industrial plantation forest concessionaries, which by 2010 were occupying approximately 1.6 million hectares, while natural forest concessionaries were occupying approximately only 300,000 hectares (Ministry of Forestry 2011). Investments were made in road construction to bring raw materials to the processing facilities. The demand for labour was fulfilled through various transmigration programmes and by setting up settlements adjacent to the plantations or processing facilities. However, smallholder involvement is quite limited, since the activity is financially unattractive (Van Noordwijk et al. 2008). Although industrial tree plantation has attracted some migrants to Riau, it has remained mainly a large-scale activity.

and areas (Ministry of Forestry 2009). All of the forest resources and forest area management activities are covered, including state forest licensing.

The state forest licensing includes state forestland released or used for other purposes, such as estate crop development, farmlands, transmigration and mining, with criteria set by regulations. This means that other sectors have possibilities to request state forestlands from the Ministry of Forestry for utilization for their own purposes. They are supported by Law No. 1/1967 as by No. 11/1970 on foreign investment, and by Law No. 6/1968 as by No. 12/1970 on domestic investment. These laws gave levy and tax benefits and/or exemptions for limited time periods, in particular to the priority sectors for economic development, namely the agriculture, industry and mining sectors. In the agriculture sector, the fishery and forestry sub-sectors, among others, became the priorities for domestic and foreign direct investment (BAPPENAS 2008). In addition to the tax benefits and exemptions, Law No. 1/1967 as by No. 11/1970 ensured that foreign investors can access land resources in certain land tenure forms, namely rights to construct and use buildings, rights to manage land for commercial uses, and rights to use lands and usufruct rights. This means foreign investors are not differentiated from Indonesian investors, although by law (BAL) foreigners cannot acquire primary landownership rights.

Along with the introduction of new rules and regulations, another complicating factor was that the forestry sector rapidly lost ground. Until the early 1990s, it was an important sector in terms of its contribution to national income, particularly through the revenues generated from the payment of fees by the concessionaries and the export values of forest products (Resosudarmo 2004; Nurjana 2007). In 1997 the total export value from the forestry sector was US$6.2 billion or about 11 per cent of the total national export value (Sumargo et al. 2010). In 2001 the forestry sector contributed approximately 20 per cent to total GDP, creating around 2.35 million direct jobs and around 1.5 million indirect jobs (Sastrosumarto et al. 2007). During this period, there was an enormous and increasing demand for forest products, which resulted in a booming wood processing industry and was followed by increasing timber prices (Banerjee 1997). It is estimated that in this period the national wood processing industry consumed 60–80 million cubic metres of wood per year (Barr et al. 2001). This kind of log consumption was well above the Indonesian average timber harvest of 25 million cubic metres per year (Ministry of Forestry 2007). Along with this rapid growth (and over-exploitation), it became increasingly difficult for the forestry sector to maintain the production level (and stop deforestation).

Regional autonomy and forestry decentralization

Following the failure of central government in dealing with the economic crisis in 1998, the empowerment of regional and local governments became one of the most urgent policy priorities. This was translated into decentralization, as mandated by Law No. 22/1999 on regional government. Related to this was the concern about how to achieve a more equitable distribution of the benefits of forest resources. To this end, Law No. 25/1999 on fiscal balancing was implemented, to ensure more equal benefit-sharing among the various provinces, especially those rich in natural resources, allowing them to obtain a larger share of the fiscal revenues generated within their jurisdictions. These laws have been supported by a variety of implementation regulations and sector-specific decentralization laws, including Law 41 of 1999 on forestry, a revised version of Indonesia's Basic Forestry Law of 1967, which outlines the division of administrative authority in the forestry sector under regional autonomy.

Within this decentralization framework, district governments were given authority to issue small-scale timber concession licences for areas up to 100 hectares (Government Regulation No. 6/1999 and Ministerial Decree No. 310/1999). As a result, district governments immediately released many small-scale timber concession licences, with minimum monitoring and field control (Resosudarmo 2004). The areas designated for this type of timber concession must fall within forest classified as convertible production forest or production forest which is nominated for reclassification to other uses. It was not

Box 7.3 Decentralization in Riau Province

Riau Province began the decentralization process in the early 2000s. In the beginning, the province was not in favour of decentralization, since the income distribution between regional and central government was not clearly regulated. However, after ten months of debate, the regional government began to see decentralization as a positive opportunity to take control of their future. Since then, it has begun to prepare for decentralization with the reorganization of jurisdiction areas and personnel and the issuance of regional regulations to secure their authorities. During that period, licences for natural resource utilization were rapidly issued by the regional government. This included small-scale forest concessions and forest conversion for oil palm plantation, rubber plantation and settlement (Potter and Badcock 2001). These activities have generated significant land use/land cover changes from natural forest into other land uses/covers.

permitted to issue small-scale timber concessions for areas already subject to other licences, in particular to large-scale forest concessionaries. Owing to the lack of, and inconsistency in, information – mainly caused by different land administration maps produced by different government agencies, with different scales and categories – and unclear physical borders in the field (Potter and Badcock 2001; Elson 2011; Brockhaus et al. 2012), this land allocation created tensions among stakeholders. In addition, Law No. 41/1999 has decentralized from central to province and district governments only the administrative functions. The real authority over forest resources remains with the central government (the Ministry of Forestry). This has made integrated and sound regional land use planning almost unattainable. The situation is exacerbated still further by the fact that many regional governments have limited institutional capacity to execute their responsibilities (Obidzinski and Barr 2003; Sastrosumarto et al. 2007), which is crucial to the successful decentralization of natural resources (Kaimowitz et al. 1998; Andersson 2006).

Responding to the confusing situation of a more decentralized management of forestland use, Government Regulation No. 34/2002 on forestry planning was issued. With this regulation, major authority over forestry planning was returned to the central government, while regional governments now have only minor authority in forestry planning. The authority of central government was extended, not only controlling timber production in production forest areas but also controlling wood processing industries. For these reasons, the regulation was seen as a recentralization of forestry administration (Barr et al. 2006).

However, forest areas had already been harvested beyond their natural re-generation capacity and have been 'degraded'. These 'degraded' forestlands increasingly compete with the main economic land-based development priori-ties of the Indonesian government. One main reason is that the forestry sector can no longer provide a substantial contribution to the national development goals, and other land-based options are much more lucrative.

Competing claims for land and natural resources

With all these dynamics encountered by the forestry sector, the sector's contribution to the national income has declined continuously, even though the livelihoods of 80–95 million people continue to depend directly on forest resources (Chao 2012). Rapid oil palm expansion has contributed to (continu-ing) deforestation, forest degradation, loss of biodiversity and marginalization of forest-dependent communities (Contreras-Hermosilla and Fay 2005). In the period 1990–2005, deforestation is estimated to have occurred at a pace of 1.8 million hectares per year (FAO 2009c). This situation worsened owing to the conflicting claims over forestland and resources (Contreras-Hermosilla and Fay 2005). Although laws on environmental management, forest protection, biodiversity conservation and spatial planning have been issued,[4] integrated and sustainable land and natural resources management has not yet been accomplished. A rapid expansion in oil palm and other forms of agro-industrial plantations indicated that a growing portion of the nation's wood supply had been obtained through clearing of natural forest rather than selective harvest-ing at multiple-rotation timber concessions (Barr et al. 2001).

In 2009, the total employment created by the forestry sector was only 321,000, while the contribution to the national GDP was 2.5 per cent (FAO 2009c). For this reason, the forestry sector is increasingly perceived as less important compared with other economic sectors, which contribute more to GDP. In light of this, the government has begun to make efforts to attract investors for resource exploitation other than forestry. Needless to say, oil palm has become a top priority with ever-increasing global demand (Brockhaus et al. 2012). This seems inevitable, since oil palm is assumed to be finan-cially more attractive compared with forestry (Butler et al. 2009). However, its development could lead to tensions with the national voluntary pledge of 26 per cent carbon emission reduction by 2020 (Forest Climate Center 2009), of which 22 per cent is expected to come from the forestry and peatland sector through reduced deforestation, controlled forest fires, managed water levels (on peatlands), land and forest (including industrial plantation forest and community forest) rehabilitation, illegal logging eradication, and community empowerment (BAPPENAS 2010).

The government is convinced, however, that it is sufficient to pursue economic development to achieve the ambitious carbon emission reduction

TABLE 7.3 The Indonesian economic corridors and their main economic activities

	Sumatra	Java	Kalimantan	Sulawesi	Bali-Nusa Tenggara	Papua-Kepulauan Maluku
Main economic activities	steel shipping palm oil rubber coal Sunda strait national strategic area	food and beverages textile transportation equipment shipping ICT Jabodetabek area – defence equipment	steel bauxite palm oil coal oil and gas timber	nickel food agriculture oil and gas cocoa fishery	tourism animal husbandry fishery	nickel copper food agriculture (including palm oil) oil and gas fishery

Source: Coordinating Ministry for Economic Affairs (2011)

goals. This perception, in combination with incompatible and inconsistent regulations and land use maps, provides ever decreasing opportunities for sustainable forest management or for promotion of a reforestation effort as part of the Indonesian climate change goals. This is even more striking as, by law, the forestry sector manages almost 70 per cent of the total terrestrial area of Indonesia; yet the sector appears unable to significantly influence land governance in favour of forestry development. In such a context, governments often lack the interest to promote sustainable forest management or forest protection in their own jurisdictions, especially since oil palm can provide much higher financial benefits. This incoherent land governance situation positions the forestry sector more as a client or land provider for other land-based sectors than as an authority in its own right.

The situation has been aggravated since the formulation of the master plan for acceleration and expansion of Indonesia's economic development from 2011 to 2025. This master plan is intended to boost economic development throughout Indonesia through the establishment of six 'economic corridors', each with its specific themes based on regional economic potentials. Table 7.3 shows that economic activities related to palm oil have an important position in three of the economic corridors. These include Sumatra, Kalimantan and Papua (in food agriculture). Forestry has become a main economic activity in the Kalimantan economic corridor, but mainly through the development of industrial plantation forest estates and through wood production and the primary timber industry (Coordinating Ministry for Economic Affairs 2011).

Although decentralization was intended to provide more responsibilities and options for land use decisions at the regional level (Kaimowitz et al. 1998; Andersson 2006), it has inevitably impacted negatively on land and forests resources (Barr et al. 2006) because regional governments tended to see land and natural resources from a financial point of view (Resosudarmo 2004), and strong institutional frameworks were absent (Obidzinski and Barr 2003; Sastrosumarto et al. 2007). This became worse where integrated national and regional planning was lacking in governing those multiple purposes that are often conflicting. In addition, complex and problematic political negotiations have heavily interfered with the planning processes, while there is also a lack of reliable, updated spatial data and unclear physical borders in the field, which makes coherent discussion and negotiation difficult for all stakeholders.

The situation has created confusion and overlapping and often conflicting claims on lands. This allows for the unregulated conversion of land, as illustrated by the example from Riau Province, where people move to the forest frontier areas to establish their new oil palm plantations and are able to do so because of these confusing claims. Although spatial planning is supposed to guide land allocation, in Riau Province such planning is virtually non-existent, since the spatial planning has not been updated for the last decade.

Concluding remarks

This chapter shows that although the global debates are focused on transnational land deals by foreign investors, in Indonesia it is the central state – in combination mainly with domestic investors – which plays a dominant role in increasing land investments and processes of land use change. State involvement – and the fact that smallholders may also benefit – does not mean, however, that the expansion of oil palm is unproblematic. The rapid expansion of oil palm plantation has led to land use conversion at the cost of forests and increasingly also at the cost of rice-producing areas. It is not only large-scale companies but increasingly also smallholders who are competing in claiming lands for their new oil palm plantations. In this process, local groups often lose out as migrants from Java are in many cases better placed to benefit and are increasingly taking over. Local governments have limited institutional capacity to execute their responsibilities concerning land governance.

The area of oil palm is expected to further increase, given the government plans, a positive market perspective and the very lucrative benefits. Given the over-exploitation of forests in previous times, sustainable forestry exploitation cannot be expected to offer an economically feasible alternative as forests are already very much degraded. Although by law 70 per cent of the Indonesian territory is still considered forest area, deforestation has already taken place in large areas while other areas are currently under threat, not least because of the lack of a clear institutional framework. Oil palm expansion is difficult to halt and there are indications that oil palm is increasingly being pushed from Indonesia to parts of West Africa.[5] At the same time, within Indonesia, the rapid expansion of oil palm is increasingly contested by groups concerned about deforestation, but also about food security and/or human rights issues. The future of oil palm expansion in Indonesia will very much depend on whether the government will be able to cope with such outside competition and inside pressures and whether it will be able to improve the regulation of oil palm production.

8 | Vietnam in the debate on land grabbing: conversion of agricultural land for urban expansion and hydropower development

Pham Huu Ty, Nguyen Quang Phuc and Guus van Westen

Introduction

Vietnam does not fit stereotypical representations of 'land grabs': large-scale acquisition of lands by foreigners are not often reported, and the country cannot be seen as easy prey for the forces of the global market. Vietnam is a strong state with sufficient means at its disposal to prevent external intrusions deemed undesirable. And yet, as this chapter aims to show, comparable processes of transfer of land to other uses and users are taking place, with important consequences for traditional users and local development. If land grabbing is a matter only of foreignization – large-scale, cross-border land deals initiated by foreign investors (Zoomers 2010) – then Vietnam does not warrant much attention as an object of such initiatives, although the country and its businesses are reported as actively engaged in the acquisition of land and other natural resources in neighbouring countries such as Cambodia and Laos (GRAIN 2012; Schönweger et al. 2012). But if we are concerned with dispossession and displacement of poor people, then Vietnam offers a specific context that shows these processes of resource transfers to be much more complex and widespread that the mainstream discourse of land grabbing seems to suggest. The current land grab discussion focuses on farmland being converted from smallholdings to large-scale agriculture for the production of food and biofuel for export. Much land, however, is lost in other ways, such as the expansion of urban areas into rural fringes, the creation of national parks, and infrastructure development (including hydropower projects) that take place in many parts of the less developed world (Zoomers 2010). It is in this sense that Vietnam experiences massive transfers of land.

The ongoing industrialization and urbanization policy in Vietnam since the 1990s has accelerated the large-scale conversion of agricultural land into other uses. This process has seriously affected rural landscapes and farmers' livelihoods and has become a contested issue on the political agenda and in mass media. This chapter makes an inventory of such agricultural land conversions in Vietnam and details two types of land conversion – those for urban expansion and those for hydropower development – in order to understand the nature of the issues at stake. The data in this chapter are derived from two main sources. General information on land conversions was gathered from secondary sources such as newspapers, academic and statistical publications, legal documents on land policy, and unpublished documents. Specifics on urban land conversions and hydro dam construction in central Vietnam are primary data collected through interviews (key informant and semi-structured interviews) with different stakeholders (government officers, headmen, mass organizations, investors and villagers) in Thua Thien Hue Province in 2011 and 2012.

The remainder of the chapter is organized into four sections. The first section presents an overview of agricultural land acquisitions and conversions in recent years. The second and third sections focus on two specific types of land conversion: those for urban and those for hydropower development. The last section concludes and discusses the material presented.

Agricultural land conversion in Vietnam: an overview

GRAIN, a Barcelona-based NGO engaged in the struggle for securing land rights for poor people, maintains a website listing media reports on cross-border land deals. Although the listings do not claim to be authoritative (i.e. tested and confirmed), the website has the merit of drawing attention to what is increasingly perceived as a major issue and offers a quick overview of what land transfers may be taking place around the world. Table 8.1 presents a summary with respect to the position of Vietnam in international land deals. While some foreign acquisitions in Vietnam are reported – largely related to forestry – the main thrust is clearly a different one: Vietnamese investors also emerge as important 'perpetrators' in their own right, picking up extensive holdings for cash crops in less densely populated neighbouring countries.

It would be misleading to conclude, however, that land acquisitions and related displacements are not an issue in Vietnam. On the contrary, the emphasis in the land grab debate on foreignization of land and on agricultural land obscures the fact that other conversions are taking place on a massive scale, with often similar consequences for rural populations. For this we need to take a closer look at what happens.

Vietnam conducts a nationwide land use census every five years, and similar data are also identified every year in each province, district and commune. Land use changes over the last decade are listed in Table 8.2. It can be seen that the total land area of the country increased somewhat, as a result of new measurements. Over the decade, there was a considerable drop in the area of unused land. Much of this consisted of upland areas subject to reforestation programmes and, as a result, reclassified as forest land, a subcategory of agricultural land. Non-agricultural land uses increased rapidly, from 1.7 million hectares in 1990 to 1.9 million hectares in 2000 and 3.5 million hectares in

TABLE 8.1 Vietnam land deals in other countries and foreign deals in Vietnam

Type of land deal	Types of investment	Area (ha)
Land deals in other countries		
Cambodia	Agriculture, industry	9,380
Cambodia	Agriculture	6,436
Cambodia	Agriculture	2,361
Cambodia	Agriculture	9,784
Cambodia	Agriculture	8,000
Cambodia	Agriculture	6,891
Cambodia	Agriculture	8,100
Cambodia	Agriculture	7,600
Cambodia	Agriculture	7,560
Cambodia	Agriculture	2,502
Laos	Agriculture, forestry, other	10,000
Laos	Agriculture	10,000
Laos	Agriculture	10,000
Sierra Leone	Agriculture	110
Cambodia	Agriculture	6,155
Cambodia	Agriculture	7,000
Cambodia	Agriculture	9,014
Cambodia	Agriculture	9,656
Cambodia	Agriculture	9,614
Cambodia	Agriculture	9,773
Cambodia	Agriculture	7,900
Cambodia	Agriculture	7,591
Cambodia	Agriculture	1,900
Cambodia	Agriculture	4,889
Cambodia	Agriculture	9,785
Cambodia	Agriculture	6,695
Cambodia	Agriculture	5,080
Cambodia	Agriculture	5,095
Cambodia	Agriculture	2,183
Cambodia	Agriculture	7,289
Cambodia	Agriculture	7,972
Total area (ha)		254,392
Foreign land deals in Vietnam		
Cambodia	Agriculture	5,345
China	Agriculture	10,000
Hong Kong	Forestry	63,000
Japan	Conservation, forestry	309
Israel	Agriculture	2,500
Switzerland	Agriculture	unknown
Hong Kong	Forestry	100,000
Hong Kong	Forestry	21,000
Hong Kong	Forestry	70,000
Hong Kong	Forestry	30,000
Hong Kong	Forestry	65,000
Japan, China, Hong Kong	Forestry	3,500
Total area (ha)		370,654

Source: International Land Coalition: Land Matrix, www.landmatrix.org/get-the-idea/
web-transnational-deals/ (accessed 6 July 2013)

2009 (GSO 2010). In relative terms, expansion of residential and special-use land was the most spectacular change observed. Special-use land increased by approximately 150,000 hectares per year, and the increase in residential areas amounted to approximately 21,000 hectares each year. However, these aggregate statistics to some extent hide what is actually happening in terms of land conversions.

TABLE 8.2 Land use change between 2000 and 2009 (1,000 ha)

Land use types	2000		2009		Change	
	Area	%	Area	%	Area	%
Total area	32,924.1	100.0	33,105.1	100.0	181.0	
Agricultural land	20,920.8	63.5	25,127.3	75.9	4,206.5	12.4
Special-use land[1]	1,532.8	4.7	2,835.3	8.6	1,302.5	3.9
Residential land	443.2	1.3	633.9	1.9	190.7	0.6
Unused land	10,027.3	30.5	4,508.6	13.6	−5,518.7	−168.0

Source: General Statistics Office of Vietnam, www.gso.gov.vn/default.aspx?tabid=426 andidmid=3

More detailed information shows that most additions to special and residential land use types (non-agricultural land) have been converted from agricultural land, especially rice fields and dry croplands. However, there is no systematic reporting on the size and nature of land conversions (Nguyen Van Suu 2009). Therefore, we have to rely on a range of different bits and pieces of information scattered over several sources. It is estimated that over 80 per cent of new urban and industrial developments affect agricultural land (Bui Ngoc Thanh 2009). Mai Thành (2009) claimed that in the period 1995–2005, over 766,000 hectares of agricultural land had been converted to urban and industrial use by the central government. This accounted for 4 per cent of the total agricultural land area of Vietnam. While this suggests that the scale of conversion is relatively limited, data from the General Statistics Office present another view: the area of rice production land, for instance, decreased from 6.7 million hectares in 1995 to 4.08 million hectares in 2009, while the non-agricultural land uses[2] increased rapidly, from 1.7 million hectares in 1990 to 3.5 million hectares in 2009 (GSO 1996, 2010). In 2009, *Báo Quân đội Nhân dân* (Vietnam People's Army Newspaper) reported that approximately 59,000 hectares of rice land were being appropriated each year for non-agricultural purposes. The central government founded 228 industrial, economic and high-tech zones between 1991 and 2010, using 49,330 hectares of land, excluding a variety of small-to-medium-sized industrial areas managed by provincial authorities. The total area of industrial zones is expected to be 70,000 hectares by 2015 and 80,000 hectares by 2020 (Nguyen Van Suu 2009: 109). On the national scale, land for infrastructure development increased from 437,963 hectares in 2000 to 1.08 million hectares in 2009 (GSO 2001, 2010).

Urban expansion entails more than just the construction of residential areas, business parks and urban infrastructure. Large areas have also been used for amenities, such as the 104 golf courses created between 2003 and 2008 alone, occupying on average 471 hectares each and thus consuming 49,000 hectares in all (Duy Huu 2008). In addition, many coastal lands, including protected forests and farmlands, have been allocated to domestic and foreign companies to build resorts. Da Nang city is an example, where dozens of luxury resorts have opened along the coast, including the Empire Residences and Resort (51 hectares) and Danang Beach Resort (260 hectares).

A particular source of land loss in Vietnam is the construction of hydropower dams. This results from a policy aiming to meet rapidly increasing demand for electricity while limiting the import bill for fuels. For instance, Hoa Binh hydropower dam was constructed in central Vietnam in 1979 and flooded 75,000 hectares of land, including 11,000 hectares of agricultural land; 11,141 households, with 89,720 people, were removed from the flooded areas (Institute of Development 2010).

Farmland loss for urban and industrial expansion is concentrated particularly in some sixteen provinces, which include the largest cities. Most land conversion takes place near very large cities such as Hanoi and Ho Chi Minh City, where prominent new urban developments have mushroomed. Increasingly similar processes also occur in secondary cities such as Vinh, Hue, Binh Duong, Dong Nai, Vinh Phuc, Hai Duong, Da Nang and others.

It will be clear that such massive reallocations of land to new uses and users must affect many people. On the national scale, land conversion influenced the livelihoods of 627,000 households and 2.5 million people between 2003 and 2008 (Mai Thành 2009). In the capital region of Hanoi, urban expansion between 2000 and 2010 entailed the conversion of 11,000 hectares for 1,736 projects. This resulted in the loss of traditional employment for some 150,000 farmers (Nguyen Van Suu 2009). Hồng Minh (2005) reports that in just five years, from 2000 to 2004, 5,496 hectares were used for 957 projects, critically impacting the life and employment of 138,291 households, of which 41,000 were classified as agricultural households.

Drivers of land conversion Changes in land use and in claims on land enjoyed by different social groups are thus observed on a massive scale in Vietnam. While part of this concerns rural transformations such as the establishment of large-scale commercial agriculture and reforestation programmes, the main thrust is of a different nature and marks the structural transformation of Vietnam from a predominantly rural economy and society to an urban one based on manufacturing and service industries. This transformation is linked to various domestic and external processes. External forces can be conveniently labelled as globalization. This entails Vietnam's progressive integration into the global economy as a suitable location for a range of globally integrated production activities and ways of organizing the economy, guided essentially by the prescriptions of neoliberalism. This globalization is reflected in an increasingly open economy, with prominent roles for foreign investment and export production, but also in the adoption of corresponding consumption and lifestyle elements – as symbolized by the golf courses and resorts mentioned above. Domestically, the globalization drive has been activated by the adoption of a comprehensive set of policies known as *Doi Moi*[3] (renovation policy) since 1986. In spite of continued adherence to the socialist foundations of the Vietnamese state, this reform process has effectively aligned Vietnam's institutional framework with those of the main capitalist economies. In spatial terms, globalization and economic transformation (industrialization) are reflected in large-scale urbanization, favouring especially those localities that have advantages in terms of connecting with the world at large. A major component of the transformation, as observed, concerns land: how it is used, who uses it, and the institutional framework of laws and procedures that guide its access and use.

Economic and social transformations put particular pressures on land, while its availability is limited because most land is allocated to individuals, family households and organizations for certain periods of time (Ngo Viet Hung 2007; Nguyen Van Suu 2009). Conversion of agricultural land to urban uses and users is seen as a major requirement to facilitate the realization of Vietnam's transformation into an urban and industrial society, and hence the institutions pertaining to land had to be modified accordingly. Four factors that define these changes will be briefly reviewed: political and economic transformation, urbanization, the emergence of 'post-productivist' green spaces, and changes in land policy.

Political and economic transformation Economics and politics are the main drivers of the transformation process, with the change from a centrally planned towards a market-oriented model of economic governance. Accordingly, central state dominance in economic and social affairs has given way to a new division of administrative responsibilities between central and local authorities. The top-down approach has been replaced by more flexible strategic planning in a number of fields. New legislation, such as the Enterprise Law (2000), the Land Law (2003) and the Investment Law (2005), has encouraged economic growth, export production and foreign investment. Vietnam's GDP growth averaged 7 per cent per year between 2006 and 2010 (GSO 2010). Foreign investment reached US$29.4 billion and exports rose from US$23 billion (2001–05) to US$56 billion in the period 2006–10 (ibid.). The industrial sector plays an increasingly important role in the economy, contributing 22.6 per cent of GDP in 1990 and 41 per cent by 2010 (GSO 2011). The transformation of political and economic structures has also significantly contributed to changes in the relationship between the central and local authorities in a number of fields, such as socio-economic development strategy, natural resources management and urban development planning.

Urbanization Urbanization in Vietnam has rapidly increased since the national economy began to be integrated with the global economy. There was a marked increase in the 2000s, with 19.4 per cent of the population living in urban centres in 2001 (Coulthart et al. 2006), compared with 33 per cent in 2010 (UNDESA 2010). At present, at least one million people are added annually to Vietnam's urban areas; the current annual 3 per cent increase in urbanization means that the urban population will constitute around 41 per cent of the total in 2030. Vietnam's future economic growth will depend on its ability to develop competitive, market-driven industrial and service sectors. These are primarily urban-based activities (Coulthart et al. 2006). The cities and towns account for approximately 70 per cent of total economic output (ibid.). The large cities of Ho Chi Minh City, Hanoi, Hai Phong and Da Nang are the focal points in the transition to a market-oriented economy (Phan Xuan Nam et al. 2000).

In the last two decades, the central government has introduced reforms that have effected urban development. The first reform was set down in the Orientation Master Plan for Urban Development to 2020, adopted in 1998 (Bộ Xây dựng 1999). This explicitly addresses urbanization by designating a hierarchy of urban settlements (Coulthart et al. 2006). However, the most important policy change was the introduction of the new Construction Law in 2004. Its main feature is increased decentralization to the three lower tiers of government – provinces, districts and communes or wards – in preparing spatial plans (still subject, however, to approval by central government).

In practice, most FDI is directed towards cities owing to their competitive advantage in terms of labour market, transportation costs and infrastructure. As mentioned above, a large number of industrial sites and export processing zones have been established in and near cities since 1991.

Emergence of 'post productivist' green spaces Recent surveys have shown that the quality of life has declined in several cities in Vietnam, as city planning does not necessarily meet citizens' needs (Ngo Tho Hung 2010). One possible reason is the decline of green spaces within urban areas, although other factors such as healthcare, education systems and entertainment are also important. In addition, air pollution is becoming a serious issue in the very large cities such as Hanoi and Ho Chi Minh City. Most urban air pollution originates from traffic, manufacturing and domestic cooking. It is estimated that 70 per cent of urban air pollution comes from vehicles, in particular motorbikes (ibid.). A healthy living space includes green urban attributes as well as socio-economic and cultural services (Mahmoud and El Sayed 2011). In recent years many Vietnamese, especially the nouveaux riches, have developed a preference for leafy residential areas where they can relax and recover from daily stress (Waibel 2006). The emergence of such new urban areas is a response to aspirations of people who have medium and higher incomes and aspire to lifestyles that differ from others. By moving into these new residential areas, such people expect to adopt an upscale Western lifestyle in secure, orderly neighbourhoods, with fresh air, green spaces and comfort. In these residential spaces, they feel part of a globalizing modern society in a setting that meets international standards (ibid. 2006; see also Van Noorloos on Costa Rica, Chapter 5, this volume).

The model of new eco-urban areas has been promoted in Vietnam (Labbé and Boudreau 2011) since the late 1990s. These urban spaces are built on agricultural land in peri-urban areas. Within these areas, high-rise apartment blocks, villas and commercial and office spaces have been built, along with education, health and sports facilities and parks. By the end of 2010, 633 new urban areas had been realized all over Vietnam, with a total area of 103,243 hectares (Sàn giao dịch bất động sań An Biên 2011). Prominent new urban developments are the Sai Gon South New Urban Area (Phu My Hung) in Ho Chi Minh City, New City in Binh Duong Province, and Ciputra International City in Hanoi. Saigon South is being developed by Taiwanese investors and occupies 3,300 hectares of former wetlands. Its population is projected to be between 500,000 and 1 million residents by 2020. The New City in Binh Duong covers 1,000 hectares and was designed by the National University of Singapore. Ciputra International City near the West Lake of Hanoi is an Indonesian investment of US$2.1 billion. It occupies 405 hectares of land with villas, commercial centres and high-rise blocks of seventeen to twenty floors. A 120-square-metre apartment can be sold for about US$100,000 (Waibel 2006: 46). In this urban residential space, inhabitants control and to some extent even shape their own territory, which may be interpreted as a privatization of part of urban space (ibid.: 47).

Changes in land policy The massive changes in use and control of land that have made the economic and urban transformation of Vietnam possible are in themselves the results of institutional changes (Han and Vu 2008). Most important of these are changes in socio-economic policy and in legal frameworks, especially land laws. With this in mind, we will now explore how these changes relate to agricultural land conversion.

The most fundamental institutional change since independence in 1945 has been the land reforms. Land is an essential productive asset and a necessary means, especially in agrarian societies, to sustain livelihoods (Bui Van Hung 2004). First, land was taken from the landlords (*địa chủ*) by the state and redistributed to 2 million households[4] (Jamal and Jansen 2000). Then, the collectivization model was applied in the North after 1959, followed by the South in 1976. By 1978, however, rice production had fallen drastically, resulting in food shortages, particularly in 1980, when 1.4 million tons of grain had to be imported (Luttrell 2001). The reason for this was that cooperatives had applied the principle of equal distribution of land, and farmers' incomes no longer depended on the quality and quantity of their work. Many villagers felt that they would not have enough to eat no matter how hard they worked. They cared little for the cooperatives (Kerkvliet 1995). As a result, Vietnam faced an agrarian crisis in the 1980s, as a consequence of collective agriculture. This encouraged the Communist Party to seek solutions. The 'first wave' of agrarian reform took place between 1981 and 1987. Household contracts, which allocated land to farm households based upon the size of their adult workforce, spread throughout the country under the so-called 'Directive 100' in 1981. Cooperatives continued to supply inputs and allocate labour for land preparation, irrigation and input distribution, while crop management, harvesting and selling products were performed by households (ibid.). As the household was recognized as the basic economic unit of the rural economy by the Land Law in 1988, agricultural land was distributed to households, for a limited period of time (fifteen years for annual crops and forty years for perennial crops). At the same time, rights of inheritance and transfer were recognized (Kolko 1997, cited in Luttrell 2001: 531).

Following advice and pressure from the World Bank and the International Monetary Fund in support of free markets for land (Kerkvliet 2006), the central government promulgated a new land law in 1993. The 1993 Land Law stated that 'all land belongs to the state, and land is allocated by the state to individuals and organizations for stable long-term use' (Land Law 1993). The remarkable change in the 1993 Land Law was that households and individuals obtained the right to rent, transfer, exchange, inherit and mortgage land use rights much more freely than before, as long as new users complied with use type and periods (ibid.). Land was then turned into a special commodity in formal markets.

The next law, the 2003 Land Law, founded formal land markets in Vietnam. The duration of land allocation was and still is the same as in the 1993 Land Law (twenty years for annual crops and fifty years for perennials). However, particularly interesting reforms in the 2003 Land Law are the following: (1) there is further expansion of the user's rights by granting these rights as a gift and as a capital contribution to business; (2) communities, religious establishments, overseas Vietnamese and foreign organizations and individuals investing in Vietnam are recognized as new land users; (3) more flexible arrangements to convert garden and pond land to residential land without levy are introduced; and (4) land can be converted for purposes of economic development by local authorities, whereby a current holder's land use rights are compensated by government and investors. The compensation fees are determined within a framework set by the provincial authority. The government will not normally be involved in acquisitions for private projects. It is involved only in large public projects – for example, projects related to public security, public welfare and foreign investment. In other cases, developers have to negotiate with residents on the basis of the government fee framework. Upon reaching an agreement, a site clearance and compensation committee is to be established at the district level where the land acquisition is taking place (Nghị Định số 69/2009/NĐ-CP).

Significant land reforms, especially the 2003 Land Law, have contributed to the emergence of a formal land market that profoundly affects land conversion processes in Vietnam.

Consequences Land conversion is an outcome of political and economic reforms and the ensuing integration with the global economy. While this process might contribute advantages for economic growth at macro level and offer development opportunities for local communities, there are also limitations and negative effects. On the positive side, land conversion is necessary to effect the socio-economic transformation towards an industrial and services-based economy and attract domestic and foreign investment. In many cases, land conversion for urban development is undertaken by a coalition of private developers and local authorities, who both stand to benefit the most. Often low compensation rates for land are proposed by authorities keen to attract investment. Land is acquired and made available to investors at prices set according to policy priorities. Most cities/provinces offer new urban land at low cost to encourage investors to set up business and facilities that help economic growth. The investors can profit from a massive margin between the acquisition cost of (rural) land and the prices paid by (urban) users, while local authorities derive considerable funds from transferring land rights in order to invest in infrastructure and other services. Land conversion and allocation charges are an important source of revenue for many local governments.

Land conversion for urban development also creates job opportunities for the local population, in manufacturing, and in services such as restaurants, hotels, retail, trading, etc. People in peri-urban areas can build apartments on their plots, for rental or sale, and thus benefit from rising land prices. In addition, land conversion brings compensation money for villagers. Villagers may use this to take up new activities or invest the money in other ways. And lastly, land conversion in peri-urban zones has increased rural–urban inter-action, with changes in livelihood strategies towards non-farming activities and urban lifestyles. In practice, however, available evidence demonstrates that conversion often creates negative effects, especially loss of traditional liveli-hoods and increased resistance. Between 2003 and 2008, 627,000 households and 2.5 million people were affected by land conversion. The Vietnam Farmers' Union reports that 67 per cent of agricultural workers remained in their old jobs and 13 per cent gained new jobs, while 25–30 per cent of farmers do not have any jobs or have unstable jobs. The report also states that over 53 per cent of households experienced a reduction in income after land conversion (Mai Thành 2009). In seeking new livelihoods, some farmers have engaged in simple, self-employed non-agricultural work, such as informal retailing and services, while others are out of work (Nguyen Van Suu 2009). The villages nearest the urban edge face a future without agriculture, increasing numbers of non-native residents, and environmental threats (Di Gregorio 2011). Some farmers leave land fallow while waiting for urban expansion in order to receive compensation money (Berg et al. 2003). It was also found that most of the middle-income and wealthy households in Thuy Duong Ward, Huong Thuy District and Thua Thien Hue Province were not seriously impacted by losing agricultural land, while the poor and the elderly, who lack social and human capital (e.g. education, skills, health and social relations), face various difficul-ties and are more vulnerable.

Land conversion thus affects different people in different ways and may be unfair in terms of compensation and participation. This has led to conflicts and resistance in many parts of the country. According to a BBC article from 2007, hundreds of angry people from various localities such as Tien Giang, An Giang, Ben Tre, Long An and Binh Thuan provinces demonstrated in front of the government buildings in Ho Chi Minh City because of unequal land com-pensation.[5] Forms of local resistance are diverse. They often involve complaints, petitions and even violent action. They can be individual initiatives or involve the community. However, they arc rarely sufficient to have much impact on state agencies (Kerkvliet 2006). According to the *Vietnamnet* newspaper, 678,000 formal complaints were sent to the government between 2008 and 2011, over 70 per cent relating to land issues. Mr Trần Phong Tranh – Inspector-General of the central government – stated that the main reason for resistance and complaints was low compensation rates.[6] People often complain that com-pensation prices are lower than market prices – sometimes only 5 per cent of the market value.

Hydropower dam development

Increasingly, land has been acquired for the rapidly increasing number of hydropower dams. Even before the *Doi Moi* renovation policy (1986), several hydropower dams were constructed, affecting a total area of 332,000 hectares. Between 1986 and 1995, over 100,000 hectares were acquired for several large dams, such as the Tri An and Hoa Binh hydroelectricity plants. However, the number of hydropower dams has grown dramatically since the introduction of the Sixth Electricity Plan for the period 2006–10. Forty-six large-scale hydropower dams[7] were completed in that period, which necessitated a total land acquisition of over 100,000 hectares.[8] Small and medium-scale hydropower dams have required an additional area of nearly 35,000 hectares for over one thousand dams built between 2006 and 2010. By 2025, thirty-five new large-scale dams and more than one thousand small hydropower plants will have been added/constructed (Ministry of Industry and Trade 2007). According to the strategic Environmental Impact Assessment report (Stockholm Environment Institute 2007) for the Sixth Electricity Plan, an estimated 25,133 hectares will be lost for eighteen hydropower dams, 45 per cent of which consists of farmland and forest. Furthermore, 'unused' land, including water bodies, shrub and grasslands, will be lost, land that constitutes valuable resources for local people's livelihoods and culture. At present, the total land loss and number of displaced people are not reported in academic and government sources. We therefore have to rely on a mosaic of sources to compile a review of people affected.

Displacement Before 1990, more than 120,000 people were displaced for the Thac Ba hydropower dam, and approximately 90,000 for the Hoa Binh hydropower project. In the mid-1990s, 60,000 people had to make way for the Ham Thuan–Da Mi dam and over 24,000 for the Yali dam respectively. By the end of the 1990s, over 400,000 people had been displaced owing to hydropower projects in Vietnam, according to the Institute of Strategy and Policy on Resources and Environment (2009). Another source (Department of Cooperatives and Rural Development 2007) reports that between 1995 and 2009, 49,000 households were affected by the construction of over twenty large-scale hydropower dams (stations with capacity over 100MW), claiming 80,000 hectares of land. For example, Son La hydro dam displaced over 90,000 people from 160 settlements (Consultation Company on Electricity I 2007). Less spectacularly, many small hydro dams also displaced a large number of people – for example, Nam Na dam (2,325 persons) and Khe Bo dam (3,482 persons). A salient feature of these displacements is that some 90 per cent of the affected people belong to minority ethnic groups living in mountainous areas (see also Nuijen, Prachvuthy and Van Westen on Cambodia, Chapter 9, this volume). Several dams actually displaced only members of ethnic minority peoples, such as Hoi Quang, Nho Que 3 and Bac Me (Consultation Company on Electricity I 2007; Stockholm Environment Institute 2007; NIAAP 2008; CODE 2010).

Resettlement policy Displacement of people requires the provision of other places to resettle them; therefore, displacement and resettlement are often planned in a single 'Detailed Plan of Displacement and Resettlement'. This plan is designed by the district authority in collaboration with the investor, with the project developer having to meet the costs. Three types of resettlement are distinguished: *in situ* (*di ven*), integrated (*xen ghep*) and centralized (*tap trung*) resettlement. The first type moves displaced people to the surroundings of the reservoir created by dams; the second relocates people to different existing communities elsewhere; and the third gathers all resettlers in a new locality. Most projects apply the third type of resettlement. In the new locality, the district authority acquires land from other users to construct a new settlement for displaced people.

Most resettled people – typically farmers (often shifting cultivators) – are not satisfied with living conditions in the relocation site. The first reason is that the farmland made available to them is invariably much smaller than the land they used to have. In the study by the Institute of Development (CODE 2010) of four large dams (Hoa Binh, Ban Ve, Yaly and Tuyen Quang), 86 per cent of respondents confirmed that their farmland in the new site was smaller than previously in their areas of origin. Only 7 per cent received more land than before. In addition, land allocations may be slow in realization, as in a case reported by the Ho Moong Commune People's Committee (2009), where after three years of resettlement ninety-nine households had still not received compensation farmland as committed to by the investor. Moreover, in many cases people are disappointed with the quality of land in the relocation area, as reported in the resettlement site of the Pleikrong dam – many people did not accept living there. This new settlement is also unsuitable for their traditional customs and religion. Most ethnic minority groups practise shifting cultivation, in the past moving around mountainous areas and selecting suitable areas to settle where the soil is rich and near the forest, which plays an important role in their religions. But at resettlement locations, all are gathered in a densely populated area far from the forest, watercourses and grassland. They can no longer access those common-pool resources to practise hunting, fishing and collecting honey, rattan and fruits from the forest. In addition, they cannot find non-farm employment in the new environment. Not surprisingly, over 60 per cent of people in our survey were very unhappy with the new destination.

Compensation policy Procedures for land acquisition and compensation for existing users are essentially the same as in the urban cases. All hydropower dams implement compulsory 'land recovery' programmes. People whose lands are situated in the reservoir areas created by dams have to move out and return land to the state. The state subsequently allocates land to the investor of the hydropower project. Forced displacement differs from cases where people voluntarily contribute land for collective purposes, such as construction of roads and public structures, or social development projects. In the case of forced displacement, people affected carefully consider the compensation they receive for land and property loss. In spite of improvements made in compensation policies, such as higher compensation for farmland, compensation for property loss at market prices, and more involvement of affected households in the property loss surveys, compensation for land often remains far lower than the market price. Surveys among people who lost land in dam projects give a clear view: for instance, 95 per cent of people affected by the Tuyen Quang dam and 94 per cent in the case of the Yaly dam considered compensation to have been insufficient. Over 91 per cent of respondents claimed that compensation, especially for perennials and crops, had been very low in the Tuyen Quang project, similar to the corresponding opinions in Ban Ve (94 per cent) and Yali (91 per cent). As a result, they could not afford to buy other land in return. For example, people received approximately 37 million Vietnamese ND[9] per hectare for agriculture land loss in Yaly, but the market price at that time was 43 million VND. In Pleikrong, compensation for farmland was 26 million VND per hectare, when the market price was actually 40 million. Other land and property losses were also insufficiently compensated, and in many cases losses have not even been estimated. Over 50 per cent of people in Yaly, 34 per cent in Ban Ve, 60 per cent in Hoa Binh and 67 per cent in Tuyen Quang confirmed that the land and property loss surveys had been inadequate. As a consequence, 88 per cent of respondents in the four projects are seriously discontented with the compensation policies (Institute of Development 2010).

Programmes of livelihood restoration and job replacement assistance Besides compensation for losses and resettlement, 'land recovery' for hydropower projects also requires programmes for assistance in livelihood reconstruction and agricultural production. These, however, provide assistance only in the short term, such as rice, fuel, healthcare and school fees, and support for festivals before moving into the new settlement, as well as agricultural tools and job training. The arrangements differ considerably among projects. Most projects support rice for a year; some do so for two years, such as the Son La and Ban Ve dams. Most households receive assistance in cash, which may be more convenient for developers but may in practice not be sufficient to compensate people for the food sources they have lost. Therefore, approximately 87 per cent of displaced people deemed this assistance in three dam projects as insufficient for stable new living conditions. In addition, nearly 50 per cent did not appreciate the agricultural extension services because they did not help much to improve agricultural production (ibid.).

In general, the most difficult problems for resettlers' livelihood restoration are lack of arable land and job replacement. The most important livelihood resource for displaced people is arable land, but resettlers tend not to receive sufficient land to recover their livelihood, in spite of commitments made by developers. For example, the household survey in the Aluoi hydropower project showed that the investor has not given 0.5 hectares of arable land to displaced people as promised. The job replacement programme also does not work for ethnic minority farmers, whose education level is low and who may also have more difficulty in adapting to wage work dominated by the Kin majority. In some cases the resettlement site is also located on farmlands that do not belong to the resettled population, except perhaps very small plots. In such cases the population cannot continue to practise agriculture as their main source of livelihood. However, other jobs are often not available, not only for resettlers but also for other residents in these rural areas. Most people enrolled in such programmes prefer to receive money because they think they cannot learn to do new jobs. In fact, the general job training programme in rural areas in Vietnam is not very successful nationwide (Labour News 2012).

Such problems are not new or of a temporary nature: even with dams constructed thirty years ago resettlers may still face the same problems, as, for example, people displaced by the Hoa Binh hydropower dam. The resettled people displaced by that dam have received several assistance programmes to mitigate the impacts of displacement, including Programmes 747 (1995–2001), 472 (2002–06), 1588 (2009–15), and Programmes 134 and 135. Although these programmes have made improvements, they have not worked as effectively and efficiently as expected. The investment is too small in scale and too fragmented to be adequate. The agricultural programme has not enabled farmers to produce competitive products for the market. Funds for infrastructure have been expanded, but about 40 per cent of communities still lack schools, healthcare and water supply systems (Nguyen Cong Quan 2011).

Consequences Displaced people thus face many challenges, including lack of farmland, jobs and access to public amenities. It is difficult to identify any evidence that shows that resettlers have a better life after relocation. Research by the Institute of Development (2010) showed that over 82 per cent of the resettled people stated they were worse off than before resettlement. These findings have been matched by our recent survey in the Aluoi resettlement site one year after relocation. As a result, the incidence of poverty has been persistently high in resettlement communities. In the Hoa Binh hydro project, the poverty rate in spite of assistance programmes remains high, moving only from 45 per cent in 2001 to 34 per cent in 2008 (see Table 8.3).

Poverty is often accompanied by hunger, as most families cannot produce enough food owing to lack of sufficient agricultural land, especially paddy fields. Therefore, they have to spend compensation money to buy food. Household

TABLE 8.3 The poverty rate of households living in resettlement sites

| Classification | Hydropower dam | | | | Average rate (%) |
	Hoa Binh	Ban Ve	Yaly	Tuyen Quang	
Poor	33.4	81.1	65.6	46.3	56.3
Near poor	20.3	3.5	0.7	20.6	11.5
Average	44.9	15.4	33.7	33.1	31.8
Better-off	1.4				0.4

Source: Management board of Programmes 747 and 472 (2009)

surveys in Binh Dien (2010) and Aluoi (2012) showed that resettlers have reduced their food intake from three to two meals per day after resettlement, and they normally face severe food shortages for three to six months a year.

Displacement and resettlement due to hydropower dam construction also result in increasing disputes among villagers because of differences in compensation and land disputes. In addition, conflicts between resettlers and established populations in destination areas are also serious: 27 per cent of resettlers in fourteen villages in the Ban Ve hydropower project said they have disputes with the local villagers. More importantly, the number of individual and collective appeals has increased rapidly in the wake of hydropower dam construction. In the resettlement sites of the Yaly, Ban Ve and Tuyen Quang dams, 62 per cent of respondents said they have sent petitions to different levels of authorities, of which 18.2 per cent were at community level, 16.8 per cent at village and commune level, 29.5 per cent at district level, 26.7 per cent at province level, and 8.95 at the central government level (Institute of Development 2010).

Discussion and conclusion

The case of Vietnam allows us to draw a few conclusions about the current 'hype' around international land grabbing and to extend the debate to other fields that are no less relevant. Seen from the perspective of Vietnam, the hype in the land grab debate consists of the emphasis on the role of foreign actors (foreignization) in land acquisitions, and on the singular attention paid to acquisition of land for agricultural production purposes. Our point is not to deny the importance of these issues; rather, it is to assert that they are only part of more encompassing processes of change. The key problems arising from land grabbing – displacement and dispossession of resident populations in addition to sustainability issues – are not confined to the land-rich and people-poor peripheries of Africa and other areas where large landholdings are converted to corporate agriculture (or held for financial speculation). They are equally features of the structural transformations experienced by Vietnam and similar countries where an essentially rural economy and society are giving way to urban, industrial and services-based equivalents. This is not an equitable process, but entails the transfer of resources (land, water, nature) in favour of stronger actors (developers, investors, state agents, etc.) at the expense of weaker ones (villagers, small-scale farmers, minority populations).

Land conversion procedures in Vietnam comply with the principle of free, prior and informed consent (FPIC) only in part. The Land Law (2003) prescribes timely announcement of a decision to convert ('recover') land, but the announcement often comes late – in practice, often just before project implementation. Compensation prices are set by local authorities; dissatisfied landholders may appeal but the decision is with the authorities, since the state is the ultimate owner of the land. In the case of private projects, compensation is in principle negotiated between interested parties; but since agreement is difficult in many cases, the authorities intervene 'in the national interest'.

Large-scale land acquisitions are often interpreted as evidence of the rise in importance of 'vertical' forces over 'horizontal', territorial ones. Typically, global market forces (prices, opportunities for gain) are thus seen to overwhelm the regulatory powers of 'traditional' territorially based governments. While this case study of Vietnam actually confirms the role of globalization as the harbinger of change, it also serves to nuance the vertical-over-horizontal discourse. Governments, horizontal actors par excellence and as such sometimes considered as creatures of the past, may very well actively implement the globalization strategies. As shown in urbanization and hydropower projects in Vietnam, the public sector assumes a leading role in bringing about these changes and reallocating land resources in favour of uses and users it deems more attractive. This is partly a logical consequence of Vietnam's socialist orientation, but it is not fundamentally different from cases observed elsewhere – for example, by Saskia Sassen (2005).

Land conversion is not a new phenomenon in development processes, but its extent and effects are. The process, on the one hand, could create massive benefits for stakeholders, such as government agencies, developers and investors, and local people. On the other hand, without a firm political commitment to protect the weak, land conversion also puts intense pressures on the livelihoods of farmers and others who have no stake in the rising industries. The changes as such need not be harmful, but the way in which they are played out may be. And that, indeed, requires a strong and committed 'horizontal' regulator.

9 | 'Land grabbing' in Cambodia: land rights in a post-conflict setting

Michelle McLinden Nuijen, Men Prachvuthy and
Guus van Westen

Introduction

Much large-scale (foreign) land acquisition is focused on sub-Saharan Africa. Two reasons often put forward for this are the perceived availability of large areas of underutilized or 'free' land, and relatively weak land governance institutions offering little resistance to external appropriations of farmland (Deininger and Byerlee 2011b). In the rather different context of South-East Asia, Cambodia presents a case of just these two characteristics. With a population of some fifteen million on its 181,035 square kilometres of land, much of it suitable for agriculture, it stands out as a country with relatively abundant land resources – certainly by Asian standards. Whether this implies that land is actually underused and available for external investors is, of course, another matter. Moreover, Cambodia presents the case of a country with weak governance. This is a logical consequence of its tragic recent history. The genocidal Khmer Rouge regime (1975–79) resulted in wholesale institutional destruction and uprooting of much of the population. This was followed by a prolonged period of conflict in which the country vacillated between a command economy (Vietnamese style) and an open market economy with a legal framework that could relate more to donor-inspired notions of democratic governance than to local traditions and experiences. This is not to say that this legal framework is bad, but some fluidity and gaps in its implementation are evident. These become particularly visible when looking at land rights. In South-East Asia, Cambodia is a prime target for land grabbing.

After successive phases of socialist regulation models, Cambodia has joined the globally prevailing neoliberal regime with a vengeance since the early 1990s. Being a country rich in land and poor in capital, it has set out to attract investment by opening its 'available' natural resources to interested investors. Particularly important in this context is the kingdom's policy on Economic Land Concessions (ELCs). These ELCs are designed to attract foreign direct investment, increase agricultural production, and generate employment and income, while minimizing adverse social and environmental impacts (Kingdom of Cambodia 2005: 4). Investors are lured by incentives, including tax breaks;

low land lease fees; GSP (Generalized System of Preferences) eligibility for market access to Australia, Canada, the EU, Japan and the USA; unrestricted repatriation of profit; and special visa conditions for employees and their families (LYP Group Co. Ltd n.d.).

The Land Law of 2001 and the Sub-Decree on Economic Land Concessions allow the Cambodian government to grant up to 10,000 hectares of land to international and domestic investors in large-scale agro-industry. The main purpose of this concession policy is to develop large-scale agricultural production by promoting investment in agro-industrial activities as well as to increase employment opportunities and diversify livelihoods in rural areas. A large-scale land concession is a lease agreement of up to ninety-nine years' duration against a yearly fee of US$2–10 per hectare, depending on the quality of the land. According to the Ministry of Agriculture, Forestry and Fisheries[1] in May 2011, eighty-six concessions had been granted since 1995 within eighteen provinces and covering a land area of about 1.04 million hectares. Approximately 52 per cent of this was granted to Cambodians while 42 per cent went to foreign investors, mainly from China, Vietnam, South Korea, Thailand and Malaysia. The largest share of these land concessions (40 per cent) is located in the north-eastern provinces, where many indigenous people live. Another source, however, reported that in 2011 roughly 2.3 million hectares had been granted across Cambodia to 225 companies, on leases of seventy to ninety-nine years (ADHOC 2012: 1). Note that these numbers do not include concessions for fifty-six mining zones and twenty-two Special Economic Zones, issued under other regulatory frameworks (ibid.). Thus, the extent of the land concession programme is in dispute, as are its consequences. While the ELC policy is considered to have made some contributions to infrastructure development, employment and export growth (GTZ 2009), it is widely reported to have negatively affected the livelihoods of many Cambodians (UNCOHCHR 2007; GTZ 2009; Deininger and Byerlee 2011b; Men 2011; ADHOC 2012; McLinden Nuijen 2012). Although data varying in quality and sources may not always concur, the evidence is sufficient to state that land grabbing is not a hype in Cambodia. According to one source (LHWG 2009: 6), citing World Bank reports that rural landlessness increased from 13 per cent in 1997 to some 20–25 per cent in 2007, over 400,000 Cambodians lost their land or homes in the period 2003–09. This is quite a departure from the start of land privatization in Cambodia in 1989, when land was distributed 'almost equally' (Loehr 2010: 1036). Now, Cambodia has the most inequitable pattern of land distribution in the region (ibid.). Land disputes regularly flare up across the country, typically pitting smallholders against large-scale agro-industrial companies backed by influential people.

This chapter seeks to explore the land rights issues in Cambodia by means of two recent empirical studies in different parts of the country. The first is a case study of ELC creation in remote north-eastern Cambodia, a heavily forested area populated mostly by indigenous peoples. The second study investigates the case of a large ELC granted for industrial sugar production in the south-western coastal part of Cambodia. By discussing these cases together, our objective is twofold. First, we aim to appraise the impact of large-scale land acquisitions by external parties under the ELC programme on the livelihoods of established local populations. The second objective is to unravel the drivers of corporate land hunger – that is, the forces and conditions leading to the invasion of rural Cambodia by external investors.

Setting the scene: Economic Land Concessions (ELCs) and local communities

The two case study areas considered here differ on many counts. North-eastern Cambodia is in many respects a typical resource frontier: a vast peripheral area of mainly forest land and low population densities. However, 'development' in the guise of logging and conversion of land into large-scale agricultural operations (often rubber plantations and cattle rearing) is making significant inroads. Not only is the region experiencing a structural transformation from subsistence-oriented, small-scale agro-forestry to large-scale commercial farming directly linked to distant markets and capital, and controlled by absentee owners; at the same time, a fundamental socio-demographic change is taking place. Through colonization, Cambodia's titular Khmer people are settling in areas so far populated by small communities of 'indigenous' peoples. Unsurprisingly in view of perceived land availability, the north-east has been targeted in a large way in the Cambodian government's policy of agriculture-led development through the attraction of large-scale corporate farming. Vast areas have been granted to foreign investors and domestic non-local residents by the government, in the form of ELCs. This is often in conflict with existing regulations that classified the north-east as a national ecotourism development zone, while some of the land is designated as protected area. This results in ecological concerns as well as concerns over what consequences the ELCs may have for the culture of indigenous groups and their traditional livelihoods, based on slash-and-burn agriculture and non-timber forest products (NTFPs) collection. Our study in the north-east focused mainly on livelihood implications for indigenous people. It included desk review of existing materials, as well as empirical data collection by means of a household survey, in-depth interviews and focus group discussions. The desk review covered legislation and policy on land tenure, forestry, protected areas and ELCs, as well as sub-decrees on land tenure and use arrangements for indigenous communities and indigenous communal land in Cambodia. The household survey was conducted among 188 randomly selected households in Kalai commune in Ratanak Kiri and Bousra commune in Mondul Kiri provinces. A further twenty-seven key informants working in the north-eastern provinces were interviewed using a semi-structured questionnaire. These interviews mainly gathered the informants' opinions on how ELCs are impacting indigenous people. One focus group discussion was organized in each of two communes of the two provinces. There were twenty-six participants in total, four of whom were women. This served as the basis for generating a timeline or community history on how indigenous peoples' livelihoods have changed over time.

Indigenous communities are not the only Cambodians suffering adverse effects of ELCs and other policies aiming to make room for corporate land uses and users, although their case has a special cultural dimension that is not necessarily involved – or not so starkly involved – in dispossessions affecting Khmer farmers. But the livelihood impacts may be equally serious for the latter. This was clear from the second case study, covering the villages of Trapaiong Kandaol and Chi Kha, which are located in the south-west coastal zone of Cambodia. There, Khmer households' livelihoods depend largely on a combination of agriculture, animal husbandry and forest and fishing resources obtained from the commons. In May 2006 farmers were surprised to find their cultivated fields being cleared with the assistance of armed soldiers and police. This is frequently the case in Cambodia – the military is actively involved in the eviction of the urban and rural poor as well as the protection of large land concessions (Brady 2010). Two people were shot and five others were otherwise injured in the ensuing conflict. As a result of plantation development, roughly 450 families lost land. Surveyed households lost a combination of cropping, grazing and forest land, as well as the associated crops and common pool resources used for livelihood support. Eviction in this case took place when, in 2006, two ELCs in the Botum Sakor and Sre Ambel districts of Koh Kong province were leased for ninety-nine years. The ELCs, applying to 9,400 and 9,700 hectares respectively, were awarded to Koh Kong Plantation Co. Ltd and Koh Kong Sugar Co. Ltd in order to develop the country's first post-conflict sugar mill and sugar plantation (UNCOHCHR 2007: 31). Both companies originated as a partnership between three other firms: the LYP Group of Cambodia; the KSL Group, the oldest sugar producer in Thailand; and KSL's partner in the food manufacturing industry since 1966, Ve Wong Corporation of Taiwan (CHRAC 2009: 16). Despite Article 59 of the Land Law, which requires ELCs to be distinct and no larger than 10,000 hectares in order to prevent large tracts of land being controlled by a single person or legal entity (Kingdom of Cambodia 2001), the ELCs are contiguous and are run as a single concession by company managers (LYP Group Co. Ltd n.d.: 42; McLinden Nuijen 2012: 83) for the production and exportation of raw sugar, mainly to the EU (CAAI News Media 2009).[2] This second case study therefore gathered important insights into the web of relations and forces driving foreignization and land grabbing in Cambodia, through desk and field research including in-depth interviews, participatory land mapping, household surveys and focus group discussions with a total of 132 farmers, NGO staff, community leaders and local government officials.

Land governance and local communities: legal and institutional framework

Given the political legacy of the country, land tenure regimes in Cambodia are characterized by significant discontinuity. Recent political instability, large-scale displacement and resettlement, and the outlawing of private landownership and subsequent destruction of land tenure documents by the Khmer Rouge regime mean that the majority of people in the country live under insecure tenure conditions (Zitelmann 2005, as cited by Center for Advanced Study et al. 2006: 1). In Koh Kong, where farmers have used a mix of community, usufruct and private tenure systems, this legacy is clearly evidenced through a general confusion regarding not only current tenure status but also the procedures required to obtain secure tenure. For example, 80 per cent of farmers interviewed reported holding title to their land despite the fact that land in the research area has yet to be adjudicated by a titling team. A total of 14 per cent reported holding no tenure document. Nonetheless, Cambodian laws protect smallholders who have sufficient proof that they are the legal possessors of the land (Center for Advanced Study et al. 2006: 65). While these farmers have a right to apply for a primary land title, discrepancies occur between the *de jure* and *de facto* situations such that protective laws are not enforced (Land and Housing Working Group 2009: 5). According to critics, ambiguous land governance policies are mis-operated by corrupt officials to benefit investor elites (Boreak and Cambodia Development Resource Institute 2000: 1; NGO Forum 2010b: 5).

Among indigenous people in the north-eastern provinces, collective management of natural resources at the community level is common practice. Therefore, it makes sense for them to register and claim land tenure rights as a collective. A range of laws, policies and international treaties have been put in place in support of such rights of indigenous peoples. In Cambodia, the Land Law (2001), the Forestry Law (2002) and the Protected Area Law (2007) have granted indigenous peoples opportunities to organize access to natural resources and land titling as collectives. In reality, however, collective registration and land titling are slow and cumbersome processes. This is because effective mechanisms are lacking and the classification criteria for state private property and for what constitutes an indigenous community are unclear. The process of registration was introduced as a pilot project in two indigenous communities by the Ministry of Land Management, Urban Planning and Construction (MLMUPC) in 2003 (McAndrew and Il 2009). While it took several years to agree on the process of collective land titling, it now consists of three main components: 1) identification and recognition of indigenous peoples and their communities; 2) by-laws stipulating the registration of indigenous communities; and 3) registration of collective land titles. Each of these component processes engages a different government agency with its own procedures. First, the Ministry of Rural Development (MRD) is charged with identifying and confirming the legal identity of indigenous peoples and their communities. In 2010, only 46 out of 139 targeted indigenous communities in Ratanak Kiri and Mondul Kiri provinces actually received a legal identity certificate from MRD (Nuy 2010; Vann and Chantrea 2010). Next, the Ministry of Interior (MoI) is responsible for approving the legal entity by-laws of indigenous communities. Each community is required to set up several consultation meetings to review their by-laws before they can be approved by local authorities and the ministry. As of 2010, only twenty indigenous communities were successfully registered as legal entities with MoI (Nuy 2010; Vann and Chantrea 2010). Only after registration is it possible to proceed to the final step of registering collective land titles with the MLMUPC. While the pilot project provided insights into how to improve the registration of indigenous communities for collective land titling, in fact this process takes considerable time and effort as well as support from many stakeholders. International agencies and NGOs have played important roles in providing such support. Nevertheless, progress was hindered by differences in interpretation of the law defining state public and state private land. Moreover, limited government time and resources have been allocated to further collective titling. As a result, ELCs have been granted on indigenous community lands by the Ministry of Agriculture, Forestry and Fisheries (MAFF), leading to numerous land conflicts.

Impact on local livelihoods

In spite of the legal frameworks in place to protect the rights of indigenous people and smallholders in Cambodia (see also Andersen et al. 2007; Nuy 2010), illegal logging and large-scale land acquisitions by outsiders have undermined the traditional ways of life. In focus group discussions, most people complained about new challenges to their livelihood, particularly regarding deforestation and land. The study found that ELCs impact indigenous groups in four main ways. Each will be briefly discussed in turn. First, in the survey, 54 per cent of respondents mentioned losing land to a concession company. The average amount of land lost was 5 hectares per family, mainly land used for shifting cultivation. However, only 34 per cent of families interviewed reported having filed a complaint against the concessionaire for taking their land. Most villagers had instead participated in demonstrations and petitions to the authorities and NGOs. This may be a result of the important role local and international NGOs play in mediating between indigenous communities and concession companies, providing legal advice, and documenting complaints for relevant authorities. Nonetheless, approximately 70 per cent of land disputes remain unresolved (NGO Forum 2010b). Moreover, at the time of research only 16 per cent of families reported actually receiving compensation from the companies involved. Most households were persuaded to sell their land significantly below market prices at US$100–500 per hectare. The majority of those who received compensation were dissatisfied, having at times been forced to accept a deal. In addition, village chiefs and local authorities tended to receive better compensation (Ngo and Chan 2010). Even when compensation is paid, the amounts are not sufficient to buy new farmland in the affected areas as the companies are gobbling up all available land.

Secondly, the survey shows that household incomes of most indigenous people have decreased since the arrival of the concession companies. Indigenous household incomes mainly depend on agricultural production and collection of NTFPs such as wild fruits, vegetables, resin, honey, vines, rattan, bamboo and herbal medicines. Rice yields in particular have decreased dramatically since concession companies cleared the forest and took over community land. Average yield decreases of 60–70 per cent were reported. Livestock production also decreased from an average of ten to twenty buffalos or cows per family to some two or three, owing to the reduction of grazing areas. NTFPs are also important in supporting livelihoods; some 96 per cent of indigenous families used to collect NTFPs from the forest prior to the concession. Here again, the availability of NTFPs has dramatically decreased since thousands of hectares of forest were cleared for rubber plantations. Interviews revealed that the remaining forest lands are occupied by the companies, which ban access for NTFP collection. For example, a male respondent in Kalai-3 village said, 'I was threatened that I would be shot when walking on the company's forest land where I usually go to find wild vegetables and to hunt.' Likewise, a distressed woman in Lam Mes village, Bousra commune, said, 'I, along with other villagers, was not allowed to walk across the company rubber plantation to another forest near Phnom Nam Leah to take care of my farm and collect food in the forest.' In the survey, 87 per cent of respondents reported a significant increase in distance travelled for NTFP collection, with an average addition of 8.4 kilometres. Some families now travel 20–35 kilometres to collect NTFPs and work on their shifting cultivation plots. In addition, resources for handicraft production, such as rattan, vines and bamboo, are becoming scarce. Handicraft production of items such as bamboo baskets (*kapha*) and rice-cooking baskets (*cha ang*) is part of the cultural traditions of indigenous people. They can also earn income by selling these products. Finally, hunting and fishing are also affected because wildlife habitat has been destroyed by the concession companies. The noise of bulldozers and tractors disturbs the wildlife.

The third impact on indigenous groups involves employment. One stated policy objective of ELCs and agro-industrial development is the creation of new employment opportunities in rural areas. However, the government's enthusiasm for job creation through ELCs is not shared by many indigenous people. While new wage work could offer alternative livelihoods and replace traditional income sources such as shifting cultivation, NTFP collection and hunting, the benefit appears limited. On average, surveyed families earn US$249 per year from wages ranging between US$3 and 5 per person per day. The focus group discussions showed that daily wages have decreased from US$5 to 3.65 or less, owing to job competition from migrant workers. In addition, only 30 per cent of households interviewed stated that they had worked with concession companies. This matches statements by a concession company representative in Mondul Kiri province, who reported that 39 per cent of rubber plantation workers are indigenous (Phnong) people from nearby villages and 61 per cent are migrants from other parts of Cambodia. NGO representatives have suggested that companies prefer migrant workers because they have more skills and accept lower pay. Resentment is clearly reflected in the survey results, where only 24 per cent of respondents indicated they would accept a job offer from a concession company and then only because they need to work to survive. For example, a woman in Bousra village said, almost in tears:

I forced myself to work for the company because I have no farm land any more, and it is hardly possible to find food from the forest now. There is no forest any more. I don't know how to find money besides working on the rubber planta-tion. I don't know how to do business. I have no idea how to protest against the company to get my land back. We have already demonstrated but without result. I want to return to work on my farm. It is hard to work on the rubber plantation.

The 76 per cent of respondents who declared themselves unwilling to work for the concession company offered several reasons. Many (26 per cent) com-plained that the work was too hard and offered too little freedom. People said that they have to get up in the middle of the night to prepare food and travel to work and that they have limited time for lunch and rest. At least 12 per cent were too angry with the company for grabbing their land and destroying their spirit forests[3] to be able to work for them. In Kalai commune, a fifty-eight-year-old man said, 'I am very angry with the company that destroyed our spiritual forest land and grabbed our farmland. I can say that I and my generation will not work for those concession companies even if we are starving.' At least 11 per cent of respondents claimed that the company cheated people when pay-ing wages and that wages were too low because of competition from migrant workers. Another 4 per cent said their health does not allow them to do such work. Health is a challenge for indigenous communities, as health facilities in the area are limited.

The fourth impact of ELCs on indigenous groups is positive. Infrastructure improvements made by the concession companies in the concession areas

TABLE 9.1 Timeline of indigenous communities, marking key events and trends

1980–93	1994–2006	2007–present
Economic	*Economic*	*Economic*
Main forms of livelihood are shifting cultivation and NTFPs collection	Shifting rice cultivation yields remain good (enough to eat)	Loss of shifting cultivation land and cashew nut farms
Good rice yields provide enough food; the remainder can be sold each year	Sufficient wildlife and fairly easy hunting	Loss of NTFPs and difficulties accessing forest because of concession companies
Abundant wildlife; hunting was easy	Main forms of livelihood remain shifting cultivation and NTFPs collection	Much less wildlife for hunting
Sufficiently available farmland in the community	Cashew nut plantations expand among communities, especially in Kalai, from 1996	Rice needs to be bought from market
	Deforestation begins, affecting NTFPs collection (especially resin production)	Need to work on rubber plantations (concession companies); wages used to buy rice from market (mostly Bousra)
		Loss of buffalos and cows: no place to raise them as companies have cleared forests and do not allow them on their land (threats of confiscation); many animals have died
		Need to work hard and get up early (2–3 a.m.); 'just work for food' (Bousra)
Environment	*Environment*	*Environment*
Landscape intact with abundant forest	Logging by powerful local people and foreign concession companies from 1998	Forest cleared by concession companies for rubber plantations, etc.
Good-quality river and lake water (pure and natural); no pollution by outsiders	Rainfall remains regular	Companies using chemical pesticides and pest controls pollute water resources
High and regular rainfall		Irregular rainfall
Vietnamese forest concession companies logging in indigenous community area in 1985, cutting large trees only		Climate change; hotter than previous years
		Company litter (plastic rubber seedling bags) not discarded properly

Sociocultural and security	Sociocultural and security	Sociocultural and security
Freedom to access land and forests anywhere in the community	Local and international NGOs and Cambodian Red Cross promoting agricultural extension, human rights, community forestry, natural resource management, literacy	Loss of traditional medicine: harder to find owing to forest clearance
Good security (no thieves)	Good security (no thieves)	Loss of spiritual forest lands and burial forest lands
Good health (natural environment)	Good health	Insufficient food to eat as wild fruits and vegetables no longer available in the forest
A variety of medicinal herbs could be collected from the forest	Still practising traditional cultural and spiritual ceremonies	More health problems
Solidarity among community members during traditional ceremonies	Belief in spiritual forests and strict ritual practices	Spiritual beliefs and traditional practices marginalized as spiritual lands are destroyed
Belief in spiritual forests and ritual practices (spiritual forest land well protected)	Some indigenous families still wearing traditional costumes	NGOs working on agricultural extension, human rights, natural resource management, literacy, credit and saving, health education, advocacy, etc.
Use of traditional costumes by some indigenous families	Some Khmer families migrating to settle in indigenous communities	Many Khmer families from other provinces in the area working with companies
Infrastructure	**Infrastructure**	**Infrastructure**
Poor or non-existent roads: difficult to travel to provincial town	Some bicycles and motorbikes	Better roads and bridges built in community
Travel by foot, elephant or oxcart	Travel across Vietnamese border possible without restriction (open border)	Most indigenous families have bicycles, motorbikes and better houses
	Roads to provincial town still in poor condition	Better access to quality water (e.g. shallow and pump wells) and electricity
	Community paved roads built from 1997	
	Open shallow and pump wells and latrines constructed by government and NGOs	

Source: Focus group interviews, Bousra, Mondul Kiri and Kalai, Ratanak Kiri, July/August 2010

mean that indigenous communities benefit from roads, bridges, schools and health centre renovations, particularly in Bousra commune. Improving infrastructure in rural areas is an important item on the government agenda in granting concessions. Interviews revealed that most respondents recognized infrastructure benefits as linked to the arrival of the concessions in their community.

One objective of the study was to determine how indigenous peoples' livelihoods have changed owing to ELCs and other forces. The group interviews revealed three important periods of change: 1980–93 (re-establishment of communities after the Khmer Rouge); 1994–2006 (rise of the free market economy); and 2007–present (introduction of ELCs). These have been presented in the timeline matrix above to show how life has changed with regard to economic aspects, the environment, sociocultural and security aspects, and infrastructure.

While the representation of past conditions may be coloured by nostalgia, the timeline in Table 9.1 clearly documents major transformations having taken place in a fairly short time span. Modernization, driven by external forces and agents, has considerably constrained traditional livelihoods and access to natural resources as well as having eroded the natural environment. Improvements in infrastructure do not compensate for the economic and cultural marginalization suffered by the indigenous groups.

Meanwhile, in the southern villages of Trapaiong Kandaol and Chi Kha, people are also facing hardship as a result of their lands being swallowed up by a new ELC. As local livelihoods are intrinsically connected to land and its resources, dispossession has consequences for income, food security, health and education. Important livelihood support obtained from forest and fishing resources has been lost: forest land was cleared and the quality of the remaining commons has been reduced. In addition, as soon as the sugar company took possession of the land, larger livestock transitioned from being a household asset to an economic liability: livestock caught on concession land has been shot or held for ransom by the company's security guards. Moreover, the ELC has reduced access to local water resources used for food and livelihood support; some resources have been lost to land use change while others have been poisoned by pesticide and fertilizer run-off from the sugar plantation. As a result of these losses, the majority of households report having less food as well as worse health. Finally, income losses have forced some households to take out loans and sell land and cattle to pay for illness in the family. Income loss has also forced some children to work more and study less. Children as young as nine years old cut, bundle and carry sugar cane, while children from the age of thirteen spray fertilizers and pesticides without instruction or protective gear. Despite significant losses outlined above, compensation has generally not been provided. In fact, the majority of households surveyed have not received compensation for any of their losses.

In cases where compensation was given, lost land was underestimated and undervalued and the process was characterized by intimidation and coercion.

Villagers have faced obstacles to participation in the development process. Few jobs have been created that are open to locals, and most work on the sugar estate is seasonal. At the time of fieldwork, fewer than fifteen farmers worked at the mill; the majority of these positions are based upon seasonal harvests and thus are part-time. In response to land loss resulting from the project, villagers have sought recognition from local to international levels. Complaints have been filed with Tate & Lyle (the buyer of the sugar produced in the area), with the Organisation for Economic Cooperation and Development (OECD), and with Bonsucro, the organization setting standards for sustainable sugar production. A complaint filed five years ago with the National Human Rights Commission of Thailand has recently resulted in a statement affirming that human rights abuses, particularly concerning the right to life and self-determination, have resulted from the development project.[4] More recently, legal proceedings were filed in the UK against Tate & Lyle on behalf of 200 Koh Kong farmers, who lost 1,364 hectares of land to the government of Cambodia through illegal land concessions. The farmers claim full ownership of the sugar cane produced on their land.

Drivers: forces leading to large-scale acquisition and foreignization of land

In the two study areas, we have seen that the ELC policy may have serious socio-economic consequences for indigenous people and Khmer smallholders alike. The discussion now turns to the drivers behind these transformations. What forces cause poor Cambodians to be evicted from their land?

The growing demand for natural resources is the main driving force behind the large-scale land acquisitions in the north-east. Especially in the north-eastern provinces of Kratie, Stung Treng, Mondul Kiri and Ratanak Kiri, much of this has to do with the production of natural rubber (Dararath et al. 2011). According to MAFF, approximately 69 per cent of ELC companies located in the north-eastern provinces grow rubber trees.[5] Latex is exported to leading rubber consumption countries such as China, Taiwan, India and Japan, although the largest rubber plantation in Cambodia actually exports to European markets. The price of rubber has doubled in recent years from US$2,500 per tonne to about US$5,400 per tonne,[6] providing a clear incentive to convert more land to rubber production. Yet it would be too simple to view the Cambodian land grab as simply the outcome of anonymous market forces, as a shifting balance between demand and supply of particular commodities. A closer look at the Koh Kong case shows that international corporate networks and policy frameworks together shape the conditions under which local communities in Cambodia are being transformed.

As mentioned before, eviction in the Botum Sakor and Sre Ambel districts of Koh Kong province took place when two adjacent ELCs were awarded to two nominally different companies, both owned by the same consortium of three investors (UNCOHCHR 2007: 31): the LYP Group of Cambodia, the KSL Group from Thailand and Ve Wong Corporation of Taiwan (CHRAC 2009: 16). The LYP Group was established in 1999 by Ly Yong Phat, business tycoon and senator of the ruling Cambodian People's Party, and conducts domestic and interregional operations in hospitality, real estate, infrastructure and utilities, and trading and distribution, as well as agro-industry (LYP Group Co. Ltd n.d.). The KSL Group is a business management group based in Bangkok and engaged in the sugar, seasonings, ceramic, trading, IT and real estate industries (KSL Group 2003). Its managing director since 1996 has been Chamroon Chinthammit (KSL 2009), who is also the chairman of the Koh Kong Sugar Company Ltd and was named by *Forbes* as one of Thailand's forty richest citizens in 2011.[7] Ve Wong Corporation is a Taiwanese company in operation since 1959 (Ve Wong Corporation n.d.), engaged *inter alia* in food production, trading and construction (ibid.).

The fate of the Koh Kong villagers can be understood only by taking a closer look at the complex web of relations linking different parties in the sugar industry. Half a world away, Tate & Lyle had signed a five-year contract to buy sugar from Khon Kaen Sugar Industry concessions in Cambodia and Laos (Campbell 2011) (Khon Kaen Sugar Industry is the sugar division of the KSL Group). However, Tate & Lyle sold all sugar holdings to American Sugar Refining, Inc. (ASR), formerly known as Tate & Lyle North American Sugars, Inc.[8] Headquartered in Yonkers, New York, ASR is a subsidiary of Florida Crystals Corporation and the Sugarcane Growers Cooperative of Florida. ASR's production capacity of 6 million tons of sugar makes ASR the largest cane sugar refining company in the world.[9] ASR owns and operates six sugar refineries in New York, California, Maryland, Louisiana, Canada and Mexico, as well as sugar refineries in England and Portugal. ASR markets products through brands such as Domino, C&H, Florida Crystals, Redpath and Tate & Lyle. ASR has been licensed to market the sugar sold under the Tate & Lyle brand name since acquiring the sugar operations of Tate & Lyle for US$314 million in cash in 2010. Included in the transaction are refineries in London and Lisbon.[10] Thus, through the Thai partner in the Koh Kong sugar consortium, sugar fields in southern Cambodia are directly linked to one of the world's largest processors and sellers of cane sugar. This is the corporate link.

In order to understand what happened in our case study villages, we also need to understand the policy links. On the domestic scene, firstly, Cambodia's policy of awarding ELCs to corporate agro-industrial interests is an attempt to pursue economic development by integrating the country's natural resource wealth into the global market economy. Thus, the country aligns its development strategy with the essentially neoliberal philosophy promoted (if not imposed) by international organizations and the donor community. Since the time of market reform and national reconstruction, this orientation has guided its development strategies from the first Socio-Economic Development Plan and the Triangle Strategy to the more recent National Strategic Development Plan (Kingdom of Cambodia 2009: 1). The United Nations' 'human development' ideas and notions of sustainability in the wake of the Brundtland report have certainly also influenced Cambodia's national development strategies, but such notions have been diluted under the dominant market formula; Cambodia unites these sometimes strange bedfellows in the National Sustainable Development Strategy (UNEP Regional Resource Center for Asia and the Pacific 2009: 45). The pursuit of large-scale corporate sugar farming is a variation on the classical model of agriculture-led development, where land and the agricultural sector, generally viewed as underutilized, are the wellspring for country-wide development (Cypher and Dietz 2009: 341, 353; Deininger and Byerlee 2011b: xv). While in itself a logical policy, agriculture-led development can undermine the opportunities for sustainable development when elite capture takes place, particularly in countries with weak institutions and tenure insecurity, such as Cambodia (Deininger and Byerlee 2011b: xxv). This has been the case with the recently re-established sugar industry in Cambodia, where the investment environment is characterized by geographical proximity to some of the region's largest sugar producers across the Thai border, cheap land and labour, few investment restrictions, and unmitigated government backing coupled with weak, post-conflict institutions unable to ensure rule of law and corporate accountability.

A second, less obvious but no less important policy driver behind the Koh Kong land grab relates directly to EU trade policy. Since 2001, Cambodia has been one of the foremost beneficiaries of a Generalized System of Preferences (GSP) trade scheme of the EU called 'Everything but Arms' (EBA) (European Commission Delegation of the EU to Cambodia 2011). Under EBA, Least Developed Countries (LDCs) can export products other than arms and ammunition to the EU without duties and for a guaranteed minimum price (ibid.). The EBA scheme is one example of the EU's approach to development within an international trade regime under the directives of the World Trade Organization (WTO). According to this approach, guided essentially by a neoliberal development paradigm, the market is viewed as the effective development mechanism par excellence: through modernization and economic growth, poverty is to be alleviated and standards of living raised (European Commission 2012).

In this case, the EBA scheme allows Koh Kong sugar access to higher-priced markets in the developed world. Without this preferential access it is doubtful that the operation could be run at a profit.

The EU sugar regime reform and the EBA

Out of all agricultural commodities sold on the global market, sugar has been considered one of the most policy distorted (Mitchell 2003: 1; OECD 2007: 9; Nyberg n.d.: 1). Protectionist markets of OECD member countries, particularly the USA, Japan and the EU countries, have traditionally severed the relationship between price and cost of production and restricted trade opportunities for those without preferential access (OECD 2007: 9). Within these markets, policies have led to increased protected market production with lower imports or higher subsidized exports. As a result, these markets have benefited from prices significantly higher than the world price, while their domestic consumers faced higher prices and world trade prices in sugar were pushed downwards (ibid.).

The EU's programme for sugar was an anomaly – it made sugar one of the most profitable crops and the one least open to reform (USDA Economic Research Service 2006: 1). Uncertainty is one reason for sugar producers to protect their markets: the sugar market in particular is susceptible to volatile prices and large variations in demand (OECD and FAO 2011: 120; Nyberg n.d.: 1). Sugar prices, at a record high in 2006, generally fell as domestic support measures in traditional importing countries increased production (Nyberg n.d.: 1). Nevertheless, with policy relatively unchanged for forty years, sugar prices three times higher than world levels and an export system operating against trade rules, criticism mounted within the EU as well as from the outside. While pressures for trade liberalization under policy reforms were met with stiff resistance in protected markets, the EU began a reform process in 2005 and adopted the new sugar regime in 2006 (OECD 2007: 9). After the ruling of the WTO in a case brought by Australia, Brazil and Thailand, the 2006 reform of the European sugar regime brought a 'radical overhaul' to sugar policy and placed it in line with the EU's Common Agricultural Policy (European Commission 2006: 2). As a result of reform, the EU transitioned from a large net exporter of white sugar to a large raw sugar importer. Benefiting from quota and duty-free access, imports mainly arrive from the African, Caribbean and Pacific countries (ACP) and the Least Developed Countries (LDCs). This sugar is refined and sold in the European market (OECD and FAO 2011: 124).

Reforms in the sugar policies of the USA, Japan and the EU were expected to result in price increases in the world market and substantial production decreases in their respective domestic markets. In turn, lower domestic sugar prices would increase demand and result in more sugar imports (OECD 2007: 40). At the international level, gains resulting from the liberalization of the global sugar market were estimated to reach between US$3 and 6.3 billion per year. In the medium to long term, the EU reform held 'potential gains for LDCs due to the implementation of the EBA initiative' (Nyberg n.d.: 1).

To a large extent, preferential trading schemes with developing countries define the market (ibid.: 1). These schemes, which are very important as they allow access to higher-priced domestic markets in the developed world, have included the ACP/EU Sugar Protocol and the Agreement on Special Preferential Sugar, EBA, the Caribbean Basin Initiative, and the African Growth and Opportunity Act, in addition to the regional trading blocs. Unfortunately, encouraging trade and releasing its catalytic effect against poverty appears to be less straightforward than the economic formula of the EC might imply. Despite preferential trading within an 'unrivalled development framework' for the ACP countries, the European Commission concluded in a 1997 review of policy that (as cited by Holland 2003: 161):

> The principle of partnership has proved difficult to carry through ... The recipient country's institutional environment and economic and social policy have often [been] a major constraint on the effectiveness of Community cooperation. The Union must bear some responsibility; its procedures have also limited the effectiveness of its aid. The impact of trade preferences has been disappointing on the whole.

This disappointment has been shared by others. Concerns over EBA and human rights abuses in Cambodia led an asset management arm of Deutsche Bank to reconsider its investment relationship with the KSL Group, the company producing sugar under its Khon Kaen Sugar subsidiary in Koh Kong.[11] In 2010, holdings of US$14 million were divested. According to spokesman Claus Gruber: 'When they set up the Everything but Arms programmes with countries such as Cambodia – countries with poor transparency, poor governance – I think the European Union is also responsible for looking into these kinds of issues.' Gruber also stated that the EU should act responsibly towards European firms by guiding them in investments abroad.

While GSP trade initiatives such as EBA at face value seem excellent opportunities for those who need them most, LDCs and their domestic entrepreneurs are often unable to use many of the preferences granted (Agazzi 2010). As LDCs lack production capacities, they continue to export commodities rather than more value-adding manufactured export products. It is difficult for them to build their production and processing capacity from scratch, against established competitors within the prevailing fairly liberal trade and increasingly integrated production networks. As a result, EBA mainly benefits more capable businesses that are well established in global value chains and therefore enjoy the right market connections – in other words, those which are not necessarily in need of a helping policy hand. At a recent UNCTAD meeting in Geneva, Rehman Sobhan, chairperson of the Centre for Policy Dialogue, stated: 'The EBA is very good, but the main beneficiaries tend to be the entrepreneurs of state-owned enterprises' – to which one may add those private business people who benefit from good relations with the public sector. Karin Ulmer, policy officer for trade and gender at APRODEV, proposes that policies such as EBA should be shaped according to the context of the specific countries and the nexus within the country between development and trade (ibid.).

Despite these limitations, the ticker keeps scrolling. In 2011, sugar prices reached a thirty-year high of US$795.4 per ton. The price increase was a result of two seasons of adverse weather and resulting global sugar deficits. Stocks of sugar were at a twenty-year low in 2010/11; prices are predicted to stabilize as production increases and stocks rebalance (OECD and FAO 2011: 120). Nonetheless, if adjusted for inflation, sugar prices are actually at the same level as in the 1980s. Facing rising costs for fuel and inputs, sugar producers are looking for ways to reduce costs and increase profitability.[12] For the big players in South-East Asia, producing sugar in Cambodia offers that opportunity.

Conclusion

The findings discussed in these two case studies in Cambodia enable some more general conclusions on global land grabbing. The first is the obvious role of well-established institutions in guiding access and use of lands. This is in line with the earlier observation (Deininger and Byerlee 2011b) that (foreign) land grabs are more likely to take place in countries with weak legal and regulatory regimes pertaining to land and human rights more generally. In Asia, Cambodia stands out as a case in point. The traumatic Khmer Rouge period in the later 1970s uprooted whole communities and destroyed whatever infrastructure in terms of regulating land rights Cambodian society had. The following prolonged period of instability and conflict has made it difficult to repair this societal destruction and produced a somewhat fluid institutional landscape that offers ample opportunities for abuse. While legislation and the institutional architecture in Cambodia seem to offer a reasonable degree of protection to ordinary people (including indigenous groups) and adhere to notions of sustainability, reality on the ground is often dictated by naked power and patronage. This was evidenced in both case studies, where land acquisitions took place in clear conflict with the laws of the land.

The second conclusion is the important trans-local link observed especially in Koh Kong, but also in the north-eastern provinces and presumably also in many other land acquisitions. It is one thing to conclude that land grabs and large-scale foreignization take place within the context of global market forces. Those are not specific, are impersonal, and may not be easily changed. It is another thing to show that villagers are driven from their land as a direct consequence of policy measures in another part of the world. It is this trans-local nature of development-induced dispossession which makes such land grabs stand out as new processes. The globalization of the sugar trade has forged trans-local linkages that are geographically diverse and include actors in Thailand, Taiwan, the EU and the USA. EU trade and development policy, in particular the EBA trade scheme within a recently reformed EU sugar regime, has created avenues of opportunity from local to international levels that elude observations 'on the ground'. Rather than fulfilling the pro-poor mandates of both the EBA and ELC policy, sugar development in Trapaing Kandaol and Chi Kha villages has resulted in marginalization of the poor as well as continued human rights abuses and labour violations. No one will be blind to the good intentions of preferential trade arrangements for LDCs, but this case study warns us, first, not to focus narrowly on conditions and stakeholders that are visible locally when analysing land issues. When context and trans-local links are not sufficiently taken into account, the core of the issue escapes analysis. Perhaps even more importantly, it also shows that 'something can be done' – not just in elusive terms of strengthening institutions in developing countries, but also in the policies of countries and groupings in major economic and political centres elsewhere, policies having a direct bearing on what happens here, there and everywhere in a globally integrating world.

Faced with adverse media exposure and pressure from donors, the Cambodian government issued a moratorium (which was soon violated)[13] on granting ELCs from April 2012.[14] In addition, some concessions have been terminated by the government. Moreover, in mid-2012 the government launched a new campaign of granting land rights to communities suffering from the adverse effects of ELCs. For example, 4,158 hectares were moved from a concessionaire to displaced families in 2012 (*Phnom Penh Post*, 30 November 2012), and according to the Ministry of Land Management, Urban Planning and Construction (MLMUPC), in June 2013, about 250,000 hectares were removed from 107 concessionaires.[15] The government also announced plans to grant about 1.8 million hectares from state land properties to 478,928 families. However, this new policy may negatively affect the process of collective land titling for indigenous communities in the north-east of the country. In Ratanak Kiri province indigenous communities are pressed to accept private instead of collective land titles.[16] Also, facts on the ground have again fallen short of the promises. According to Human Rights Watch the land titling campaign in Kompong Speu and Koh Kong provinces was being carried out successfully in some areas, while land was being taken from villagers in others through a 'non-transparent and extralegal process'.[17] Land rights remain a matter of serious concern in Cambodia.

10 | Beyond the Gulf State investment hype: the case of Indonesia and the Philippines

Gerben Nooteboom and Laurens Bakker[1]

Introduction

After the groundbreaking report *SEIZED!* (GRAIN 2008) – which sought attention for the sharp increase in large-scale transnational investments in land – alarm bells rang among NGOs, activists, researchers and policy-makers who were concerned about the social consequences for the global South of these large investments in land. In this narrative, Gulf states were depicted as one of the three main players (besides Western and Asian investors) and a major driver of the global rush for land. First, the reports on land deals caused unrest among NGOs fearing displacements and among peasants fearing to lose land. Secondly, the report sparked protests by critical scholars, activists and journalists who put emphasis on the intrinsic inequalities of the deals proposed, based on rumours of Memoranda of Understanding (MOUs) already signed. And thirdly, the deals provoked a wave of critical debate in mainstream media (e.g. Guardian 2008), through new NGO reports (Daniel and Mittal 2009; Oxfam 2011), through institutional inquiries (Cotula et al. 2009; Von Braun and Meinzen-Dick 2009), and in academic journals.[2] The debate mobilized people, power and money and challenged others to engage in the debate and counter those who stressed possible positive effects of land deals (Cotula et al. 2009; Von Braun and Meinzen-Dick 2009; Borras and Franco 2010b). The strong reactions to the 'massive' transnational investments in land in policy, activist and academic circles, with Gulf states as one of the major perpetrators identified, constitute what we now call the global land grab hype, discussed in this volume's Introduction.

In this chapter, we focus on the narrative of Gulf states' (GCC[3] countries') investments in land[4] and analyse the main reasons why many of the investments did not materialize. For this purpose, we take the cases of Indonesia and the Philippines as pivotal. GCC states were described by critics as rich in oil but lacking in arable land: as 'natural' land grab investors aiming to gain control over fertile land, water resources and food production in an attempt to sustain food security at home. Major investment countries mentioned were Sudan, Pakistan, Ethiopia (GRAIN 2008; Woertz et al. 2008a) and South-East Asian nations such as Indonesia, the Philippines, Cambodia and Vietnam (GRAIN 2008; Woertz et al. 2008a; NTS 2010; Montemayor 2011). Between 2008 and 2010, six deals involving GCC investors were announced in Indonesia, covering 2.6 million hectares, and nine in the Philippines, covering 863,500 hectares (see Table 10.1). Yet by 2013 none of the announced GCC deals has materialized in Indonesia and only four deals covering a modest 3,550 hectares in the Philippines – mainly based on previously established business cooperation. Why did the GCC deals not materialize in Indonesia and only partly in the Philippines?

In order to answer this question, we look at the narratives and expectations regarding GCC investments since the start of the global surge for land in 2007/08. Our analysis consists of three parts: 1) an overview of dominant narratives around potential GCC investments in Indonesia and the Philippines; 2) an overview of reasons to invest from the perspective of GCC states; and 3) an overview of reasons why the GCC investments did not materialize. By doing this, we aim to show the mobilizing power of the global land grab hype in terms of resources, policies, research and protest, and, consequently, the causes of stagnation of the GCC states' agrarian investment in Indonesia and the Philippines.

Data on actual land deals are scarce and often unreliable, while some information is never made public;[5] therefore triangulation is important. Material for this chapter and Table 10.1 has been collected through the study of media reports, available data sets such as the Land Matrix and the GRAIN database, 'grey' (not commercially published) literature, local newspapers, reports from the field, and interviews.

The GCC investment narrative

The narrative on Gulf investments is characterized by several key elements. First, the need to establish food security for the domestic population is an acute issue for GCC states, as they are poor in both arable land and water resources (GRAIN 2008; Woertz et al. 2008a, 2008b; Smaller and Mann 2009). Attempts to produce food at home have proved to be unsustainable. Since 2005, GCC countries – most notably Saudi Arabia – have been changing their agricultural policies from attempts at self-sufficiency through subsidized domestic production to investments overseas (Woertz 2007, 2011; Shepherd 2010). GCC states have the financial power to purchase food on the world market, but since the 2008 food crisis, in which food-producing nations limited or discontinued their exports, GCC states have become aware of the market's capriciousness and have preferred to increase dedicated crop production abroad over market dependency (Lippman 2010: 92; Shepherd 2010: 3). These developments are part of a global trend towards investment in arable land and food production. Since 2008, governments, sovereign wealth funds and private companies have been looking for investments in farmlands, which are believed to offer stable and reliable returns. GCC states are believed to be major investors in farmland in Asia and Africa.

Secondly, the GCC states depend on a huge migrant labour force from Asian countries to maintain their developmental model (Regt and Moors 2008; Fofack 2009), which makes GCC states' economies and political stability dependent on capital, migrant labour and cheap food imports. The huge labouring classes in Gulf states are primarily foreign contract workers (in construction, the oil industry and the services and retail sectors). As non-citizens, they profit little from the clientelist politics of the state. Gulf states are 'sitting on a class time bomb' (GRAIN 2008: 4). Investments in farmland thus also have a political dimension because they would allow GCC states, and most notably Saudi Arabia, to increase their political influence in the target countries (Daniel and Mittal 2009; Shepherd 2010).

Thirdly, national governments of developing and middle-income countries in Africa and Asia are eager to attract investments from abroad to revive their rural sectors and stimulate their economies. Despite favourable growth figures over the last decade, the middle-income countries are still facing mass unemployment, poverty and a stagnating rural development agenda. GCC states, in conjunction with East Asian investors, are believed to be a viable alternative to the diminishing investments from the crisis-struck North. In line with this thinking, the Indonesian and Philippine governments have actively been attracting GCC investment capital since 2007.

GCC perspectives GCC perspectives on land investments have hardly been discussed in depth in the academic literature.[6] A nationalist policy of food self-sufficiency has long been attractive to GCC states to limit their dependency on the world market, food-producing countries and power blocs. The Second World War drove home the message. In that period, '300,000 people in Saudi Arabia could have perished without food supplies from the Allied Middle East Supply Centre in Cairo', while on the other hand, 'the grains coming from traditional suppliers like India were not sufficient, because the Allies needed them for their war effort' (Reilly 2010). In 1973, 'there were open threats from Kissinger that the USA could stop food supplies in retaliation to the oil embargo' (ibid.). This was one of the reasons Qatar opted for food production in greenhouses using solar-based desalinated water and Saudi Arabia established an agricultural sector of its own. The spectre of 'political blackmail' has been haunting GCC states in their food security projects since then (Guzman 2010).

In 2011, the news site Qatar Today posted 'Food: the big fright', which reiterates the Achilles heel of GCC states' development policies: 'Of the region's total land area of approximately 259 million hectares, only 1.7 per cent is currently under cultivation, mainly with groundwater irrigation.' Though the region's citizens are 'among the world's richest peoples in terms of per capita wealth' given the estimated $35 trillion oil and gas reserves, the GCC countries 'are the world's most water insecure and food deficient, importing 60–95 per cent of their food requirements', according to a high official of the Qatar National Food Security Programme.[7] Growing domestic and migration popula-tions will increase the demand for food in the future.

GCC state sources mention three options to obtain food security: achieve self-sufficiency in staple-food production, depend on the world market, or directly invest in farmland abroad. The first (nationalist) option increases national economic independence, but it requires enormous state subsidies for irrigation schemes and other infrastructure while depleting the freshwater reserves and is financially and ecologically unsustainable for water-intensive crops like wheat (Shepherd 2010) and potatoes (Lippman 2010). The market option, as we have seen, involves a deep and risky dependence on the world market and on food-exporting countries. Some voices argue to extend this option and store more food in Gulf countries, but storage is expensive and does not ultimately solve the problem (Woertz 2013). This makes the third option of direct transnational farmland investments a crucial strategy to lessen world-market dependency and the (political) vulnerabilities it creates.

The GCCs use their financial resources to make these investments. In Saudi Arabia alone, the 'King Abdullah Initiative for Agricultural Investment Abroad' is supported by a government fund of $5.3 billion in seed capital (Shepherd 2010: 12). The large agricultural corporations that dominated Saudi's domestic food-crop production are themselves also shifting to farmland investments overseas. Previously the recipients of large state subsidies on domestic agricul-ture, they are now attracted by the new subsidies on food imports and agro-investments abroad (ibid.). '[Almost all of the] nationwide listed agricultural conglomerates ... have either been reported to be directly investing in foreign agriculture or have subsidiaries or joint ventures that are' (ibid.). For Saudi Arabia alone, there is a total estimated budget of over US$5 billion available for agricultural investments in food.[8]

Nevertheless, the possibility of investment in foreign farmland also attracted internal criticism. Lippman (2010: 96) cites Saudi businessman Fawaz Al-Alamy, who points out the problem of securing investments against political risks or natural disasters, and the WTO rules that permit countries to halt agricultural exports in times of shortage. Other concerns came from the side of GCC-based multinationals and executives of domestic food and beverage industries, who are already tuned in to global corporate food-market chains. They tend to favour secure, long-term trade agreements with suppliers and not direct investments in land.

Indonesian and Philippine perspectives Since the economic crisis at the turn of the millennium (1997–2000), the governments of Indonesia and the Philip-pines have tried to attract GCC investors in order to obtain the capital funds supposedly waiting to be tapped. Both countries are fairly stable democracies characterized by a relatively weak central state, deep socio-economic inequalities, a considerably liberalized agricultural sector, and a welcoming national governmental outlook towards foreign direct investment in agro-industry. Land and investment policies, as well as their actual implementation, are in both countries influenced by political decentralization, strong business elites and top-down ideas on idle lands capable of accommodating much-needed foreign investments. In addition, broader cultural and social ties are frequently brought forward to substantiate collaboration. When Indonesian president Yudhoyono addressed the World Islamic Economic Forum in Jakarta in 2009 on the impact of the economic crisis, he said:

> The Muslim countries with vast reserves but without a real agricultural sector can come to the rescue. By gearing their investment policies to support agriculture in the Muslim world, the countries of the Gulf Cooperation Council can directly improve the welfare of the Ummah and also help solve the world's food security crisis. And since they are food importers, they will also be securing their own food supply needs.[9]

The Philippines' Arroyo government had in 2004 already announced the preparation of 'at least 2 million hectares of new land for agribusiness' to be one of its main development goals. These lands were designated as 'underutilized farm lands which can be made more productive', 'idle and marginal lands, including denuded upland areas', 'agrarian reform lands', and 'public alienable and disposable lands'.[10] Much of the designated land is concentrated in Mindanao, and Mindanao is to be the 'agribusiness hub' of the country. Attracting foreign investors is part of the policy, and since 2005 several high-ranking officials, including the president, have visited the GCC countries.

A win-win discourse A win-win discourse masks the possibly opposed food security interests of investors and target countries. State actors on both sides typically justify the desired investments in terms of mutual benefit, the huge potential of untapped resources or unused land, the importance of international cooperation, the strengthening of mutual relationships, peace-building, and Muslim brotherhood (Indonesia at the national level, the Philippines at the regional level of Muslim Mindanao). The parties further meet in a neoliberal discourse of 'modernization', global competitiveness, the benefits of capital and advanced technology, and agribusiness and foreign investments as development tools (Salerno 2010). GCC states and GCC private investors speak of 'shared benefits' for investors and target countries, 'fair deals', partnerships and win-win solutions: investors bring capital and technology and invest in infrastructure; target countries will profit from substantial agricultural growth, economic development and job creation.

A crucial argument is that the food security of target countries will not be threatened: 'The Saudi government argues that the relationship benefits both parties; if Saudi investors quintuple the food output of these countries, the host country would have more agriculture revenue and food for itself and they could increase exports to Saudi Arabia.'[11] The CEO of an investment company in UAE stated that the negotiations 'are based on fair deals that reach beyond a business transaction to social responsibility'; an 'upgrade in ... infrastructure, a transfer of new technology, capital, and new school and hospital buildings' are often cited by UAE investors.[12] 'We're not talking about a land grab, we are talking about investment in food supply,' said a participant in the Saudi government's food-security programme. 'You invest, buy from local farmers and produce there. This includes investment in infrastructure – irrigation, farm-to-market roads – and thus creates jobs' (Lippman 2010: 93).

Why deals did not materialize

In 2008/09 GCC investors announced various large deals in land and food crops in Indonesia and the Philippines, most of which have so far not materialized. We discern political, economic and legal reasons for this discontinuation of intended deals. Below we discuss the most important reasons we found in Indonesia and in the Philippines.

Indonesia Indonesian–Gulf trade relations go back at least four centuries. Arab traders settled in the Indonesian islands and gave rise to a minority population group of Arab ancestry. Moreover, trade relationships lay at the root of the spread of Islam in Indonesia in the fifteenth and sixteenth centuries (Cribb 2000: 44, 79). The Arab traders never managed to emulate the trade networks of the Chinese or Indian entrepreneurs, probably owing to a lack of power and influence during the colonial era (McVey 1992: 2). Later, this historical distance from the colonial power-holders stood them in good stead with Indonesian nationalists and political Islam. In present-day Indonesia, political Islam argues for greater unity and collaboration among the Muslim *Ummah* and is represented in politics by – among others – the Prosperous Justice Party (PKS). In government continuously since 2004, the PKS maintains strong links with the Middle East, the Gulf states in particular. Most of the PKS leadership were educated there, and popular opinion has it that Middle Eastern charities and the Egyptian Muslim Brotherhood funded the party's establishment. The PKS propagates transnational Islamic political and social collaboration in order to diminish 'Western domination' (see Muhtadi 2012: 184–6, 193–7), as well as the boosting of national rural investment and development in order to increase the quality of life of the rural population. Visiting Saudi Arabia in 2010, Indonesian minister of agriculture Suswono (of the PKS party) announced that his government had altered investment regulations in order to facilitate Saudi land investment projects, which had been stalled in the previous year owing to regulatory complexities (Saudi Economic Survey 2010; Woertz 2011: 124).

From 2004 onwards, Indonesia worked hard to become a more attractive destination for foreign investors. In 2007, a new Investment Law (Law 25 of 2007) came into effect that replaced the previous Investment Law of 1967 and its amendments. The new Investment Law applies to all direct investments in all sectors and awards foreign investors equal legal status to that of Indonesian investors. Also, the law decrees that dispute settlements between international investors and the Indonesian government may be reached through (international) arbitration. The government hence appears to have loosened its hold on the business sector and allowed for greater internationalization of its dispute settlement.

Closer links to the countries that saw the birth of Islam and house some of its most holy places are deemed commendable by the propagators of Indonesian political Islam. Among these groups, Arab nations and their inhabitants often enjoy a reputation as pious and truer in their observation of Islam than South-East Asians, who live in secular states and frequently maintain a relaxed or even lax outlook towards their religious duties. In this view, Indonesia, with its corruption and other vices, would benefit from a stricter implementation of Islamic principles in its politics. By contrast, the GCC countries are strong examples of the successful combination of religion and politics. The recent 'war against terrorism' and the wars in Iraq and Afghanistan have damaged the image of Western nations and their tolerance of Islam among many Muslims worldwide, bringing the insight that Islamic nations would do well to unite and support one another's development and needs.

This line of thought was paralleled by increased criticism in Indonesian public opinion vis-à-vis Gulf states as a result of turmoil over Indonesian female migrant workers being maltreated, raped or deprived of their earned salaries by their employers there. From 2010 onwards, the issue became a matter of national politics after considerable media attention devoted to the large number of Indonesian citizens held in (mainly Saudi) Arab prisons without trial or contact with their families or compatriots. The issue came to the boil after the unannounced execution in 2011 of a domestic worker for the killing of her employer, who, according to her statements in court and widespread popular opinion in Indonesia, had maltreated her. As a result, President Yudhoyono temporarily forbade the departure of new female migrant workers to Saudi Arabia. Commentators and some politicians suggested to us that this attention to the situation of Indonesian female workers in the Gulf states was no coincidence, but was part of a political agenda of PKS opponents aimed at stemming the rise of political Islam by problematizing relations between Indonesia and the Gulf states. The fact that this would negatively influence the national economy by potentially diminishing GCC investments and decreasing migrant remittances was, they felt, subservient to this political goal.

Indonesian law contains elements which can be considered obstructive to foreign investments in land or in agrarian production. The 2007 Investment Law states that investors are obliged to respect the cultural traditions of the community at the investment's location. This could open up a pathway to custom-based land claims, while fast land titling procedures are not possible if the investment goes against the population's sense of justice or disturbs the 'public interest'. Furthermore, foreign investments in Indonesia's agricultural sector are limited by a 'negative list' of business fields closed to investments or only conditionally opened. In the cultivation of staple food crops in areas of 25 hectares or more, for instance, foreign shares' ownership is limited from a previous maximum of 95 per cent to a new maximum of 49 per cent. Although this limitation is not applicable to indirect investment (e.g. through portfolio investments and the stock exchange), the limitation is likely to curb foreign direct investment in agriculture.

Moreover, the 2010 Horticultural Law deals specifically with rice and vegetable oil, both of which are among the types of agrarian produce that the GCC investors seek to invest in. This law states that foreign investments in these products are possible only on a 'grand scale', that foreign interests may represent a maximum of 30 per cent of a horticultural enterprise, that a foreign investor should deposit a sum with a national bank equal to the investments made, and that foreign investors may not use the credit facilities of the Indonesian government. These fairly strict regulations appear to be in line with the 2004 Plantation Law, which stipulates that foreign investors should work through an Indonesian counterpart and require permission from the ministry responsible, which is a long and arduous bureaucratic process discouraging potential investors.

Butt (2011) points out that Indonesia has a major problem of legal uncertainty that is not only discouraging to investors but also difficult to solve, as the Indonesian legal system is complicated, contains many vagaries in its texts, and is strongly subject to political influences at all levels of government. Moreover, many lands supposedly available for investment turned out to be in use and legally contested.[13] The International Finance Corporation and World Bank's 2012 *Doing Business* report on the practicalities of business ranks Indonesia as 129 out of 183 countries, just below Honduras and just above Ecuador and the West Bank and Gaza (IFC and World Bank 2012: 6). Investment conditions may be improved through more customized conditions regulated in Bilateral Investment Treaties (BITs), several of which have been signed with Qatar (2000) and Saudi Arabia (2003), although neither BIT has come into force as yet. At the same time, the legal complexities discourage investors from GCCs and give domestic investors a comparative advantage.

The Saudi Ministry of Commerce and Industry identified missing infrastructure and lengthy bureaucratic procedures as major reasons for the sluggish implementation of overseas investments (Woertz 2011: 124). Qatari state-owned Hassad Food, for instance, announced that it would aim to invest in existing agro-companies rather than acquiring land rights and building up farming operations from scratch (ibid.: 125).

The main issue is whether Indonesia aspires to attract foreign direct investment in agrarian production. Tambunan (2011: 76–9) argues that FDI leads to much more effective knowledge transfer than with the government constantly in between parties, and that the government therefore should promote this type of international economic activity. Sussangkarn et al. (2011: 9) find that FDI positively impacts local firms' productivity and employment, but that Indonesia's industry focuses on raw or intermediate materials and needs to produce capital goods. They conclude that Indonesia should stimulate FDI in developing domestic industries and human resources instead of producing agrarian staples. Interviews with regional and local politicians in East Kalimantan, for instance, underscore this point. Foreign investors who invest only money, such as GCC investors are expected to do, are not preferred. 'We are interested in foreigners who bring us knowledge.'[14] There are plenty of Indonesian companies which now have the money to invest; they are preferred and know better how to deal with local conditions and business relations, as they share more financial benefits among stakeholders.[15]

In contrast to the Philippines, as will be discussed below, Indonesia does not possess a well-organized nationwide civil society that is capable of protesting and withstanding land allocations to investors, even if lands made available for investment are not vacant in reality or are legally contested. Protests are mainly local and rarely manage to attract major attention from the press or government officials. In general, farmers who stand to lose their land tend to hold out for as much recompense as is obtainable, but tend to agree to abstain from further claims.

Whereas initially announced deals were driven by the apparent availability of Indonesian agricultural lands to meet GCC food supplies, changing public opinion and a deeper understanding of local circumstances revealed considerable obstacles and risks that hampered actual realization.

The Philippines As in the case of Indonesia, Arab traders have established connections with the south-west of the Philippines since the fifteenth century, most notably in western Mindanao and the Sulu Islands. The areas occupied a strategic position at the centre of the shipping route between the Far East and the Malayan world. Arab trading led to the spread of Islam and the establishment of the marine-based Sultanate of Sulu in 1450. Today, most announced GCC deals focus on Mindanao. Of the nine deals announced on food or fruit production, seven were in Mindanao and two were unspecified. Malaysia and Saudi Arabia have been actively involved in the peace negotiations between the government and armed Islamic separatist movements in Mindanao, promising more development and economic aid with the attainment of a peace pact. The agricultural potential of Mindanao certainly plays a role. Mindanao is an attractive investment area, and this will only increase once lasting peace is established.

Since the period of American colonial control, the island of Mindanao, with a current population of over eighteen million people, has served as the agricultural hub of the Philippines, with a long tradition of foreign investment. Resistance to central control (fuelled by resentment at the increasing number of Christian settlers, as well as the logging and mining activities that had become important sources of export earnings) was initially organized by the Moro National Liberation Front (MNLF). Formed in the late 1960s, it was largely accepted as representing the interests of Mindanao's Muslim population until the 1990s. Despite the formation of the Autonomous Region in Muslim Mindanao (ARMM) in 1989 and a peace agreement with the MNLF in 1996, the armed conflict continued. A breakaway faction of the MNLF, the militant Islamist Moro Islamic Liberation Front (MILF), emerged as the government's main opponent. The MILF maintains contact with the Organization of the Islamic Conference,[16] but it has also been accused of maintaining relations with the terrorist group Abu Sayyaf and the Indonesia-based Jemaah Islamiyah. However, in the context of the peace negotiations, the MILF has officially distanced itself from those organizations. Saudi Arabia has regularly offered assistance in peace negotiations with the separatist groups and in 2012 an initial peace accord was signed.

For decades, some fruit companies in Mindanao have been establishing trade relations with GCC countries.[17] In May 2009, the groundwork was laid for declaring some areas in Mindanao 'Special Economic Zones', with favourable tax conditions and other privileges for Saudi agro-investments.[18] Ending the Muslim separatist insurgency in Mindanao is a major concern for which Saudi assistance is requested on both the diplomatic and economic fronts. As part of the effort to support the economic development of Mindanao after the signing of an initial peace pact between the MILF and the government in late 2012, the growing of staple foods for the Gulf market is being planned.[19] The production of staple foods in the Philippines for export to other countries has an ironic side to it. The Philippines is a major importer of rice and maize to meet its domestic needs. The FAO estimates that 15 per cent of the population (12.7 million people in 2006) are chronically undernourished (FAO 2009a). About one third of the Philippine population lives below the poverty line, according to the Philippine National Statistics Board.[20] Despite a large agricultural sector, which employs one third of the national workforce, the

Philippines is not able to grow enough food for its domestic population, and it is not likely to do so in the near future. Foreign countries pursuing food security by using Philippine rice fields is thus difficult to justify.

Like Indonesia, the Philippines is a major supplier of labour to Gulf countries. It has over 1.4 million contract workers employed in Saudi Arabia, who sent home some US$1.6 billion in 2010.[21] Trade relations are also important. Saudi Arabia is the Philippines' major supplier of oil. This invites trade-offs. Philippine presidential visits to Saudi Arabia have intensified in recent years. Parallel to the president's lobbying for Saudi farmland investments in the Philippines, such visits include negotiations for a secure Saudi oil supply and for the release of Filipino contract workers jailed for minor offences. As an advocacy NGO put it, the president was 'practically demanding' the release of the workers 'as the "concessions" for the land grab deals'; this is 'how global land grabs are being done and allowed in exchange of not just the freedoms of some overseas Filipino workers but the sovereignty of nations' (Guzman 2010: 36–7).

TABLE 10.1 Announced and realized foreign investments in food crops in the Philippines

Investor country	Announced			Realized		Status
	Deals	Hectares	Value of deals (US$, m)	Deals	Hectares	
Saudi Arabia	5	303,500	1,580	2	3,500	2 realized 1 contested
Bahrain	2	30,000	300	0	0	1 contested
United Arab Emirates	1	400,000 (in 5 countries)	50	1	50	1 realized
Qatar	1	100,000	?	0	0	general agreement
Oman	1	10,000	?	0	0	cancelled
Kuwait	1	20,000	?	0	0	general agreement
Total	11	863,500	> 1,930	3	3,550	

A host of tangled and overlapping laws in the Philippines may put off an investor, especially when large tracts of land are involved. Foreign ownership of land has always been a touchy issue in the Philippines. The provision of the Philippine Constitution on 'protection of national patrimony' bans the acquisition by 'aliens' and 'alien-owned' entities of public and private lands. But foreign investors can now lease private lands for up to seventy-five years by virtue of the 1993 Investors' Lease Act (Republic Act 7652). This law amended the four-decades-old Presidential Decree 471, which had fixed the maximum period of leasing as only fifty years.

A 100 per cent foreign equity may be allowed in some areas such as manufacturing in export processing zones; but in investments in land for the exploration, development and utilization of natural resources, and in the culture, production, milling, processing and trading of agricultural products, a maximum of 40 per cent foreign equity is in place, while rice and corn industries should be wholly Filipino controlled.[22] Foreign corporations may acquire land in the Philippines provided that such land is held under private land title. Most of the land involved in announced GCC deals, however, has the legal status of agricultural land, ancestral land, protected area or public land, or consists of lands subject to distribution to landless farmers under the 1988 Comprehensive Agrarian Reform Programme (CARP). Most of these are legal categories different from private land.

Moreover, the CARP seeks to distribute public and private agricultural lands, except landholdings with an area of 5 hectares or less, to landless tenants and rural workers. By 2014, 1.6 million hectares of agricultural lands will be fully acquired and distributed to 1.2 million beneficiaries.[23] This scenario tells us that Gulf investors and their Philippine partners will at some point have to deal with small farm-holders in order to acquire sufficient land to plant agricultural crops.

In addition, a strong lobby for the protection of indigenous peoples' rights and the environment exists. NGOs, civil society organizations, the Catholic Church and indigenous communities often invoke provisions of the Integrated Protected Areas System (NIPAS) Act and the 1997 Indigenous Peoples Rights Act (IPRA), which recognizes native title for indigenous peoples. The Philippines hosts hundreds of self-defined 'indigenous peoples', who claim ancestral domains. Lands targeted for GCC investments are frequently subject to such claims, making their availability to international investors uncertain.

Despite these legal ambiguities, successive Philippine leaderships, notably the previous government of Gloria Arroyo, have actively sought GCC money to invest in agriculture. Several trips to Gulf countries were made to discuss these investments. Some deals were announced, coupled to the signing of memoranda of understanding (MOUs) between the Philippines and the Arab country involved. Usually, the deals start with MOUs that signal the willingness of the Philippines to host the investments. But MOUs are just the start of the lengthy process of hurdling legal ambiguities, not to mention the long and winding road of identifying suitable land for the deals announced.

Then there is the issue of decentralization. The Local Government Code (RA 7160) gives local government units (LGUs) such as provinces, cities and municipalities their own power to attract foreign investments and deal with investors as part of their development plans and to create their own sources of revenue. The LGUs have the power to authorize the reclassification of agricultural lands and to decide on how to utilize and dispose of these; however, these processes must be subject to public consultation and appropriate local laws.

The national government's MOUs with GCC investors frequently do not comply with one or more elements of the laws mentioned above, and this has led to various protests and legal procedures by NGOs and church groups, as well as by political parties and members of parliament, and has attracted wide criticism in the media. The various land laws are often used to counteract foreign investments in land, whether still at the announcement phase or with contracts signed. Legal complexities somehow become useful tools for resistance. This may deter Gulf investors, who often want legislative guarantees to protect their investments.

Philippine civil society is highly developed and well organized. NGOs and advocacy groups often resist, if not block outright, potential foreign land investments. Along with a relatively independent media and an increasing number of activist legislators in parliament, they serve as the watchdogs of foreign land deals. Together they develop (some) opportunities to influence government policies on foreign land investments.[24]

Lawmakers representing labour groups and farmers proposed House Bill 6004 in Congress in 2012, which would limit large-scale foreign investments in land. The Bill proposes that all contracts, agreements, negotiations, talks and deals relating to foreign investments in land exceeding an aggregate of five hectares shall be publicly disclosed and should be approved by the National Regulatory Board on Foreign Land Investments, a newly-to-be-created institution, before being implemented. The Bill makes 'Foreign Land Grabbing' a criminal offence that is punishable with a penalty of US$1,000,000 and confiscation of assets in the Philippines. Persons or corporations found guilty of violating any provision of the Bill may furthermore face individual penalties of up to 1,000,000 Philippine pesos as well as prison sentences of up to six months.[25]

The Catholic Church is also a strong force when it comes to advocacy of land rights, and it has long been seen as actively lobbying against foreign investments that adversely affect local communities. The Church recently led protest marches against the construction of a 12,427-hectare foreign-funded export processing zone and free port in Aurora province that would displace thousands of farmers, fishermen and indigenous peoples from their ancestral domains.[26] With a strong backing from the Church and the NGOs, the president agreed to personally meet the protesting affected communities and promised to investigate the proposed project.

Conclusions

So far, hardly any of the announced land deals between Gulf states' investors in Indonesia and the Philippines have materialized. Above, we have identified a number of issues which jointly offer an explanation for these deals' failure to materialize.

The incumbent Yudhoyono government of Indonesia and the Philippine Arroyo government (2001–10) actively tried to attract foreign investors in order to obtain the capital funds to boost economic development and to create jobs. An important part of this strategy was oriented towards rural development through large-scale capital and technological investments. Gulf states' investments were expected to play an important role in this development strategy, even more so after the price hikes in food which began in 2007. At the same time, in some Gulf states – most notably Saudi Arabia, Qatar and Bahrain – the need was felt to move away from domestic food production or dependency on the world market for food towards direct investments in food production overseas. Whereas Saudi Arabia created large investment funds to acquire land and to outsource food production, for the Qatar government the agricultural investments were part of a general diversification of its economy. The assumed policy shift and the funds made available for foreign investments, as well as the global rise in food prices, sparked the simplifying GCC investment narrative.

This dominant GCC investment narrative, however, obscured a number of facts: the GCC countries did not have similar needs or a common foreign agenda. Moreover, the policy changes in GCC countries met with internal opposition by parties preferring the security of long-term trade agreements over direct investments. Moreover, policy alternatives, such as food storage and strategic reserves, are seriously considered (Woertz 2013). National governments of Indonesia and the Philippines, which favoured transnational land deals and actively tried to attract foreign investment and Gulf investments, changed coalitions or were replaced. In Indonesia, the reformist Islamic party in government (PKS), which favoured connections with Gulf countries and stimulated Gulf state investments, lost ground. In the Philippines, the new Aquino government cancelled deals that the previous Arroyo government had made with GCC investors, while ongoing parliamentary investigations into the negotiations of these deals suggest that they will not be reinstated.

An important obstacle to the process of foreign investment was the presentation of marginal lands being available for investments which were, however, contested and not freely available at all. News – or even rumours – of GCC investment plans revealed overlapping claims on property and insecure legal complexities. These in turn sparked protests by local peoples, competing government departments and farmer organizations. As a result, investors pulled out before they had even started. In Indonesia, the general opinion towards Gulf states and most notably towards Saudi Arabia changed unfavourably as a result of the several cases of abuse, torture and even murder of migrant domestic workers.

Notwithstanding the promises of national governments to foreign investors, complex legislation and unclear procedures make it difficult for investors to directly invest in agriculture in Indonesia and the Philippines. Central government authority is obstructed or contested locally by lower-level officials, non-governmental organizations and civil society groups advocating local interests – such as the tenure security of the population and recognition of existing land use arrangements – over the central government's emphasis on developing the national economy. While existing national legislation fails to provide international investors with the security they require and new proposals in the Philippines clearly favour local people, international investors can gain access to agricultural production only by establishing joint ventures or by minority share-holding, which denies them full or majority control in the enterprise. Moreover, at least in Indonesia, we discern economic nationalism to be at play. Announced deals are regularly taken over by domestic investors or seriously scaled down. Gulf investors are offering only money and not the knowledge and technology transfers local governments are interested in. In Indonesia, domestic investors are better equipped to deal with legal, social and economic complexities, and are generally favoured by all parties along the commodity chain as they offer more possible benefits in terms of bribes, fees and profit sharing, and they know the system. Whereas economic nationalism and regional business protectionism as a means to spoil foreign investments seem to be more at play in Indonesia, in the Philippines legal and open protests turned out to be critical. With its strong civil society and political grassroots mobilization, protests were quickly taken up in the media and issues were put on the political agenda, leading to inquiries in parliament. In Indonesia, protests gained little attention beyond the immediate region and remained case specific.

The migrant worker connection, which was brought forward initially as an existing example of ongoing good collaboration, seems to have generated insufficient trust to support agrarian investment as a new line of economic collaboration. Announced deals in the Philippines were made in return for work permits in Gulf countries, and in Indonesia the media exposure of cases of mistreatment of young migrant women to the GCC countries (especially Saudi Arabia) transformed the image of helpful fellow-Muslims into that of arrogant exploiters of national resources.

The GCC land grab hype had its disappointments. Investors and international financial institutions which expected high returns on investments in countries enthusiastic over the win-win solutions reached saw their initiatives thwarted by opposition in the field, legal uncertainties and massive critical international media exposure. Yet the critical and alarmist style of media reporting, as well as the unreliable and overlapping content of many of the databases put forward as proof, now run the risk of overshooting their purpose and endangering the credibility and reputations of these global critics.

11 | Tracing the dragon's footsteps: a deconstruction of the discourse on China's foreign land investments

Peter Ho and Irna Hofman[1]

Introduction

China's socio-economic and political rise in the world seems to incite either fear or euphoric expectations. A 'global magnifying glass' is placed over China's every move in the world, moves which – regardless of their specific effects – are influenced by the perceptions and associated fears – 'the yellow peril' – or expectations of China as an emerging global power or as the 'booming billion consumers' market'.

The discourse on China's emergence, in fact, applies equally to China's role in the 'global land grab' debate. The alleged merits or threats of 'land grabs' have resulted in various studies over recent years (see, for example, Bush et al. 2011; De Schutter 2011; Deininger 2011; Borras and Franco 2012). In short, it boils down to the question of whether land acquisitions are entirely negative for poor and socially vulnerable groups, or whether they might also entail positive effects – or might even be a necessity to feed the world.[2] China's role in the global 'land grab' is part and parcel of this debate. Is China a 'neocolonial power in the making' (Adem 2010: 335), or does China also aim to espouse economic prosperity in recipient countries?

The array of China's global agricultural activities has not been studied in an inclusive way, neither in a solid qualitative nor in a quantitative sense.[3] Although providing definite answers and conclusions is impossible, our aim in this chapter is to go beyond vague guesstimates and to illuminate the difficulties of assessing the quantity and impact of China's foreign land acquisitions. Through analysis of the discourse and the available material on these investments, we aim to arrive at a better understanding of Chinese land-based investments, with specific regard for the empirical complexity.

Against this backdrop, we have probed the development and magnitude of Chinese land-based investments over time and place. For this purpose, we made an inventory of the available data, drawing on a large variety of sources, varying from scientific databases and portals to NGO reports and newspaper articles. Instead of 'land grabbing' or 'land grabs', we prefer to use the more neutral terms 'overseas land-based investments' or 'land acquisitions'. In fact, a definition of a 'land grab' is non-existent, as researchers and organizations apply different standards. In contrast with the other chapters in this book, we exclude Chinese domestic 'land grabs' (or domestic land acquisitions). Our focus is exclusively on Chinese acquisition of land use rights abroad for an area of over 1,000 hectares in order to produce agricultural commodities.

We start with a description of the constitutive elements in the discourse on China's 'land grabs'. This is followed by a discussion of the actors behind China's foreign land investments. The subsequent empirical section provides an overview of Chinese land-based investments in terms of their incidence, size and geographical dispersion for the period 1949–2011. Where relevant and possible, the investor, investment type, reported size, data source and outcome of the investment are also reviewed. Thereafter we proceed to illuminate the motivation to invest overseas of the various Chinese actors involved. The final section briefly discusses the quality and reliability of the data.

Unpacking the discourse: China's global emergence and its hallmarks in foreign affairs

The discourse on 'land grabs' was from the outset split into opposing camps, in which those regarding China's land-based investments as neocolonial exploitation are pitted against those who see investments as possibilities for local development through 'economic diplomacy' and 'soft power'. Without passing judgement on either side of the discourse, it is clear that China's overseas investments have sparked a heated debate, a substantial proportion of which focuses on its land acquisitions in developing countries. The discourse on China's land-based investments was virtually non-existent before 2000. Only gradually, from the mid-2000s, did articles and reports on Chinese 'land grabs' begin to seep into the international literature. However, it was not until 2008, with the publication of GRAIN's *SEIZED!* report, that the debate took off. In this sense, the discourse is a recent discourse.

At the forefront of China's 'land grab' discourse is China's allegedly neo-colonial approach – i.e. the use of economic and political means to continue or extend influence in developing countries. The country's global resource-seeking activities and concerns over domestic economic development, food security and the opening up of new markets will supposedly infringe on the food security of the recipient countries. This issue plainly came to the fore in 2011, when a German official attacked China for having caused the famine in the Horn of Africa (Szent-Ivanyi 2011).

As part of the third Forum on China–Africa Cooperation (FOCAC), in 2006, the Chinese government initiated the establishment of agricultural training centres in several African countries. Chinese experience and know-how are highly welcomed by many governments, in particular with an eye to recent food crises (Shun 2008; Sudan Tribune 2010). In the training and extension centres, teams of Chinese agronomists and other staff educate local farmers and conduct research on the adaptability of Chinese seed varieties and crops to the African climate. As such, Chinese teams working in Africa may enhance food security in host countries (Shun 2008; Rubinstein 2009; Buckley 2011).

A related component of the 'China land grab discourse' touches on the effects of the land acquisitions on the local labour market. When large-scale monoculture production replaces small-scale farming, there is less demand for (local) employment, with negative outcomes for social equity (Murray Li 2011; Bush et al. 2011). Diana (2008), however, points out the multifaceted nature of exchange between Chinese entrepreneurs and Laotian farmers. If employed and implemented in a proper way, contract farming can be a means to provide farmers with a secure income and access to new knowledge and expertise, while retaining ownership of the land (see also McCartan 2008). Nevertheless, Chinese investments regularly entail the influx of large groups of Chinese workers, which creates grievances at the local level.

At a more generic level, a recurrent theme in China's international relations is the prominence of China's 'soft power' policies[4] (Kurlantzick 2007) in international relations (Breslin 2009; Strauss 2009; Power and Mohan 2010; Wang 2010). Remarkably, the perception of different Chinese as opposed to Western interventions in developing countries has a longer history. As early as the late 1940s, Furnivall noted: 'But in the tropics the European who, from humanitarian motives or through enlightened self-interest, treats his employees well, risks being forced out of business by Indians or Chinese with different standards' (1948: 312).

China's present approach in foreign affairs has a historical parallel with the policy principles issued by Mao Zedong, which were mutual respect for territorial integrity and sovereignty, mutual non-aggression, mutual non-interference in internal affairs, and equality and mutual benefit (Alden and Alves 2008: 47). The policies of non-interference and non-conditionality in political terms are China's current hallmarks in foreign affairs. Some argue that these policies are used by China to justify the opacity around its land deals with foreign governments (Alden and Hughes 2009). Moreover, the country's unconditional aid and investments may allow regimes to better their position without pressures to change their political system (Alden 2005, 2007; Strauss 2009; d'Hooghe 2010).

On the other hand, there are those who maintain that China's 'soft power' may entail a 'new economic diplomacy' that may have a greater effect in good governance and the rule of law than Western aid programmes. Alves (2006: 7), for instance, noted that since the establishment of the FOCAC in 2000, 'China has reduced and exempted a total of 1.3 billion USD (10.5 billion RMB) of debts owed by 31 African countries', while 'trade between both parts has rapidly increased since then'. In early 2005, China also exempted trade tariffs for a total of 190 commodities from twenty-five of the least-developed African countries (ibid.). China also invests in the training of human resources, for instance through establishment of local training centres and scholarships for African students in China.

It is at this point that China's 'soft power' accords with the international debates on a 'new economic diplomacy' and the impact that China's rise may have on that (Woolcock and Bayne 2007). In response to the international critique of trade with 'no strings attached', the Chinese leadership points to its own development trajectory as a potential way out for the least-developed nations. As argued elsewhere, China is increasingly emboldened to claim a development model of its own, owing to its successes in meeting the Millennium Development Goals, including in health, primary education and reducing rural poverty (Ho 2009). Implicitly, China feels justified in rebuffing the critique, as it once felt caught in the same developmental net as Africa and much of the developing world – occupied and exploited by 'colonial and imperialist' powers.

Leaving the aforementioned discourse largely aside, we would rather draw attention to the inherent complexity and contradictory nature of global land-based investments, and of Chinese land-based investments in particular.

China's role in the global 'land grab' is, as described, considered significant. As GRAIN's report stated: 'From Kazakhstan to Queensland, and from Mozambique to the Philippines, a steady and familiar process is under way, with Chinese companies leasing or buying up land, setting up large farms, flying in farmers, scientists and extension workers, and getting down to the work of crop production' (GRAIN 2008: 3). This quote could be nuanced; but the reality is that over time, particularly in the last decade, there has been a significant growth in Chinese foreign agricultural land investments, which increasingly are found all over the world. Investments vary significantly in terms of size, purpose and the actors involved.

Who are these Chinese? Disaggregating Chinese actors in overseas land acquisitions

What characterizes Chinese overseas investments is the mix of private and public interests: an ambiguity in terms of 'public' or 'state' versus 'private' (Wang 2007; Kaplinksy and Morris 2009). This 'institutional ambiguity' (Ho 2005) has everything to do with China's economic transition, during which the state gradually privatized state and collectively-owned assets, resulting in a confusing hybrid mix of semi-public/semi-private entities. As a result, the precise association with and influence of the Chinese state are difficult to identify.

Concerning actors, there is also a tendency to simplify matters. For example, 'China' is seen as a monolithic agency – a single actor on a worldwide quest for natural and mineral resources. Yet the term 'China' in fact denotes a wide variety of state, semi-state and private actors. Chinese state-owned enterprises (SOEs) operating overseas are particularly closely followed and criticized by foreign observers because of the supposed governmental backing (Gu 2011). However, *private* enterprises operating overseas also receive governmental support to enhance their global expansion, resulting in a situation where state-guided investments intermingle with private enterprise goals (Tang and Li 2010).

In order to understand better the overseas activities of different Chinese actors, we distinguish five different categories of Chinese actors that engage in overseas land investments:

1 *National companies* with direct linkages to the central government. Their investments have a global outreach; these SOEs operate under formal state– state agreements and are expected to further the state's strategic objectives (Kaplinsky and Morris 2009). The primary state agribusiness company is the China State Farm Agribusiness Corporation (CSFAC), which closely collaborates with the Chinese Ministry of Agriculture. Regional branches of the CSFAC (the SFAC) frequently operate in conjunction with the national CSFAC (Freeman et al. 2008). Note that non-agricultural SOEs also engage in land investments, such as the Chinese telecom company ZTE. Although the SOEs have strong linkages with ministries, they have become more independent corporations with international subsidiaries (Jiang 2009).

2 *Provincial state-owned companies* backed by provincial, and sometimes also national, authorities. Initially they operated primarily in neighbouring countries; today they invest globally. The regional companies are expected to operate in accordance with provincial policies of decentralization and experience pressure to make profits (Kaplinsky and Morris 2009). As a result, their activities have become increasingly commercially oriented (Freeman et al. 2008). A prominent example of this category is the Beidahuang (BDH) Group, one of China's largest agricultural enterprises, with various branches and subsidiaries. The company is a former (military) state farm, previously set up to reclaim the wastelands and forests of what was once Manchuria (today administratively divided into Liaoning, Jilin and Heilongjiang provinces). As a former state farm, the BDH Group – in Chinese, the 'Vast Northern Wasteland Group' – is closely linked to the provincial government of Heilongjiang and the People's Liberation Army.

3 *Private small and medium-sized enterprises* (SMEs), which in fact largely escape Chinese governmental control. It is a reasonable consequence of the global expansion of SOEs that private enterprises have followed suit in overseas investments (Cheung and Suny 2009; Kaplinsky and Morris 2009). In pursuit of profit, they determine their own development path abroad (Wang 2007; Gu 2009; Kaplinsky and Morris 2009).

4 *Financial institutions*, most notably the China Development Bank (CDB), responsible for the China–Africa Development Fund, and the ExIm Bank (Export Import Bank) (Freeman et al. 2008). These enable and extend credits for Chinese investments. In addition, there are various sovereign wealth funds, of which the most important is the China Investment Corporation (CIC). Together with the CDB and ExIm Bank, the CIC manages substantial Chinese foreign exchange reserves and provides venture capital for projects overseas. Detailed information about CIC's investment portfolio is scarce.

5 *Chinese individual expats* dispatched in teams by the state to work in agricultural training centres. Most teams are employed for a period of two years and replaced thereafter (Buckley 2011). Some expats dispatched in development aid projects later benefit from their experience, such as in Africa, and prolong their stay independently from the government, sometimes even to become owners of a former research farm (Bräutigam 1998; Buckley 2011).

China's land acquisitions in time and place: what is new and what is true?

As we set out in our introduction, apart from describing the discourse we also aim to assess the available data on Chinese overseas land acquisitions. This has been done by reviewing and analysing a wide pool of sources.[5] The analysed data have been depicted in a series of world maps along four dimensions: i) the incidence of Chinese overseas investments, i.e. the number of *new* cases; ii) their development over time; iii) the size and range of investments; and iv) their geographical dispersion.

It is extremely difficult to assess how many new projects have been committed to at a given time and place, as the information on Chinese investments is notoriously unreliable. As Scissors (2011: 3) writes: 'Host countries boast of and the media breathlessly report investments that might never occur (such as in Nigeria) or huge but largely unused loan facilities (such as in Venezuela). Legitimate transactions are re-announced again and again.' Moreover, a substantial proportion of Chinese land-based projects might be rejected at a later stage by regulators, or run into problems during the execution phase.

To stay on the safe side, we have depicted investments on the map with limits set at below ten and more than ten investments. However, how far more than ten investments cannot be estimated without making unfounded guesses. Owing to the limitation of space and the inconsistency of data, we could include only a rough classification of size.

Based on evident shifts in the incidence of Chinese overseas investments over time, we have distinguished three consecutive periods: 1949–99, 2000–08 and 2009–11. The last period runs until the end of 2011 and also includes announced investments for 2012 and beyond. The potential investments have been depicted separately in the maps (Figures 11.1 to 11.3).

The period 1949–99: aid, not investments What is immediately apparent from the first map is that before China's official proclamation of the 'Going Global' strategy in 2000, Chinese overseas agricultural investments were few and geographically scattered over a handful of countries. In terms of incidence, most land-based investments were in Africa. However, in terms of investment size, the bulk of Chinese land-based investments was actually found in Cambodia. Here a total of six confirmed investments accounted for over 105,000 hectares, whereas all African investments accounted only for approximately 11,000 hectares. One major investment in 1989 (of 43,000 hectares) was reported for Australia, of which details are yet unknown (Callick 2008). Finally, two investments in Cuba (1996) and in Mexico (1998) together accounted for a minimum of 1,200 and a maximum of around 6,000 hectares.

On the basis of this material, it appears that before overseas investments were set as national policy in 2000, China concentrated its land-based investments in the South-East Asian vicinity. This is not to say that China was not active on the African continent, but it would be misleading to identify the earlier development aid activities as land-based investments.

Starting from the 1950s, China engaged in a variety of development aid projects in Africa. These projects were predominantly driven by geopolitical goals and to create a sense of 'Third World' solidarity (Bräutigam 1998). Mao's newly independent China urgently needed international legitimization after 1949. Coupled with fading support from the Soviet Union after the 1950s, the Chinese government had to find other, new international allies (ibid.; Alden

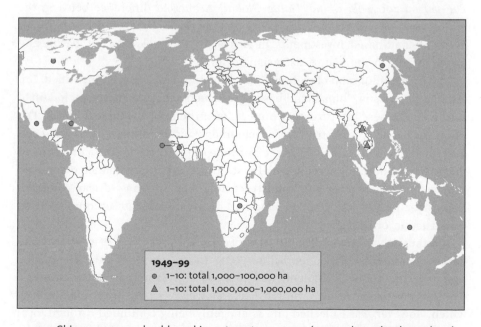

11.1 Chinese overseas land-based investments, 1949–99 (*source*: drawn by the authors)

and Alves 2008). The 'one-China' policy was a core aspect of China's international partnerships, and the government continuously strived to solidify its international position (Bräutigam 1998). Interestingly, a number of Chinese projects in different African countries were actually founded on bases formerly in the hands of the Taiwanese state.

Over the years the number of projects fluctuated in accordance with China's domestic political winds and related socio-economic upheaval. Political campaigns such as the Great Leap Forward (1958–62) and the Great Proletarian Cultural Revolution (1966–76) affected the availability of resources for foreign aid (ibid.; Alden and Alves 2008). On the whole, there were over 120 agricultural development projects in 44 countries from the mid-1950s to mid-1980s, accounting for approximately 15–20 per cent of China's African aid (Bräutigam 1998: 5, 43). These projects generally took the form of small-scale research farms and remained under the ownership of local people (ibid.).

The beginning of Chinese president Deng Xiaoping's economic reforms in 1978 marked a shift in China's development aid rationale. The political strategic imperative of foreign aid was replaced by a more economic rationale by which projects became more commercialized (ibid.). Between the 1980s and the 1990s many Chinese acquired formal ownership of the farms. As the farms became more profit-oriented, the Chinese managers benefited from their knowledge in the African setting, which they had accumulated over the years (Yan and Sautman 2010).[6]

The period 2000–08: China 'Going Global' A marked difference between the period 2000–08 and the preceding period is the rise in the incidence of China's overseas land-based investments in Africa, in the Mekong river basin, and farther south in the South-East Asian region.

In Africa a minimum of eighteen new investments have been identified. Important catalysts in China's land-based investments in Africa in the period up to 2008 were Chinese infrastructure projects over the previous three decades. The marriage between infrastructure development and land investment has been described by Adem (2010: 339) as the 'formula of resources for infrastructure' or the 'Angola mode'. Chinese financial institutions are prime financiers for such projects. Simultaneously, the 'infrastructure deficit' of many African countries is a major reason why Chinese land-based investments are accompanied by construction of infrastructure.

Another new development in 2000–08 was the extension of China's land-based investments farther south into South-East Asia. Apart from Cambodia, new investments were implemented in Laos and Myanmar. Furthermore, a Chinese investment of 1.24 million hectares was reported in the Philippines, which, however, was cancelled and is allegedly being continued through local contractors (GRAIN 2008). Also notable are new investments in Indonesia and

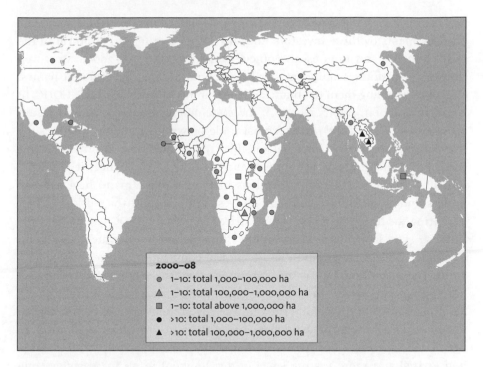

11.2 Chinese overseas land-based investments, 2000–08 (*source*: drawn by the authors)

Papua New Guinea. Here Chinese companies involved in the energy sector became involved in a 1 million hectare investment for cassava, palm oil and sugar production in 2007 (McCartan 2008).

This figure seems to contradict the popular perception, which regards China as having concentrated its land-based investments in the African continent. For the whole of Africa, the confirmed size of Chinese land-based investments is 3.2 million hectares, as opposed to 2.24 million hectares[7] in South-East Asia, and approximately 800,000 hectares in Laos, Cambodia and Myanmar. These figures apparently confirm the image that China invested heavily in Africa after 2000. However, a major problem with the statistics is that the high African figure is caused by a single investment in 3 million hectares in Congo by the Chinese telecom company ZTE. Even more problematic is that different sources mention a different size for this investment, varying from 10,000 hectares (Bräutigam and Tang 2009: 697) to 3 million (Gray 2009). Based on the conservative figure, the land-based investments in Africa would amount to around 200,000 hectares, significantly lower than in the whole of the South-East Asian region together.

Complicating matters is the fact that several sources have reported that the figures for the Mekong river basin may be understated for a number of reasons. First, Chinese private companies and individual entrepreneurs in general appear to be the main investors[8] in the Mekong river basin (Frost 2004; Humphrey and Schmitz 2007; Shi 2008; UNCTAD 2009). Owing to the relatively small scale of investments by these investors, they do not require formal approval in the host countries and thus escape official statistics (UNCTAD 2009). Moreover, Chinese companies acquire smaller land concessions under different names, effectively enabling them to obtain larger amounts of land in total (UNCOHCHR 2007). In addition, the incidence of investments may be understated because an unknown part of the intra-regional trade between China and the Mekong river basin countries is informal (or illicit) and thus goes unnoticed (Frost 2004; Frost and Ho 2005; Humphrey and Schmitz 2007). Hence, it is crucial to deal with the statistics in a cautious manner if one aims to have a better understanding of China's land-based investments around the world.

During the third Forum on China–Africa Cooperation (FOCAC), in 2006, the Chinese state launched a US$5 billion China–Africa Development Fund and a package of debt cancellation and technical cooperation (Power and Mohan 2010). These combined measures effectively paved the way for increasing Chinese public and private land-based investments in African agriculture (Yan and Sautman 2010). Shortly before, the Chinese government issued its first African Policy Paper, in which the main elements of the renewed Chinese approach in Africa were specified. Furthermore, roughly by the mid-2000s, Chinese SMEs had arrived at a more mature stage of development in an increasingly competitive domestic market. As a result, they were ready to look for greenfield opportunities in less developed markets abroad (Gu 2009).

However, despite these events and developments there was a drop in the incidence of investments in the two years following the FOCAC. It is likely that this was due to the outbreak of the 2007 global credit crisis. The crisis hit China hardest in 2008, when GDP growth dropped by 4 per cent to 9 per cent, and exports dropped by 40 per cent. The turning point for the country, however, came as early as February 2009.

The period 2009–11: exploring new areas After a short-lived period when Chinese land-based investments slowed down, they picked up again from 2009. Since then, approximately thirty to thirty-five new and announced investments account for a total that ranges between 350,000 and 2 million hectares. Remarkable is the diversification in geographical terms, as China has started to explore areas which hitherto had not, or only rarely, been targeted for investments. Notably, there were few incidences of new investments in areas where previously China had been active. Negative experiences in Africa, where some investments did not materialize, may have caused China to redirect its investments towards less volatile and more mature markets in the industrialized and emerging economies: Latin America, the Pacific and European countries. This is not the sole explanatory factor, as the changing consumption pattern in China is also visible in these investments in vineyards (Australia, Bulgaria

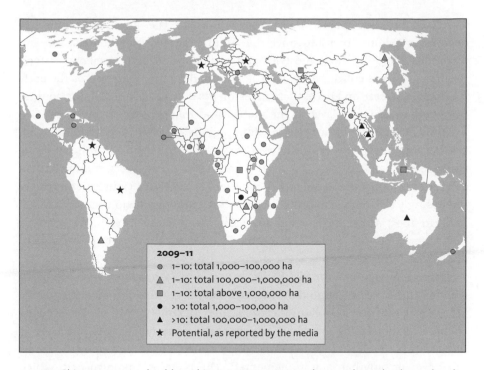

2009–11
◉ 1–10: total 1,000–100,000 ha
△ 1–10: total 100,000–1,000,000 ha
▣ 1–10: total above 1,000,000 ha
● >10: total 1,000–100,000 ha
▲ >10: total 100,000–1,000,000 ha
★ Potential, as reported by the media

11.3 Chinese overseas land-based investments, 2009–11 (*source*: drawn by the authors)

and France), and cattle, dairy farms and orchards (Australia and New Zealand). While rising domestic demand for wine and beef has obviously driven the investments in vineyards and cattle farms, the investments in dairy may also have other motives. Recent food safety scandals, such as the 2008 San Lu infant milk incident,[9] have had and continue to have a significant impact on the Chinese dairy sector.

The impetus for China's foreign land investments: state guidance and private interests

The primary explanatory drives behind China's foreign land investments are food insecurity and the nutrition transition of the Chinese population.

It is evident that China's sustained economic growth has exerted a rising pressure on the country's domestic natural resources. The oft-cited numbers portraying the country's dire situation are that China boasts 21 per cent of the world's population, while the country possesses only 8.5 per cent of the world's available arable land, and 6.5 per cent of the world's water reserves (UNOHCHR 2010). To complicate matters, China lost 8.2 million hectares of arable land between 1997 and 2010 owing to urbanization and environmental degradation (ibid.). The country became a net food importer by 2004[10] (Humphrey and Schmitz 2007).

To fuel its economic development, China compensates for its domestic shortfalls in other countries and regions abroad. The stimulus for this has become even more pressing since the country's growing middle class began to pursue more luxurious lifestyles and consumption patterns. Popular food products, such as coffee, cacao, wine and animal products, are more efficiently produced overseas and necessitate investments abroad. As a result, the country has become a major player in the global land market over recent years.

However, the significant rise in China's global activities in agriculture cannot be seen separately from the country's global expansion in other sectors. Chinese companies are also involved in infrastructure projects, mining and oil extraction around the world, while smaller-scale private Chinese enterprises increasingly also engage in overseas investment and production activities (Frost and Ho 2005; Alden 2007; Wang 2007; Gu 2011). These investment activities may intertwine and coalesce in terms of interests, timing and government objectives.

Chinese foreign investments between 2006 and 2010 comprised US$215.9, of which agriculture[11] accounted only for a small proportion of total investments, i.e. 4.2 per cent (US$9 billion) (Scissors 2011: 3). Moreover, of all investments considered (pertaining to various sectors of the economy), 60 per cent were in fact unknown or 'troubled' investments: cancelled, or announced by the media but never or only partially implemented. The issue of unknown or troubled investments is a problem that we also encountered in preparing the above paragraphs. A substantial part of Chinese investments that are agreed upon or announced in the media never materialize.

The pace of Chinese investments in the last decade, discussed in the above paragraphs, follows the state's 'Going Global' strategy (Alden 2005, 2007; Freeman et al. 2008; Cheung and Suny 2009). The first formal policy to enhance the global expansion of different sectors of the Chinese economy was launched in December 2000 in the 10th Five-Year Plan. In a broad sense, the government initiated the strategy to enhance global expansion of Chinese companies. For agricultural production, this pertained particularly to natural rubber, oil-bearing crops, cotton, vegetables and timber (Freeman 2008: 5).

In 2008 the Ministry of Agriculture further spurred the global expansion of Chinese agribusinesses (Ping 2008). Its new policies identified investment potential for SOEs, with a special focus on edible oil-bearing crops, in Central Asia, Russia, Africa, South-East Asia and South America. Moreover, the ministry issued principles on which foreign farm investments should be based: locations should be situated in countries on *good terms* with China, which are rich in *resources* and *human capital*, while being *politically stable* (ibid.). Earlier attempts to expand global activities by Chinese companies failed owing to absence of state support. Chinese agricultural experts, entrepreneurs and officials therefore urged the government to maintain oversight of overseas land investments to manage the risks involved in investments, related to trade, diplomacy, security and manufacturing. The Ministry of Agriculture recommended that its companies establish cooperative agreements in order to avoid criticism of a 'neocolonialist' approach (ibid.).

In light of the above, one could see China's overseas land-based investments as part of 'developmental outsourcing'. Outsourcing is associated with the contracting out of a business function to an external party, owing to comparative advantages in labour costs or economies-of-scale (Yourdon 2004). Yet in the Chinese case the higher supply of natural resources abroad – here, agricultural land – is the driving force. In contrast to the classical economic view, by which free markets and 'invisible hands' determine flows of commercial production, we see that the state is a central actor. Domestically, the Chinese state has been typified as a classic example of an East Asian 'developmental state', i.e. featuring highly autonomous and strong macroeconomic planning, intervention and regulation. Strikingly, what may be learnt from Chinese land-based investments is that the state plays a critical role at the global level, in the same way as it does at the domestic level.

However, the impetus for private companies to go overseas should not be underestimated. Although the Chinese state is an assumed principal actor steering and determining the land investments, profit-making and market expansion might be no less important for Chinese private companies and individual entrepreneurs. Even more, geopolitical motives instigate further expansion of companies in many countries – for instance, the recent relatively small-scale Chinese land investments in the neighbouring Central Asian republic of Tajikistan, which is relatively rich in land resources (Hofman 2013). These particular investments are thought to add leverage to the Chinese presence in the politically unstable but natural-resources-rich Central Asian region. The acquisitions are also motivated by the importance of developing the bordering Xinjiang Uygur Autonomous Region. The region is an important bridge between Tajikistan and China, and social stability in the region is of utmost importance for the Chinese government (Laruelle and Peyrouse 2012).

Going beyond the hype: rethinking the Chinese 'land grabs' discourse

The discourse over China's 'land grabs' has become highly politicized and split over issues of 'neocolonialist' exploitation versus 'win-win' opportunities and 'new economic diplomacy'. We postulated that this discourse is in contradiction with, and not sufficiently informed by, the available empirical data. To validate this postulate, we started out by describing the camps that are pitted against each other. Rather than choosing sides in the 'land grabbing' discourse or jumping to definitive conclusions, we wished to fathom and capture the complexity of China's global land-based investments.

An interesting feature of China's overseas land-based investments is the developmentalist nature of Chinese outsourcing, which is apparent in spatial-temporal ways. State measures, in particular the 'Going Global' policy and the establishment of the FOCAC, both in 2000, have played a major role in driving Chinese overseas land-based investments, which were few and fragmented before the policy's proclamation. Moreover, evident geographical waves can be distinguished over time, most recently to regions hitherto untargeted by Chinese land-based investments. The marked rise in the incidence and investment size of China's overseas land-based investments shortly after the proclamation of its 'Going Global' policy in 2000 is without doubt. However, besides and beyond domestic food security, geopolitics and profit-making, there may be equally important drivers behind China's foreign land acquisitions *today*.

Furthermore, contrary to the common perception, the bulk of Chinese investments over the years 2000–08 did not go to Africa, but to South-East Asia. There is a clear rise in the incidence of Chinese land-based investments in Africa; however, the picture in terms of investment size is murkier. According to Oxfam, internationally 'as many as 227 million hectares of land ... has been sold or leased since 2001' (Oxfam 2011: 2). At the time of that report, 67 million hectares of reported land deals had been cross-checked and it was concluded that half of the 'grabbed' area was on the African continent. When this figure is juxtaposed with our findings of a maximum size of 3 million hectares by Chinese investors, the question arises: who 'grabbed' the remaining 30 million or so hectares in Africa? Even when taking into account updated figures from the Land Matrix (July 2013), it should be acknowledged that there is a huge gap between the area included in Chinese land deals and the total area subject to large-scale land acquisition in Africa.

These observations have two possible implications: for one, we may have to rethink the dominant discourse that the Chinese are among the prime agricultural land investors worldwide; or perhaps we should start to cast serious doubt on the rigour of the current calculations of foreign land acquisitions. The blurring of factual numbers and guesstimates of land investments requires us to be cautious, 'when one number is quoted by one source, then requoted, retweeted, put on Facebook, and so on until it becomes public truth' (Oya 2012). Exact investment sizes are difficult to determine, given that a substantial number of announced investments do not materialize for a variety of reasons, such as management and implementation problems, unused loan facilities, and opposition driven by fears of 'China taking over' (see also Bräutigam and Tang 2009; Yan and Sautman 2010; Scissors 2011). In fact, China ranks second in announced and expected land investments; yet when it comes down to actually implemented deals, Chinese investments are ranked only twenty-first after a range of other, thus larger 'land grabbers' (Anseeuw 2012). China is not the sole actor in land-based investments, since other economies face similar problems of food and energy security. Equally important in the recent wave of land acquisitions are domestic elites and intra-regional corporations, resulting in 'land grabbed land grabbers' (Borras et al. 2012: 859).

Neither fears nor euphoria about China as an economic powerhouse that can rewrite development and save the Euro-zone in one go (Grammaticas 2011) are helpful when it comes to understanding China's global role and impact. For one thing, what is portrayed as property theft may boil down to an amalgam of different legal-institutional arrangements varying from (long) leases to concessionary rights and preferential loans. Furthermore, while China is seen as a monolithic, homogeneous actor in land-based investments, it is in fact composed of a variety of actors ranging from state-owned to collectively owned, private and individual entities with different activities and interests.

Moreover, it remains to be seen whether newly announced Chinese land investments will be implemented in Latin American countries, or whether a scenario similar to the African case will unfold. As Scissors forecast (2011: 3): 'a previous rush into Sub-Saharan Africa saw promised investments and contracts that did not materialize. To some extent, this will happen in South America as well.'

The phenomenon of worldwide land-based investments is like other processes of globalization, likely to feature multiple layers that constitute highly complex and, at times, markedly different unfolding outcomes on the ground. Accounting for complexity, rather than thinking in terms of simplistic metaphors – whether they be 'win-win opportunities' or 'neocolonial, expansionist land grabs' – might be a better way to get to grips with that reality. Understanding motivations and the actors behind China's 'resource grabs' would benefit from a more nuanced starting point, rather than the hype that such metaphors have so far brought us.

12 | Conclusion: beyond the global land grab hype – ways forward in research and action

Annelies Zoomers and Mayke Kaag

The 'global land grab' revisited

This book has reviewed the global rush for land in various countries. Taking the 'land grab hype' as a starting point, it has provided a systematic analysis of how large-scale land acquisition takes shape in different institutional settings and analysed its outcomes on the ground. A comparison of the cases brings to the fore a number of issues that together show the need for further research and action.

The case studies first of all invite us to revisit current definitions of land grabbing. While the term 'land grabbing' primarily has the connotation of something illegal – land theft – the chapters show that in many countries much of what happens today is *not illegal* at all. In most of the cases, host governments play an active role in supporting or enabling these deals and consider them as a sound way to obtain foreign exchange and as potentially having positive effects on infrastructure, rural job generation, technology transfer, export crops and food security. Evidently, not all large-scale land acquisitions should be labelled as 'land grabs'. We would like to reserve the term for those practices that in the narrow sense of the term could be legal, but nevertheless severely threaten the rights of local people without offering them something in return: land deals can be legal but *unfair*.

In almost all countries treated in this volume, large-scale land acquisition was legal and part of formal state policies, with official goals varying between economic growth, modernization and/or food security. But human rights issues also play a role in all countries under view. In fact, the cases show that land deals per se may be legal (the *fact* that these lands are being acquired), but that in the *process* of acquisition, illegal things may often occur. The examples in this volume are numerous. In Ethiopia, for instance, activities began before the required formalities had been completed. In Tanzania and Vietnam, local communities were not informed properly, or compensation has not been given (or not as had been promised). In this sense, the process often involves a cost for local groups that are not strong enough to protect their rights. This hints at the importance of accountability in processes of large-scale land acquisitions – we will return to this later in this chapter.

Diversity of form, similarity in outcomes While the term 'the global land grab' has been part of the hype surrounding the current wave of large-scale land acquisitions in the global South, our book shows that the reality is diverse. In this sense, *'the'* global land grab does not exist: large-scale land acquisitions take plural forms and various actors play a role in the way large-scale land acquisition takes place. Focusing more closely on the diversity of large-scale land acquisition, the chapters in this volume make it clear that several typologies are possible. One could, for instance, classify 'land grab' practices by types of actors: foreign or external 'grabbers' (as in the case of the chapter on Tanzania and the chapters on the Gulf states and on China) versus domestic 'grabbers' (such as in the chapter on Kenya). Alternatively, actors can also be divided into public actors (such as in the chapter on Vietnam) and private actors (for instance, in the chapter on Costa Rica).

Our chapters show, however, that static typologies will not help us to understand reality: actors are not operating in isolation but form mixed and blurred categories which are difficult to disentangle. Understanding the global land grab requires that we understand better how various types of actors collaborate in making deals possible. Land grabs are often combinations of public and private capital (joint ventures), involving foreigners, state actors (national- and local-level) and a multitude of other actors at different levels of society. It is not possible to draw clear conclusions about 'whom to blame for land grabbing'. Rather than isolating actors and making static typologies, it seems more useful to try to understand how alliances are being made and how interactions are taking place. The cases suggest that it is the presence in particular of mechanisms for checks and balances which makes a difference for the outcome of large-scale land acquisitions, not the type of actors.

Land grabs can also be characterized on the basis of their uses: for growing food crops, crops for fodder or biofuel crops, but also for tourism, urban expansion or large infrastructural works such as dams. Then there is land grabbing and grabbing of other resources such as water. However, once again, perhaps more interesting than distinguishing between categories would be an analysis of the dynamics – for instance, how land grabbing and water grabbing may be related, and how initial land grabs for biofuel over the years may have turned into land for food production because of changing markets.

Looking at the results, we see that in spite of the diversity in the features of large-scale land acquisition, the *outcomes are surprisingly the same* (see also Schoneveld 2013). The state, for the sake of rapid modernization and economic development, is opening the doors to large-scale investment, and the result is the expansion of land occupation for agricultural and other purposes. Large-scale land investments for agriculture generally lead to monocultures – often contributing to environmental degradation and in many cases to deforestation (as is shown in the chapters on Indonesia, Costa Rica and Vietnam). As a consequence of the land rush, rapid transformations are taking place without much involvement of civil society; and to the extent that local groups are not incorporated, they are forced to move, while the cleared land is taken up in a process of land use intensification. Irrespective of the geographical and institutional settings, processes are often not transparent, not even in countries praised for 'good governance', such as Ethiopia, and not even in cases of Western companies boasting of their corporate social responsibility policies (see the chapter on Tanzania).

Focusing on the type of land involved, we see a bias towards fertile areas with access to water and preferably also with good road access (markets), as well as towards low-density areas in subtropical zones often in use as extensive pastureland and forest areas. Technological innovation and the saturation of fertile areas have led investors to increasingly target more marginal and often also vulnerable areas, as for instance illustrated by the invasion of peatlands in Indonesia (Susanti and Budidarsono, this volume), the occupation of the Chaco and the Delta region in Argentina (Goldfarb and Zoomers, this volume), and the use of marginal areas in Ethiopia (Schoneveld and Shete, this volume). The chapter on Argentina also shows that investors in soy, in making a selection of new investment sites, often attempt to disperse risks and spread their production over various agro-ecological zones. The question of the type of area targeted can also be answered from an institutional/political perspective. The chapter on Cambodia suggests that investors from abroad may intentionally target weak institutional settings, where they have ample room for manoeuvre. On the other hand, the chapter by Ho and Hofman shows that Chinese investors may have a preference for stable political environments as investment settings.

Where entrepreneurs have taken over land, it is often for long periods (up to ninety-nine years) and the process is irreversible, in the sense that it may be returned to the state but not to the population who were removed. The benefits in terms of employment are relatively small (such as in the case of soy); and to the extent that employment is generated (e.g. in Indonesia), local groups are often bypassed by outsiders who have better education and are better positioned to benefit from job opportunities. After acquiring the land, investors are often relatively free to change their plans, and there is no or very little control on their business operations. More generally, given the lack of information and the fact that many of the deals are made behind closed doors, investments are difficult to control. Local people are usually bypassed, displaced and/or enclosed, without receiving compensation. After displacement, people do not have much choice other than to move to cities and/or more marginal localities, becoming more vulnerable to the adverse effects of climate change. As the authors of the Kenya chapter argue, people in urban areas also are often affected and even displaced by large-scale land acquisitions for urban development and speculation.

Summarizing the effects, the land rush is in many countries leading to 'foreignization' (Zoomers 2010), in the sense of local groups losing their territorial control and external actors taking over, often in legal ways and with the support of the state. Land is suddenly fenced and local people are excluded not only from access to land and other resources such as water, minerals and forest products, but also from possible benefits resulting from large-scale land investments, such as employment and technology.

What is the size? Looking at the tip of the iceberg One of the issues that has been given much attention since the beginning of the hype on land grabbing is the question of how much land is involved. Our analysis shows how difficult it is to make a reliable estimate. Whereas in the debate much emphasis is given to agricultural lands, we are now aware that we are looking only at the tip of the iceberg. Land investments are not restricted to food or biofuels: enormous areas of land are used worldwide for non-agricultural purposes, including residential tourism (Costa Rica, for instance, but also South Africa and Indonesia), urbanization (Vietnam, but also Ethiopia, Kenya, Senegal, China and Indonesia), and dam construction (Vietnam, for instance, but also Peru and Ecuador). In each of these cases, land acquisition goes hand in hand with displacements and enclosures, often without compensation and in ways quite similar to the case of food and biofuel expansion. It follows that pressures on local land markets are currently much higher than suggested in existing databases, which most often focus mainly on agricultural land.

In addition, in making an assessment of how much land is involved, and making decisions about compensation, it is not sufficient to look only at land. Attention should be paid also to 'underground' realities (how much water or minerals are involved), as for instance is convincingly illustrated by the chapter on water grabbing in the Andes. What the implications are in terms of losing access to other resources, such as forest products including wood, fruits and wildlife, should also be taken into account.

Finally, the global land rush is much more extensive than suggested, not only because of the multitude of drivers (see above), but also because of translocal effects: investments at location A will generate a chain of spatial effects in other locations (B, C and D). In Indonesia, new opportunities for oil palm expansion attract people from faraway areas, which has an impact not only on the place where investments are being made but also on the area affected by outmigration. In Argentina, soy expansion has direct repercussions for cattle ranchers who are forced into more marginal regions such as the Chaco. Our book thus shows the importance of also taking into account translocal effects (see also Zoomers and Van Westen 2011). No conflicts might appear within the area in which land acquisition takes place (e.g. the pampas in Argentina), but negative effects are often externalized towards more distant areas. In Ethiopia (Schoneveld and Shete, this volume), for instance, inter-ethnic conflicts were reported when a community of pastoralists was forced to migrate outside of their territory in search of new pasture when their pastureland had been included in a large-scale land investment project. Such translocal effects should be taken into account in development plans and in decisions about compensation.

Ultimately, the translocal effects of current large-scale land acquisitions may often not remain confined to the national context but become transnational in character (we return to this later in this chapter), among other things because they involve a restructuring of global supply chains.

The relevance of taking into account history and past policies and experiences The land grab is often presented as a sudden and unexpected issue that arose as a consequence of the food price crisis of 2007/08, but in reality it is a logical outcome of earlier policies and ways of governance. Thus, it is interesting that from the early 1990s onwards, and with the aim of furthering neoliberal policies, donors began to play a direct role in land-related issues, something that had long been taboo. Donors began to invest increasing amounts of money in measures aimed at the liberalization of land markets, titling programmes, and the creation of cadastres (De Soto 2000). According to the adherents of land titling, well-defined, secure land rights are crucial for creating incentives for investment and sustainable resource management: they facilitate low-cost transfers of land and credit access as the rural non-farm economy develops, and they allow for the provision of public services at minimum costs (Deininger 2003). Donors consequently pushed governments to liberalize land markets, often in combination with decentralization policies. In addition, in the context of the 'good governance' agenda, governments were pressed to create an enabling and stimulating business environment, as attracting foreign investment was seen as a necessary condition for pro-poor growth.

In other words, it is not merely the food crisis or the demand for biofuels but the whole set of earlier policies which is responsible for the current trends, and donors played an active role in helping to create the conditions in which land grabbing could flourish. The reasons why large-scale land acquisition took place can only be explained by the fact that a number of conditions were fulfilled simultaneously. We see this in almost all chapters of this volume: the availability of large tracts of underexploited land (owing to neglect of agricultural policies for more than two decades); the emphasis by donors on attracting foreign capital (and the availability of an FDI-friendly business environment); the emphasis on the need to create a modern land market (buying and leasing land became much easier in many countries); and the facilitating presence of institutional weaknesses. In the context of decentralization, the national governments were supposed to step back in favour of local government while also making room for market forces. However, as soon as FDI began to come in, local governments were often not strong enough to deal with the new outsiders. In other cases, they are, or are considered as, extensions of national political elites rather than representing local interests, such as in the Ethiopian highlands (this volume), Tanzania and Kenya.

When the food crisis occurred in 2007, additional land claims were generated by the simultaneous hype about the climate crisis (and need for biofuels and reforestation), which triggered rapid growth in new investments in renewable energy. Finally, the hype on land grabbing was further strengthened by speculative investments. In Costa Rica, owing to residential tourism, land prices are currently so high that buying land for nature conservation is no longer feasible (see the chapter by Van Noorloos). In addition, the coincidence of the financial crisis in the EU may have had some impact on the speed of expansion: European investors are more interested than before in opening new market outlets in Africa, Asia and Latin America; however, owing to the crisis, investment flows in particular areas may also have gone down.

In addition to the importance of looking at past sets of policies, including the role of international organizations such as the World Bank, this volume also shows the importance of placing current events concerning large-scale land acquisitions in the historical context of the countries and localities where they are taking place. In many countries, what is happening today is to a large extent a continuation of history. In countries such as Argentina or Costa Rica, large-scale land acquisition and 'foreignization' have been taking place for centuries. Furthermore, responses to land grabs – in particular, protests or the absence thereof – are influenced by local and national histories. In countries with a strong history of civil society and protests in land matters, such as Kenya, protests may be very different from, for instance, any that occur in Tanzania, whose history is marked by the *Ujamaa* policy and associated relocations. In Ethiopia and in Vietnam, where mainly marginalized groups are affected by current land grabs, the low degree of protest can be partly explained by histories of marginality.

Large-scale land acquisitions, particularly the related processes and problems at the local level, cannot be adequately understood without a proper understanding of local land governance from a historical perspective. Focusing in more detail on the relevance of earlier experiences, several chapters (Kenya, Tanzania, Argentina) illustrate convincingly that large-scale acquisition (and horizontal expansion of the occupied territory) is not new, but has happened before. Similar processes took place during the colonial period. Part of what is happening today happened in the 1960s during the 'green revolution' (the introduction of new crop varieties, mono-cropping, mechanization); it happened during the 1960s and 1970s, when land reform was high on the agenda; and it happened during the 1970s and 1980s, when much attention was given to agricultural colonization (countries with considerable areas of 'empty' land trying to expand their cultivated area through settlement schemes). It is striking how little attention is given in current policy debates to the lessons that can be learned: the green revolution (1950s) showed the strength of capital-intensive technology (new varieties, irrigation, rapid agricultural growth), as well as the dangers and risks (salinization of irrigated areas, growing inequality). Land reforms (mainly in the 1960s and 1970s) showed how difficult it is to change property relations, how politically sensitive the land issue is, and how creative large landholders can be in undermining or bending the rules (e.g. transferring land to their children in order to prevent expropriation). Finally, agricultural colonization (1970s–1980s) exposed the myth of empty lands, as well as the devastating environmental impact of horizontal strategies which led to deforestation and environmental degradation (e.g. in the Amazon and Indonesia). It also showed how difficult it is to control spontaneous mass migration (large-scale land investment followed by rapid processes of spontaneous colonization by people looking for land, leading to rapid deforestation and other environmental problems).

But even in countries where large-scale land acquisitions may not have taken place before, what occurred in the domain of local land governance in earlier times may often be very similar to what is currently occurring on a large scale: client relationships shape opportunities and barriers to land access for people or categories of people. Strikingly, there is little connection between the literature on local land use and land management – literature which was so plentiful in the 1990s – and the current debate on land grabbing. It is important to conduct research into the political micro-processes underlying 'successful' land grabbing and to examine what history can teach us about the current dynamics of land claims (including land grabbing), the ways land conflicts are resolved, and the implications for tenure security for different categories of the population. This means a plea to build on past research on land use and land governance in order to understand current dynamics, and to have debates on land governance from the 1990s inform the current debate on land grabbing.[1]

Looking behind the scenes: understanding the geopolitical implications The various chapters show that besides looking at the direct and indirect effects 'on the ground', it is relevant to look behind the scenes and try to understand current processes from a more geopolitical perspective. Here also, our conclusion is that *the* global land grab does not exist. The world is not a levelled playing field, and it is worthwhile to critically review which countries are the hot spots and what kinds of countries are bypassed in processes of large-scale land acquisition. Not all countries are equally targeted by investors, and it is useful to gain a better understanding of the differential roles of countries, either as countries of destination or as countries of origin.

Based on our country studies, we can indeed make a distinction between countries of origin (playing a role as 'land grabbers', e.g. China, the Arab states and also investors from the EU) and the host countries (those often presented as the 'victims' of land grabbing, such as Cambodia or Ethiopia). Reality, however, is much more complex. Several countries do not belong to just one of these categories but play a double role: people in China and Vietnam, and also in Brazil and South Africa, are victims of large-scale land acquisitions within their own territories, while their country is simultaneously 'grabbing' land in other countries – so, in contrast to the hyped narrative, the world cannot be divided into simple categories of 'perpetrators' and 'victims', or, in more neutral terms, investing versus investment countries.

The importance of the global land grab can be described in terms of area involved or number of affected people. But it might be more important to analyse the implications for transnational connections and power relations. Our case studies show how in Indonesia and the Philippines, political, social and religious relations with the Arab world play a role in shaping land grab realities. In Argentina, through soy production, linkages with the EU and the USA, and also China, play a dominant role, while Argentina is also becoming a hub for expanding soy production towards Africa. Investments in Ethiopia by China, Saudi Arabia, Italy and the Ethiopian diaspora are influenced by, and a reflection of, historical connections, but in their turn will also have implications for Ethiopia's geopolitical position. Current patterns of land grabbing cannot be understood without also taking into account the role of long-established diasporas in the various countries (e.g. Indians and Chinese settled in Africa), who nowadays play important roles as brokers and investors.

The current global land rush thus plays a role in reshaping geopolitical realities. In its manifestations in different countries, it builds on prior existing relationships, may revive old ones that had been neglected, and may change the content of existing relationships (religious linkages can add an economic dimension) while it is also building new ones. We observe a shift from the dominance of neocolonial North–South relationships to an increasing importance and density of South–South economic linkages (with new interactions taking place between Africa, Asia and Latin America). In this way, current large-scale land acquisitions are manifestations and building blocks of a so-called emerging multipolar world (Dietz et al. 2011). Grevi (2009) coined the term 'interpolarity' to indicate that the current world order is characterized not only by multiple poles but also by a growing interdependency between them. This volume offers snapshots of how, through the global land grab, interdependencies are not only increasing at a global level, but are also reinforced and shaped from 'below' – having repercussions for the very outlook of the multipolar world.

The land grab hype from a cross-continental perspective In view of what has been argued in the foregoing on the plural forms and the history of the current land grab, it is interesting to note how in the various continents the land grab discourse is very much shaped by historically rooted narratives (which show important differences between Africa, Asia and Latin America).

In Africa, the popular media discourse on land grabbing has been very much rooted in received ideas on Africa as the ultimate victim of history: media expressions of 'the new scramble for Africa' have portrayed non-Western powers like China (see also Ho and Hofman, this volume) and the Gulf states as the greedy 'ultimate Other' plundering the continent's resources, while the agency of Africans (as protester or as collaborator) has largely been ignored. Policy, research and activist arguments to a large degree build on ideas about African smallholders as knowledgeable caretakers of the environment – as they appeared in the 1980s in publications such as *The Greening of Africa* (Harrison 1987) and *Farmers First* (Chambers et al. 1989) – whereas large-scale external investors would lack this local knowledge and sense of responsibility.

In the context of Latin America, the tone of the land grab debate is different. Land grabs are perceived much more as a continuation of earlier land struggles in many countries, especially in the Andes and the Amazon regions, with their strong tradition of 'social movements', including indigenous groups, peasants and landless people, but also environmental movements (which is also reflected in the chapters about Peru and Ecuador). In comparison with Africa, in discussing the implications of the land rush, there seems a stronger focus on the role of indigenous/environmental groups: consequences are described in terms of 'foreignization' (which in a sense could be seen as the revival of old *dependencia* debates). Despite the strength of social movements, however, the chapter by Boelens et al. shows that smallholders and indigenous group are not strong enough to stop the expansion of agro-industries, not even in Ecuador with its new pro-indigenous Constitution. Argentina (Goldfarb and Zoomers, this volume) and Costa Rica (Van Noorloos, this volume) are examples of countries where social movements have not been powerful enough to turn developments in new directions.

In Asia, to the extent that attention is given to the global land rush, it is interesting to see that – in comparison with Africa and Latin America – current 'grabs' are framed as a direct consequence of rapid urbanization and economic growth. In addition, reference is made to the green revolution in the 1960s and 1970s, which helped the continent to become more food secure. The chapters on Vietnam, Cambodia, Indonesia and China show how national governments placed much emphasis on rapid economic growth and satisfying energy needs, which appear more prominently on the agenda than poverty alleviation and/ or food security. Indigenous groups (minorities) are less represented by NGOs and other organizations than in Latin America.

12 | Conclusion

209

Finally, carrying our cross-continental perspective to the global North, it is striking that – in spite of the fact that, for instance, China is increasingly involved in land deals in Europe and Australia (Ho and Hofman, this volume) – large-scale land acquisition in this part of the world is usually not framed in terms of 'grabbing'.[2] Why would one not speak so easily of land grabbing in these latter cases? Is this because better legal provisions prohibit real 'grabs' and ensure that ordinary land users/owners do not become victims of these deals? Or is it because people and agriculture have already become part of larger global chains – in other words, the fundamental changes have already occurred in the North? The answer is not so clear, but we would like to suggest that the predominant focus on the global South in the current land grab debate deserves a more critical treatment than it currently receives.

The land grab hype is 'human made', not only in terms of 'mere facts' but also in terms of framing and making interpretations of what is happening on the ground. In considering who helped to create the land grab hype, we see a highly heterogeneous group of actors, each having their own reasons for raising their voices: anti-globalist movements, development NGOs, environmentalists and indigenous peoples' groups; local farmers' groups fighting for improved land governance and against the negative effects of neoliberal policies; media looking for breaking news (for which the African narrative particularly, as elaborated in the foregoing, was very attractive); and researchers, who on the one hand were concerned about these new developments, but who on the other hand also realized that this topic could be good for raising research funds. For others, the land grab hype served to call attention to the need to improve governance and/or promote corporate social responsibility. The land grab debate thus represents a melting pot of various interests, narratives and experiences, and the claims it advances are not coherent. The frictions involved can be illustrated by referring to environmentalists who have used the hype in their struggle against deforestation but have been accused by others of 'green grabbing' (Fairhead et al. 2012). Rather than seeing the land grab hype as a neutral and uniform 'global' event, it is important to look at the narratives behind it (which, as we have seen, may differ for different continents and settings) and the plurality of voices and interests involved.

Ways forward in research and action

New policy domains – strengthening institutions Analysing the situation in the various countries, it is interesting to see that in most of the chapters the land grab is very much presented as the outcome of institutional weaknesses. To the extent that large-scale land acquisitions produce negative results, donors place much emphasis on the need to 'strengthen institutions'. Current attempts to improve land governance include the 'Voluntary Guidelines on the Responsible Governance of Tenure of Land, Fisheries and Forests in the Context of National

Box 12.1 The Voluntary Guidelines

On 11 May 2012 the Committee on World Food Security (CFS) officially endorsed the 'Voluntary Guidelines on the Responsible Governance of Tenure of Land, Fisheries and Forests in the Context of National Food Security' (hereafter cited as Voluntary Guidelines).[3]

The Voluntary Guidelines (based on consultations in various countries and with different stakeholders searching for 'national' consensus)[4] are intended to provide a framework for responsible tenure governance that supports food security, poverty alleviation, sustainable resource use, and environmental protection. They set out principles and internationally accepted practices that may guide the preparation and implementation of policies and laws related to tenure governance, and much emphasis is placed on protecting tenure rights to land, fisheries and forestry; on resolving conflicts; and on legal recognition of indigenous and other customary tenure rights, as well as of informal rights (not only for land, but also other natural resources, including gathering rights).

The Voluntary Guidelines declare that states should protect tenure right-holders against the arbitrary loss of their tenure rights, including forced evictions that are inconsistent with their existing obligations under national and international law; and they should promote and facilitate the enjoyment of legitimate tenure rights and provide access to justice to deal with infringements of legitimate tenure rights. They should also provide effective and accessible means.

The Voluntary Guidelines seek to improve governance of tenure of land, fisheries and forestries for the benefit of all, 'with an emphasis on vulnerable and marginalised people, with the goal of food security, poverty alleviation, sustainable livelihoods, social stability, housing security, rural development, environmental protection and sustainable social and economic development' (p. 1).

Guiding principles for responsible investment, as formulated in the document, are the following: *Respect* (recognizing and respecting tenure right-holders and their rights, whether formally recorded or not); *Protection* (safeguarding tenure rights against threats – human rights are thus taken as a starting point, with much attention paid to consultation and participation); *Transparency* (providing information about rules and current situation); and *Accountability* (holding people and public agencies responsible for their actions and decisions).

Food Security', endorsed by the FAO in 2012 (see Box 12.1). In addition, in many countries, much attention is given to the need to provide people with land titles[5] and to the creation of modern low-cost land administration systems as a way to help people to protect their rights.

In practice, however, there are several reasons why the importance of institutions (and transparency) should not be overstated. The comparison of practices in various countries showed that processes of land acquisition and their outcomes are surprisingly similar in spite of important differences in institutional settings. The problem is often not so much the rules and regulations, but the lack of control and practical implementation. In many countries – owing to capacity problems among other things – policy implementation is limited; local authorities as well as civil society, which are assumed to execute and control land policies, are often too weak, opening the door to corruption and non-authorized transfers.

Donors and governments generally are currently placing much emphasis on improving land administration systems and land titling as a tool to improve land security. Land titling programmes may generate some security (to those who obtain a title to their land), but the fact that traditional land rights are often family rights is frequently ignored, while land titling programmes generally concern individual land rights. This conversion of communal rights to individual rights often creates problems in families and communities (see, for instance, Kaag et al. 2011). Land titles might help the 'head of household' (male and/or female heads of households) to improve; but this is not a solution for the landless, or for the youth who still rely on inheriting land (before inheritance, they do not have options other than to work family plots).

In the case of large-scale land acquisitions, providing local people with land titles may mean that they can stay on their lands, but this does not mean that they will benefit: land titling will not automatically translate into enhanced production capacity, owing to the lack of credit facilities, technical assistance and/or fertile land. In addition, immigrant groups of newcomers are often more successful in benefiting from the newly generated employment because they are better qualified. The local population (who could stay if their rights were acknowledged) are in many cases bypassed by newcomers – immigrants with higher levels of education, and opportunity seekers who bring more capital and have better opportunities to benefit. In Riau in Indonesia, for example (see the chapter by Susanti and Budidarsono), it is mainly the immigrants who are the 'winners' in development.

Responsible business and codes of conduct In addition to improving land governance and protecting local groups through the provision of land titles (see above), there are also initiatives focusing on controlling the behaviour of investors by applying notions of corporate social responsibility. The World

Bank has been working on a 'code of conduct' (or 'Principles') together with appropriate land policies (Deininger and Byerlee 2011a). In addition, there are initiatives to create more responsible conduct on the part of large investors, initiatives such as the Roundtable for Sustainable Oil Palm or the Round Table for Soy Production (supported by donor organizations). In the discussions thus far, there has been a tendency to place much emphasis on the need for more consultation and mechanisms for benefit sharing, including compensation (ibid.).

Developing 'codes of conduct' may help to prevent exploitative relationships, but there are many limitations (Meinzen-Dick and Markelova 2009). First, codes of conduct may work (i.e. individual enterprises are forced to stick to the rules), but the outcomes (and the developmental impact) will very much depend on the negotiating power of the various stakeholders and on their capacity to control. Interestingly, codes of conduct and/or the promotion of 'responsible investments' stimulate investments in the social sphere (e.g. schools, medical services, housing) that are very similar to the 'old-fashioned' (and isolated) development projects. Whereas development organizations decided to turn away from the project approach (in favour of 'sector-wide approaches'), there is now a risk that old-fashioned development projects will return – leading to a patchwork of 'development', which is not sustainable in the long run.

In addition, there is the risk that investors will use social projects such as schools as a 'wild card' to continue their business as usual, as they will already have 'performed their social duties'. Codes of conduct may help to control the negative effects of large-scale land acquisition, but the impact will be limited to 'enlightened' investors who are willing to adhere to these principles. It is clear that not all investors will be equally interested in or capable of following such principles (especially not at times of crisis). Even if investors adhere to principles – or accept new rules – they cannot be imposed on the whole sector, and free-riding cannot be prevented (Zoomers 2013).

Finally, it is striking that in the debate about responsible business, until now not much attention has been given to the question of the 'responsible scale of doing business'. Many investors have more land than they need or than they are capable of cultivating. It is not so clear what the optimal scale of operation would be. It seems that investors are stimulated in many countries to acquire as much as they can – land prices are low and governments are often not very demanding – while the hype has also contributed to businesses not wanting to miss out.

Beyond the hype: working towards translocal private and public accountability It is clear that new legislation, guidelines for policy-makers and governments, land titling programmes and/or codes of conduct for investors alone will not bring sufficient progress in stopping land grabbing and turn land investments, be they large-scale or not, into vehicles for inclusive and sustainable development. The case studies have shown that large-scale land acquisitions represent important stakes for investing states and private investors, as well as for national and local governments and other land gatekeepers in the host countries. The stakes exceed private/public divides as well as international/national/local distinctions: large-scale land acquisitions are often conducted in private–public collaboration and weave webs across localities by linking distant producers and consumers in transnational value chains, by creating translocal effects through the movement of people and resources, and by linking local and external businesses and governments. The importance of the stakes (making it attractive *not* to adhere to guidelines and rules) and the complexity of the field of stakeholders (making it easy to 'free-ride') call for strong mechanisms of accountability. As elaborated elsewhere (Kaag et al. 2012), accountability in land governance concerns the ways in which governing bodies and their representatives – responsible for decisions concerning land claims, settling land disputes, and making development plans for their territories (at national, regional and local levels) – are accountable to the citizens they represent and serve. Are the latter able to control those who govern them? In other words, this is about the effective societal mechanisms of checks and balances concerning land matters. One could elaborate this in the same way for private actors such as land investment businesses and their representatives. In what way can they be held accountable, on the one hand to the local population and other partners in the investment country, on the other hand to their clients (the consumers at the other end of the chain)?

As has recently been elaborated by Polack et al. (2013), one line of thinking about strengthening accountability has focused on legal measures ('accountability as rights'), while another line of thinking, which has been less prominent in policy and research circles, focuses on how people can actually control their governors ('accountability as power'). We would here particularly underline the importance of this latter in transforming 'land grabs' into more positive opportunities for inclusive development. The case studies have shown that legal provisions are most often in existence: in theory, 'land grabs' would not occur and large-scale land acquisitions would foster development. That this does not work out in practice is importantly related to the fact that there is little control over the public and private stakeholders.

The interdependencies between a multitude of stakeholders and between different parts of the world created by current large-scale land acquisitions represent challenges for reinforcing accountability, but they also offer opportunities. In view of the foregoing, we would like to argue that for creating an effective accountability framework for large-scale land acquisitions, it will not be sufficient to limit oneself to private companies only, or merely to public actors such as governments or to only one stakeholder level (international/

national/local). Such a framework should rather be thought of as an integrated system of checks and balances covering different types of actors and plural sites. Looking at the private businesses engaged in large-scale land acquisition, it is clear that both the national and local governments of the countries in which they invest, as well as the local populations, have a role in controlling their practices. As we have seen that local stakeholders in particular often do not have sufficient power to do so, we may resort to the consumers at the other end of the production chain (who may live on the other side of the globe) to add their consumer power in order to reinforce checks and balances. Consumers are an important force in stimulating businesses to adhere to their corporate social responsibility policies, and media and civil society organizations have a role to play in stimulating them to take their responsibility as consumers seriously (as is currently happening in the case of the textile industries). In the same vein, citizens are supposed to control their rulers, but in this they can be helped by local, national and international civil society and consumer groups, as well as by socially responsible enterprises.

The problem of accountability cannot be resolved in a day. The challenge is to produce responsible and assertive citizens. This requires a sufficient level of basic education (people should be able to check information for themselves) and civil education (what are my rights and how can I enforce them?). In addition, the problem of poverty presents itself in many cases throughout this volume. It is clear that poor farmers who have to struggle to survive will be able to think only about sowing and what they are going to eat tomorrow, and not have larger horizons of reflection or be able to engage in emancipatory action (see Sen 1997; Bebbington 1999). This evidently holds also for the poor in urban areas. Considering the governors, often it is not a lack of knowledge about rules that is the problem; in the end, it is to a large extent about political ethics. Reinforcing this calls for training other than courses on legal issues and technicalities. Finally, civil society organizations and action groups, local or otherwise, may help each other in a translocal and transnational land coalition.

For the problem of land grabbing, no magic bullet or easy fix is available: the problem is complex and multifaceted, comes in many forms, and yet has massive outcomes. But we believe that taking a more political, a more translocal and a more historically sensitive perspective than has hitherto generally been taken will help to promote progress in research and action.

Final reflections: why the land grab hype was good

The global land grab can be characterized in terms of number of land deals and/or the area and people affected by land grabbing. But this volume has shown the importance of looking at the larger picture and underlying processes.

At the beginning of the hype, when the media began to report on 'millions of hectares of land being grabbed in Africa', people's initial response was to 'look for facts'. Observers have now begun to report that 'reality has not met the expectations', emphasizing that many of the announced land deals actually did not take place (which may be a source of relief to some and of disillusion to others). There are disappointing results with miracle crops, and investors have often changed plans in response to falling short in expected returns, frequently without informing stakeholders about such changes. In addition, there are disappointing results in terms of employment and technology transfers. We can conclude that there is underperformance in terms of positive effects and a growing consensus that the negative impact for local groups should not be underestimated.

The hype has been very effective in bringing the phenomenon of large-scale land acquisitions into view and prompting people to investigate the 'facts in reality', while it has also prompted people to develop nuanced views. It helped to speed up the process of data collection, but also went hand in hand with 'naming and shaming', which has exerted pressure on several actors to change practices and stimulated the debate about responsible business.

The excessive media attention has helped to mobilize considerable funding, facilitating new types of collaboration, including public–private partnerships on a world scale and transnational civil society linkages. Thanks to the availability of social media, now policy-makers, practitioners and academic researchers can respond more quickly than before to perceived urgencies, and local activist groups – dispersed as they are – have increased possibilities to communicate and ally. It should be remembered, however, that between activist groups and local populations a large gap may still exist – the chapters have also shown that local populations most often are still outside these newly formed knowledge networks concerning land deals.

Finally, the hype about land grabbing should be evaluated not only in terms of its contribution to the land grab debate. The land grab debate is not 'just about land'; it is the manifestation of reshuffling international relations and a restructuring of global connections. The hype has helped the Western world to become aware of the more dominant role of South–South relations, even though European and US firms also play important roles in the global land rush – and the latter is an aspect that, because of the hype, has remained underexposed. It also marks the return of the African state, which for a long time was forced to 'step back' in the context of neoliberal reforms but is nowadays playing a marked and visible role in making land deals. The hype was also a wake-up call – after two decades of neglect – that more priority should be given to agricultural development.

Notes

Introduction

1 www.landmatrix.org.

2 For examples, see www.grain.org and www.landcoalition.org.

3 We would like to thank Gerben Nooteboom and Laurens Bakker for their valuable reflections on the phenomenon of 'hype' and their literature suggestions on this topic. A large part of this section is based on their input.

1 Schoneveld and Shete

1 Unfortunately, the authors were unable to access regionally disaggregated data for these projects.

2 The other EIA documents that the authors were able to peruse, from Karuturi Gambella and the nearby 27,000-hectare BHO Bio rice project, were submitted only in July 2011 and October 2011, while cultivation activities had already commenced, and leasehold contracts were signed as far back as October 2010 and May 2010, respectively.

3 In 2010 the Ministry of Federal Affairs embarked on the villagization programme, which aims to resettle 1.45 million people in Ethiopia's lowland areas of Benshangul Gumuz, Gambella and SNNPR into new villages by the end of 2015 (HRW 2012). The programme seeks to consolidate scattered (agro-)pastoralists into larger, better-equipped villages in order to promote sedentarization, reduce food insecurity, and improve the efficiency and effectiveness of modern services delivery (Teklemariam 2012). Resettled households will receive land certificates for 2–5 hectares of land.

4 Although the Constitution (1995) does recognize the free right of pastoralists to pasture (Section 40(5)) and peasants' right to compensation in the case of expropriation (Section 40(8)), in practice these provisions are not extended to landholders without land certificates. Proclamation 455/2005, for example, defines a landholder in the context of expropriation only as one 'with lawful possession of the land' (Section 2(3)).

5 A resettlement site has yet to be determined – although, according to the resettlement plan, it will be located within a 10-kilometre radius of the farm to minimize the trauma to the population of a second resettlement.

6 According to a district administrator, the company even requested the district government to assist in recruiting children specifically. This type of labour is, however, not necessarily illegal in Ethiopia. The most explicit reference in Ethiopian law to child labour is the rather arbitrary Article 36(1d) of the Constitution, which specifies that 'every child has the right not to be subject to exploitative practices, neither to be required nor permitted to perform work which may be hazardous or harmful to his or her education, health or well-being'.

7 The Codes of Conduct are also relatively limited in scope. For example, besides the provision that 'the local community gets an opportunity to acquire knowledge of the project so that peoples around provide sustainable support to the project' and 'care should be taken to protect historical relics and burial sites' (p. 5), the 'social component' focuses entirely on labour conditions and makes no reference to livelihood reconstruction obligations. The AISD acknowledged that the Codes of Conduct was developed largely to appease donor concerns.

8 Although district government is

217

the sole beneficiary of land rents, most of the contracts have a three-to-six-years payment exemption. With most companies still in their exemption period, few district governments have yet collected any rents.

2 Abdallah et al.

1 Reducing Emissions from Deforestation and Degradation.

2 www.tic.co.tz/ticwebsite.nsf/2e9cafac3e472ee5882572850027f544/729d4c075f2b03fc432572d10024bea6?.

3 No. 5 s. 33 (I) (a).

4 The ranch is located about eighty kilometres north of Dar es Salaam, west of the Makurunge–Sadani road, bounded by coastal mudflats to the east, the Wami river and Saadani Game Reserve to the north, and the Ruvu river to the southeast.

5 TZS: Tanzanian shillings.

6 Tanzania ratified the Minimum Wage Fixing Convention of 1970 (No. 131) and has adopted the Labour Institutions Act of 2004, which prescribes minimum wages on a sectoral basis, and the Employment and Labour Relations Act, which provides the modes, formulas and timing of payment of wages. It has also established wage boards, which make recommendations on the cost of living, among other things.

7 *Daily News*, 27 March 2013, daily-news.co.tz/bunge/?n=22827.

3 Klopp and Lumumba

1 This was a double crisis for Kenya since the country experienced large-scale post-election violence in the same period, which saw the displacement of approximately 650,000 people, many of them farmers from the food basket region of Rift Valley. This violence helped plunge the country into a domestic food crisis that served as a rationale for improving food security via modernization, rather than by providing adequate support for displaced and dispossessed farmers.

2 To this day, families working in the Mwea Rice Scheme face very serious human rights violations and controls over their produce and land use.

3 *Forbes* magazine ranks Kenyatta's son Uhuru, who inherited his father's wealth and political mantle, as one of the richest men in Africa. His wealth is derived from 200,000 hectares of land that his father accumulated. He has just been elected president of Kenya, which may not bode well for land reforms in the country.

4 One calculation of some of the monetary losses linked to lost parastatal and protected land gives 'a cumulative estimate of the value of land grabbed at an astounding Ksh 53 billion [approximately $725 million or 4 per cent of the GDP for the entire country that year]' (KNCHR and KLA 2006: 4, www.kenyalandalliance.or.ke/publications). Note that the many recommendations from this commission have not yet been adopted.

5 At a National Symposium in April 2007, 600 participants approved the final draft with the Law Society of Kenya and the Kenya Landowners Association expressing concern (USAID 2009: 4).

6 This description was taken from the KLA website: www.kenyalandalliance.or.ke/.

7 The following development partners have been participating in the DPGL: USAID, Sida, DfID, the Finnish embassy, NALEP, UNEP, UN-Habitat and the World Bank. Currently, USAID and Sida along with the government of Kenya are funding the next stages of the Land Policy implementation process.

8 This description was taken from the UN-Habitat website: www.unhabitat.org/content.asp?cid=5941&catid=283&typeid=13.

9 One reason for this is that Kenya's complex land issues are often politicized depending on the circumstances (often the coalition) at multiparty elections (see Klopp 2001 for a detailed case study). There is no simple link between election violence and land. However, it is safe to say that without reforms, land problems will continue to be selectively used by politicians and movements to justify

violence and displacement. In 2007/08 this became very evident, which is why land was included as an agenda item needing reform within the National Accord.

10 See the description by Pearce (2012) and also analysis by FIAN (2010). The case was also profiled in the documentary *Good Fortune*.

11 National Environment and Management Authority.

12 The plan to build a port at Lamu continues, and there are still concerns as to whether land is being offered as part of compensation to financers.

13 See North Energy (2011) and Ngotho (2012) for the emerging research and critiques of jatropha and carbon emissions.

14 One report on pre-election violence in Tana River Delta in August 2012 points to these enclosures as a contributing factor in the violence (KNCRH 2012: 39).

4 Goldfarb and Zoomers

1 This chapter is based on Goldfarb and Zoomers (2013).

2 Monsanto produced genetically modified glyphosate (herbicide)-resistant soy.

3 Today, Argentina is the second-largest producer of GM crops in the world after the USA, with a total cultivated area of 22 million hectares (soy, corn and cotton, among others).

4 'Brazilian farmers bought the illegal seeds (from Argentina) on such a scale that the official ban on GM crops became meaningless and was revoked by President Lula. Similar tactics were used to spread GM soy into Paraguay and Bolivia' (GRAIN 2009).

5 The authorization of the commercialization of Monsanto GM soy and inputs such as glyphosate was conducted in obscure circumstances by the Secretary of Agriculture in 1996, without public debate and with scientific evaluations performed by directly interested private actors. The report from the Secretary of Agriculture – which did not include a bio-safety assessment, was not made public, and lacked a

peer-reviewed assessment – was approved in eighty-one days and included a large section in English, which was written by Monsanto (Verbitsky 2009; Robin 2010).

6 Estación Experimental Agroindustrial Obispo Colombres is an autonomous entity of the area of the Ministerio de Desarrollo Productivo del Gobierno de Tucumán, province of Tucumán.

7 Popularly designates non-cultivated land with native vegetation – which may include a range of types and density of trees, bushes and plants, but also designates a full ecosystem – and is constitutive of peasant livelihoods in northern Argentina.

8 Red Agroforestal Chaco Argentina is a group of seven organizations, among them NGOs, universities and individual researchers, devoted to investigating topics related to development in the Argentine Chaco region.

9 In August 2012, the entrepreneur and pilot responsible for one of the cases of fumigation was taken to court and was condemned for the first time to a probation penalty, this being a world precedent for future legal processes.

10 Initiative for the Integration of the Regional Infrastructure of South America.

5 van Noorloos

1 The data and analysis presented in this chapter are available in a much more extensive version in Van Noorloos (2012).

2 The phenomenon has also been termed lifestyle mobilities, lifestyle migration, amenity migration, international retirement migration, and second home development in the literature (see, among others, Williams and Hall 2000; MPI 2006; Gustafson 2008; Benson and O'Reilly 2009; Janoschka 2009; McIntyre 2009; Hoogendoorn and Visser 2010). By using the concept 'residential tourism', I locate my research in the debates on the implications of this phenomenon in local destinations, especially because I focus on a region in the global South.

3 See Van Noorloos (2012) for a detailed methodology.

4 By 2030 the US population over the age of sixty-five will total almost 71.5 million, meaning an increase of almost 80 per cent from 2010 (US Census Bureau projections).

5 A Gallup Poll in 2011 found that 53 per cent of US non-retired inhabitants do not think they will have enough money to live comfortably in retirement (Gallup 2011).

6 The law on the maritime–terrestrial zone (Law No. 6043, *Ley sobre la Zona Marítimo Terrestre* [ZMT], of 1977) establishes rules for the use and protection of the first 200 metres of coastal land: the first 50 metres are inalienable public land, and the remaining 150 metres are restricted zone–government property, where land concessions can be issued (five to twenty years renewable) and construction can be allowed under strict conditions. Concessions cannot be granted to foreigners who have lived for fewer than five years in Costa Rica, or to companies with more than half of their capital derived from foreign sources.

7 This is related to gaps in the law (e.g. the possibility of establishing *Sociedades Anónimas* or 'corporations', whereby foreign capital and multiple concessions held by the same person can be hidden), but it is also a result of the lack of adequate control by municipalities and the Costa Rica Tourism Board – and in some cases, the involvement of powerful political figures (Salazar 2010).

8 The Costa Rican government has created advantageous conditions for investment in large-scale tourism and real estate development in various ways, such as through infrastructure and direct involvement in investment deals (Van Noorloos 2011a, 2011b).

6 Boelens et al.

1 Research for this chapter was conducted within the framework of the international Justicia Hídrica/Water Justice Alliance (www.justiciahidrica.org) and the Netherlands Organization for Scientific Research (NWO), under its programmes

'Struggling for water security: social mobilization for the defence of water rights in Peru and Ecuador' and 'The transnationalization of local water battles. Water accumulation by agribusinesses in Peru and Ecuador and the politics of Corporate Social Responsibility'.

2 According to Falkenmark's indicator, availability below 1,700 cubic metres/ inhabitant/year is considered to be a situation of water stress (Falkenmark and Widstrand 1992).

3 See: www.ana.gob.pe/con%C3%B3 cenos/proyectos-vigentes/programa-de-formalizaci%C3%B3n-de-derechos-de-uso-de-agua.aspx.

4 In the last three years, PROFODUA has almost stopped operating, so the number of water licences for agricultural use grew only marginally, to 377,470. See: www.ana.gob.pe:8080/rada/wfrmCons DUA_xCD.aspx.

5 The irrigation module assured to buyers of this land is normally 10,000 cubic metres/hectare/year. This water security shows preference over water users in the 'older valleys', who are subject to potential rationing and prorating periods according to (random) water availability at the source.

6 Transitional Provision 27 of the Constitution, established by the Constitutional Assembly of Ecuador in 2008.

7 According to the National Irrigation Plan, the irrigated area is about 1.5 million hectares, i.e. about 20 per cent of total farming area.

8 For example, according to separate estimates made in 2012 by two Peruvian Congress members, each hectare under irrigation on the Peruvian coast has been subsidized by the government to the tune of an average of either US$7,000/hectare or US$15,000/hectare (*La Revista Agraria*, 137).

7 Susanti and Budidarsono

1 In the recent administrative structure, it covers North Sumatra, Riau and Riau archipelago provinces (Cribb 2010).

2 'The New Order' was a term coined by

the second Indonesian president, Suharto, to characterize his regime (1966–98).

3 The issuance of the Basic Forestry Law No. 5/1967 gave an exclusive position to the forestry sector to manage the state forest areas, which seemed to supersede the Basic Agrarian Law No. 5/1960 in terms of state forestland governance.

4 Law No. 4/1982 as by No. 23/1997, Government Regulation No. 28/1985, Law No. 5/1990, and Law No. 24/1992.

5 www.bloomberg.com/news/2013-04-03/asian-palm-oil-planters-head-to-west-africa.html (accessed July 2013).

8 Ty et al.

1 According to the land use classification system of the Land Law 2003, special-use land includes land used for construction, transportation, irrigation, public structures, commercial and non-agricultural production purposes, special-use water bodies (hydropower, irrigation reservoirs, waterways), cemeteries and religious use, and other non-agricultural land.

2 The non-agricultural land uses include resident land (rural and urban region) and special-use land (security land, land for infrastructure development and other public purposes, and others).

3 *Doi Moi* refers to the set of reforms implemented by the Vietnamese Communist Party since 1986. These reforms departed from the model of centralized economic planning by giving market mechanisms a greater role in the domestic economy.

4 According to the first land reform between 1953 and 1955, the 'poorest peasants' (*bần cố nông*) were allocated 4 *sào* of land; 'lower-middle peasants' (*trung nông dưới*)were given 4 *sào* 2 *thước*; while a 'middle peasant's' family (*trung nông trên*) was given 4 *sào* 12 *thước*. (1 *thước* = 24 square metres; 1 *sào* (in the North) = 15 *thước* = 360 square metres; 1 *mẫu* = 10 *sào* = 3,600 square metres).

5 Source: www.bbc.co.uk/vietnamese/vietnam/story/2007/07/070718_viet_protests.shtml (accessed July 2007).

6 See vietnamnet.vn/vn/chinh-tri/70551/thu-tuong--lam-hai-hoa--dung-de-them-khieu-kien-dat-dai.html (accessed 5 August 2012).

7 A large-scale hydropower dam is defined as a dam having a power generator greater than 100MW.

8 Land area is estimated on the basis of the website of the Vietnam Committee on Large Dams and Water Resources Development: www.vncold.vn/en.

9 This amounts to 1,360 euros; 1,000 Dong = 0.037 euro (March 2013).

9 McLinden Nuijen et al.

1 www.maff.gov.kh/en/ (accessed March 2012).

2 See also Khon Kean's letter to the Stock Exchange of Thailand: www.settrade.com/simsImg/news/2007/07043155.pdf.

3 A spirit forest is a restricted forest used by indigenous people for celebrating ritual ceremonies or for praying purposes. It may include dense forest, mountain, lake, river, etc.

4 To read the statement, see www.boycottbloodsugar.net/wp-content/uploads/2012/07/NHRC-Findings-on-Koh-Kong-25-July.pdf.

5 www.maff.gov.kh/ (accessed June 2012).

6 www.tpd.gov.kh/cambodiaproduct/index.php.

7 '#22 Chamroon Chinthammit', www.forbes.com/lists/2011/85/thailand-billionaires-11_Chamroon-Chinthammit_WG0B.html.

8 ASR company overview: investing.businessweek.com/research/stocks/private/snapshot.asp?privcapId=787462.

9 'American sugar refining completes purchase of Tate & Lyle Sugars', www.prnewswire.com/news-releases/american-sugar-refining-completes-purchase-of-tate-lyle-sugars-104075823.html.

10 'Domino Sugar parent completes acquisition', articles.baltimoresun.com/2010-09-30/business/bs-bz-domino-sugar-parent-acquisition 20100930_1_domino-sugar-american-sugar-refining-acquisition.

11 'Major Thai producer among businesses facing land-grab allegations in Cambodia's lucrative sugar industry', www.bangkokpost.com/print/255018/.

12 Nominal World Price of Sugar: www.sucre-ethique.org/Statistics-on-World-Sugar.html.

13 www.phnompenhpost.com/20120 62557006/National/hun-sen-grants-elcs. html.

14 www.maff.gov.kh/kh/ (accessed November 2012).

15 www.mlmupc.gov.kh/ (accessed July 2013).

16 www.hrw.org/news/2013/06/12/ cambodia-land-titling-campaign-open-abuse (accessed July 2013).

17 Ibid.

10 Nooteboom and Bakker

1 We thank Rosanne Rutten and Jofelle Tesorio for their valuable input and comments.

2 Most notably the *Journal of Peasant Studies*, which became a forerunner in publications from 2010 onwards on land grabs, green grabs and peasant protest.

3 Gulf Cooperation Council. The GCC is an economic and political union of the Arab States bordering the Persian Gulf and located on or near the Arabian Peninsula, namely Bahrain, Kuwait, Oman, Qatar, Saudi Arabia and the United Arab Emirates (see www. gcc-sg.org/eng/).

4 We focus only on announced deals which target food crops such as rice, maize and fruits. Excluded are investments in land for the production of biofuels (e.g. palm oil, jatropha) or for infrastructure and mining, as GCCs are not particularly interested in biofuels (Woertz 2013: 92).

5 Saudi officials recently stated, for instance, that they had prepared a list with twenty-one countries which they targeted for investment, but without disclosing details on the countries, projects and scope (Eckart Woertz, personal communication, 26 March 2011).

6 Exceptions are the work of Woertz (Woertz 2011, 2013), Fofack (2009) and Lippman (2010).

7 'Food: the big fright', Qatar Today, 23 February 2011.

8 Woertz and Shepherd, personal communication during a workshop in Davao City, Philippines, August 2009.

9 'Muslim nations seek closer ties in economic crisis', *The Irrawaddy*, 2 March 2009.

10 The Medium-Term Philippine Development Plan (MTPDP) for 2004–10, www.neda.gov.ph/ads/mtpdp/MTPDP 2004-2010/PDF/MTPDP2004-2010.html.

11 Eckart Woertz, Thomas Lippman et al., 'Food security in the Arabian Peninsula', Carnegie Endowment for International Peace, Washington, DC, 14 January 2010.

12 Theodora Tsentas, 'Land grabbing: the losers in the "win-win" situation', 16 November 2009, thisisdiversity.com/ contributor/Theodora-Tsentas/1371.

13 See, for instance, the history of the MIFEE (Merauke Integrated Food and Energy Estate), described well by Savitri (2010) and McCarthy et al. (2012).

14 Interview with East Kalimantan provincial government official, Samarinda, 11 June 2012.

15 Group discussion with agrarian policy specialists, Bogor, 2 March 2012.

16 Now called the Organization of Islamic Cooperation.

17 Examples are the Nader and Ibrahim S/O Hassan (NEH) and its Philippine partner, AMA Group Holdings Corp., and the Middle East-based Tabuk Agricultural Development Co. (TADCO) with AgriNurture of the Philippines (Montemayor 2011: 16).

18 'Kingdom, Philippines bound by strong ties', *Arab News*, 12 June 2010.

19 'In December 2008, the Philippines government made a proposal to the Qatar Investment Authority for an agricultural project involving 100,000 ha for the production of rice' (GRAIN 2012: 40).

20 Press release, Philippine National Statistical Coordination Board, 2008, www.nscb.gov.ph/pressreleases/2008/

PR-200803-SS2-02_pov.asp (accessed 7 September 2012).

21 'OFW remittances up 7.6 per cent to $1.48 billion in January', *Filipino Reporter*, 19 March 2011, www.filipinoreporter.us/business-and-finance/economy/692-ofw-remittances-up-76-to-148-billion-in-january.html.

22 See Foreign Investment Act (RA 7042, 1991, Amended by RA 8179, 1996).

23 Comprehensive Agrarian Reform Law (RA 6657); 'Arroyo signs law extending CARP', *Philippine Daily Inquirer*, 8 August 2009.

24 An example of a GCC deal that has met resistance is the US$500 million joint venture between Bahrain's Nader and Ibrahim S/O Hassan (NEH) and its Philippine counterpart AMA Holdings Corp. to plant rice, corn, sugar, pineapple and other vegetables on 10,000 hectares of leased land in Davao del Norte, Mindanao. (See, for instance, 'AMA Group, Bahraini partner to develop banana farms in Mindanao', *Manila Times*, 10 September 2010; 'KMP scores land lease denial', *Tempo*, 10 February 2012; 'House to probe AMA Group holdings on the $50-M farm deal', House of Representatives press release, 26 March 2012.)

25 The House Bill 6004 (Large-Scale Foreign Investment on Land Regulatory Act), proposed in Congress in March 2012, was still pending in July 2013.

26 Tonette Orejas, 'Aquino extends review of Angara's pet project', *Philippine Daily Inquirer*, 22 December 2012.

11 Ho and Hofman

1 This chapter is partly based on Hofman and Ho (2012) 'China's developmental outsourcing: a critical examination of the Chinese global "land grab discourse"', *Journal of Peasant Studies*, 39(1): 1–48. The authors thank the editor of the journal for granting permission to use part of the original article.

2 See also the ongoing discussion on the Voluntary Guidelines on Responsible Agriculture Investments (RAI) prepared by the FAO, together with IFAD, UNCTAD and the World Bank (Borras and Franco 2010a; Borras et al. 2012).

3 To date, research on China's foreign agricultural activities has primarily been geared towards Chinese projects in Africa in recent decades. For an overview, see Bräutigam (1998), Bräutigam and Tang (2009) and Yan and Sautman (2010). Other studies have zoomed in on resource extractive industries and other sectors; see, for instance, Alden (2005, 2007), Humphrey and Schmitz (2007), Wang (2007), Adem (2010) and Gu (2009, 2011).

4 See, for instance, the classical definition in the introduction of Nkrumah (1965).

5 The figures are based on a wide variety of references that were published in recent years, mainly since 2008. These include media publications and articles, NGO reports and information circulated by international agencies. Only three of the over ninety sources are scientific sources, and two of these three have been published in ISI-rated journals. Many of the sources are also available at the database farmlandgrab.org, hosted by the NGO GRAIN.

6 Yan and Sautman (2010) describe this as the shift from a 'socialist mode of production' to a 'capitalist mode of production', which in fact mirrors the gradual move in China's domestic situation at that time towards a more market-based economy (see also Bräutigam 1998).

7 Or 1 million hectares if the cancelled investment in the Philippines is not included.

8 One of the exceptions reported over this period is the land-based investment by the Chinese state through an opium cultivation replacement programme in Myanmar, Cambodia and Laos. Most of the private investments originate from adjacent Chinese provinces, particularly Yunnan province. Their investments and operations are initiated relatively independently from the Chinese government (Diana 2008; McCartan 2008; Shi 2008).

9 We refer to the 2008 Chinese milk scandal, in which several large Chinese

dairy producers, including San Lu, added melamine to milk products to mask a diluted concentration of milk. It caused severe health problems for primarily young children and resulted in the death of six infants.

10 The status of 'net importer' does not imply that export of food commodities does not take place. The policy changes initiated since 2000 have motivated Chinese farmers to change their cropping patterns to more profit-making produce. Both imports and exports have risen sharply since that time, further influenced by China's WTO accession in 2001. Of all food commodities concerned, soybean is one of the major crops steering foreign land investments and topped the list of agricultural produce imported to China in 2008 (FAOSTAT 2008; Lohmar et al. 2009). See also Ping (2008).

11 This figure also includes US$0.2 billion or 2.2 per cent of total investments for agricultural construction contracts (Scissors 2011: 3).

12 Conclusion

1 See also Behrman et al. (2011), who argue that earlier studies on gender impacts of colonization and commercialization are not taken into account in the debate on land grabbing, whereas they would be very useful for analysing the gender dimensions of the current global land rush.

2 The Transnational Institute's recent study 'Land concentration, land grabbing and people's struggles in Europe' (2013) is one of the very few exceptions.

3 www.fao.org.

4 In 2009/10, global and regional concerns regarding tenure governance were identified through an inclusive process of consultations. Regional consultations were held in Brazil, Burkina Faso, Ethiopia, Jordan, Namibia, Panama, Romania, the Russian Federation, Samoa and Vietnam. These regional consultations brought together almost 700 people, from 133 countries, representing the public and private sector, civil society and academia. The consultations showed a strong consensus for an international instrument to deal with the governance of land, fisheries, and forests (also in line with the Millennium Development Goals).

5 In Africa, but also in Asia and parts of Latin America, to the extent that people have access to land, this is often on the basis of informal and customary rights and without formal titles. Tenure security is often assumed to depend on having formal titles and transparent land administration systems.

About the contributors

Jumanne M. Abdallah is senior lecturer in the Department of Forest Economics at Sokoine University of Agriculture, Tanzania. He is currently lecturing to postgraduate and undergraduate students on natural resource economics, land use policies and legislation, entrepreneurship, project management, and research methods. Through engaging in various research, he has gained a broad experience in social and economic issues related to natural resources governance, laws, policies, guidelines and regulations.

Laurens Bakker is a lecturer and researcher at the Institute of Cultural Anthropology and Development Studies (CAOS) and at the Institute of Sociology of Law of Radboud University Nijmegen, and at the Department of Sociology and Anthropology of the University of Amsterdam. His research interests include land conflict and natural resource management, discourses of rights, and the dynamics of law and normativity as guiding principles for social and economic communities. He works on these issues in South-East Asia, notably Indonesia, and the Netherlands. His publications include articles and book chapters on tourism, land tenure and militias (Indonesia), transitional justice (the Philippines and Vietnam), and specialized and sharia-based courts of law (the Netherlands).

Rutgerd Boelens is associate professor in water management and social justice, Wageningen University, Netherlands, and visiting professor at the Catholic University of Peru. Currently he holds the chair in Territorial Studies with the Mexican Science Foundation and El Colegio San Luis, Potosi, Mexico. His research focuses on water rights, legal pluralism, cultural politics and political ecology in Latin America and Spain. He directed the Water Law and Indigenous Rights (WALIR) programme, is coordinator of the international Justicia Hídrica/Water Justice alliance, and directs the programmes 'Struggling for water security' and 'The transnationalization of local water struggles' of the Netherlands Organization for Scientific Research.

Suseno Budidarsono is a PhD student in international development studies at the Department of Human Geography and Planning, Faculty of Geosciences, Utrecht University, Netherlands. He is also a researcher at the World Agroforestry Centre (ICRAF). His research aims at an understanding of the environmental and ecological dimensions of agro-forestry and other land use systems and focuses on the linkages between land use systems and people. He holds an MSc degree in Rural and Regional Development Planning (1991) from the School of Environment, Resources and Development, Asian Institute of Technology, Bangkok, Thailand.

Linda Engström is a researcher at the Nordic Africa Institute in Uppsala, Sweden, and a PhD student at the Swedish University for Agricultural Sciences within the research project 'Large-scale land investments in Tanzania – impacts on smallholder land access and food security'. She holds an MSc in ecology from Uppsala University and has a background in animal, forestry and development research in, for example, Indonesia, Tanzania and Ethiopia. She has worked as adviser to the Swedish Development Agency (Sida) on environmental and social issues and has work experience with various Swedish and international NGOs.

Antonio Gaybor has been a professor at the Central University of Ecuador in Quito since 1982, and director of CAMAREN, a training institution on natural resources. He has written on subjects related to agrarian questions and natural resources, including water resources and irrigation issues in Ecuador and other parts of Latin America.

Lucia Goldfarb earned an MA in development studies with a minor in environment and development from the Institute of Social Studies in The Hague in 2006. In 2007/08 she joined the Transnational Institute as a Next Generation Scholar. Goldfarb regularly consults with TNI's Agrarian Justice team and is a founding member of the Dutch section of the Foodfirst Information and Action Network (FIAN-Netherlands), where she co-authored a report on agrofuels in Brazil in 2008. She is currently a PhD researcher in international development studies at the University of Utrecht.

Kjell Havnevik is senior researcher and professor at the Nordic Africa Institute, Uppsala, and the University of Agder (UiA), Norway. He has nearly four decades of experience in research and education at universities and research institutes in Norway, Tanzania and Sweden. He has published a number of books and articles on African development issues, with a special focus on rural development and natural resource management, including the co-editing of *African Engagements – Africa negotiating a multipolar world* (Brill, 2011) and *Biofuels, Land Grabbing and Food Security* (Zed Books, 2011).

Jan Hendriks graduated in 1982 with an MSc in agricultural sciences from Wageningen University, Netherlands. From 1983 to 1988 he was coordinator of a Small Communal Irrigation Programme in the Cuzco region (Peru). Subsequently he worked as water management adviser for the Netherlands Development Organization (SNV) in Peru. For several years he worked in the north of Chile, in charge of the rural component of an EU project. For the last decade, he has operated mainly as a private consultant on irrigation and water management in the Andean region (Peru, Bolivia, Chile, Ecuador).

Peter Ho is Chair Professor of Chinese Economy at the University of Delft and director of the European Research Council (ERC) project on Land Policy and Administration in China (RECOLAND). Ho has written extensively on institutions and property rights, sustainable and rural development, poverty and social inequality, and environmental policy and management in China. He has published widely in the leading SSCI/SCI-rated journals of development and environmental studies with impact factors ranging from 3.0 to 8.25. He has also published more than ten books, including books with Oxford University Press, Routledge and Blackwell.

Irna Hofman is a PhD researcher and research assistant at the Institute for Area Studies, Leiden University. She holds an MSc in environmental sciences from Wageningen University, Netherlands. Her specialities, work and interests are focused on agrarian and social change, rural and development sociology, and transition economies. Earlier research focused on agrarian reform in Uzbekistan, and her current PhD research focuses on the rural politics of Chinese agricultural land investments in Tajikistan.

Jacqueline M. Klopp is an associate research scholar at Columbia University. Previously, for many years she taught the politics of development at the School of International and Public Affairs at Columbia University, where she remains affiliated. Klopp has written extensively on Kenyan politics, including on violence, displacement and land, and is also a founder and board member of the Internal Displacement Policy and Advocacy Centre (IDPAC) based in Nakuru, Kenya. She received her BA from Harvard University and her PhD in political science from McGill University.

Odenda Lumumba is a leading public advocate-cum-activist on land and natural resource rights in Kenya and a founding member and national coordinator of the Kenya Land Alliance. He served as a commissioner on the Presidential Commission of Inquiry into Illegal and/or Irregular Allocation of Public Land in Kenya, from July 2003 to June 2004, and as a member of the Technical Committee on Land, Property, Natural Resources and Environment at the National Constitutional Conference from 2003 to March 2005. Mr Lumumba also led the Land Sector Non-State Actors Secretariat, which championed the adoption and endorsement of the National Land Policy in December 2009 and eventually the approval and promulgation of the Constitution of Kenya 2010, with a progressive 'Land and Environment' chapter. Mr Lumumba, who has also written extensively on land matters, holds a BA from Makerere University in Uganda and is currently enrolled for an MPhil in Land and Agrarian Studies at the Institute for Poverty, Land and Agrarian Studies (PLAAS), School of Government, University of the Western Cape.

Michelle McLinden Nuijen earned her master's degree in international sustainable development from Utrecht University in the Netherlands after conducting field research on development-induced displacement in Vietnam and Cambodia. As a lecturer and PhD fellow within the International Development Studies group of Utrecht University, McLinden Nuijen continues to research sustainability issues in South-East Asia and Africa related to international political economy, rural development, dispossession, climate change adaptation, and conflict, as well as corporate social responsibility. She also has a consultancy business, Nuijen Research.

Nguyen Quang Phuc has been a lecturer in the College of Economics (HCE) at Hue University, Vietnam, since 2002. Currently, he is doing a PhD in international development studies at Utrecht University, the Netherlands. His main research interests include sustainable rural development, rural–urban relations, urban expansion and peri-urban transformation, regional and local development, and land governance. He has been involved in various development projects funded by the World Bank, the government of Finland, the FAO and the Vietnamese government.

Gerben Nooteboom is a lecturer and researcher at the Department of Anthropology and Sociology at the University of Amsterdam, the Netherlands. He teaches courses on state and society, social science and Asia, and the anthropology of development. As a researcher, he has worked on issues of poverty and livelihood, social security, ethnic violence, and human adaptation to environmental change in Indonesia. Currently, he is coordinating (with Rosanne Rutten and Erwan Purwanto) a comparative research project (2011–15) on 'Transnational land deals in Indonesia and the Philippines: contested control of agricultural land and food crops'. This project is financed by the Netherlands Organization of Scientific Research (NWO/WOTRO).

Men Prachvuthy is a lecturer at the Department of Tourism, Royal University of Phnom Penh, and director of the Mekong Institute of Cambodia (MIC). Prachvuthy has sixteen years' experience in serving community development programmes and conducting research. He earned an MA in sustainable tourism development in 2003 from the Royal University of Phnom Penh in collaboration with the University of Technology, Sydney (UTS), Australia, and the University of Bologna, Italy. He has completed a number of research projects for international agencies and local government institutions. His research interests include tourism marketing, community-based ecotourism, pro-poor tourism and value chains, and land governance and livelihoods.

Lennart Salomonsson is professor at the Division of Rural Development,

Department of Urban and Rural Development at the Swedish University of Agricultural Sciences. His research focus is on interdisciplinary aspects of agro-ecology in the rural development context. He has an agronomy under-graduate background, a PhD in agricultural chemistry, an associate professor-ship in crop science, and since 1998 he has been working in interdisciplinary research networks on agro-ecology and rural development.

George Schoneveld is a scientist at the Centre for International Forestry Research, based in Nairobi, Kenya. He has a master's degree in international business economics from Maastricht University, a master's degree in inter-national development studies from Utrecht University, and a PhD in land governance also from Utrecht University. His work focuses on the dynamics of customary rights and access regimes, political economy and ecology of investment-led rural modernization, alternative agricultural business models, land use change dynamics linked to global commodity markets, and trans-national governance architectures.

Maru Shete is a PhD fellow at the Netherlands Academy for Land Governance for Equitable and Sustainable Development (LANDac), hosted by the African Studies Centre in Leiden, Netherlands. He is also a faculty member of St Mary's University College in Ethiopia with the rank of associate professor. He holds an MA degree in regional and local development studies from the Addis Ababa University in Ethiopia and a MSc degree in development and resource economics from the Norwegian University of Life Science in Norway. His main areas of research interest include poverty, food security, land tenure issues, impact studies and economic development in Africa.

Ari Susanti is a PhD researcher in international development studies at Utrecht University. She obtained her bachelor's degree in forestry from the Faculty of Forestry, Gadjah Mada University, Indonesia in 1999. She continued her studies at the International Institute of Geo-Information Science and Earth Observation (ITC), the Netherlands, and obtained her master's degree in geo-information science. She has been working for the Faculty of Forestry, Gadjah Mada University, since 1999. She is interested in multidisciplinary research related to forestry and natural resources management.

Pham Huu Ty is a lecturer at Hue University of Agriculture and Forestry, Viet-nam, on water and land resources management. He is also a PhD candidate in international development studies at Utrecht University. His research concerns the displacement and resettlement of affected communities as a consequence of hydropower dam construction in Vietnam. In particular, the research concentrates on land acquisition issues, livelihood impact, vulnerability and resilience of land losers, migration, and land accumulation.

Femke van Noorloos is a social science researcher with a broad interest and experience in international development, land issues, food security, sustainability, tourism, migration, climate change and responsible business. She finished her PhD on residential tourism and its implications for development at the International Development Studies group (Human Geography and Planning, Faculty of Geosciences, Utrecht University) in 2012, and she is currently working as a postdoc researcher in the same research group. In addition, she is a coordinator of LANDac, the IS-Academy on Land Governance for Equitable and Sustainable Development.

Guus (A. C. M.) van Westen is a human geographer with the International Development Studies section at Utrecht University, Faculty of Geosciences. His research focus is private sector development and local economic development, with a specific interest in the role of local institutions and in 'responsible business'. He is also the deputy chair of LANDac, the Netherlands Academy on Land Governance, a platform of Dutch organizations and their Southern partners interested in issues of investment and land rights in developing countries.

Bibliography

Achterhuis, H., R. Boelens and M. Zwarte-veen (2010) 'Water property relations and modern policy regimes: neoliberal utopia and the disempowerment of collective action', in R. Boelens, D. Getches and A. Guevara (eds), *Out of the Mainstream: Water Rights, Politics and Identity*, London and Washington DC: Earthscan, pp. 27–55.

ActionAid (2009) *Implications of Biofuels Production on Food Security in Tanzania*, Dar es Salaam: Action Aid.

Adem, S. (2010) 'The paradox of China's policy in Africa', *African and Asian Studies*, 9: 334–55.

ADHOC (2012) *The Report on Land and Housing Rights in 2011*, adhoc-cambodia.org/?p=1627.

AfDB (2012) *Executive Summary of the Environmental and Social Impact Assessment for Bagamoyo Sugar Project*, Tanzania: African Development Bank Group.

Africa Report (2011) 'Ethiopia injects US$4 billion into sugar factories', 21 December, www.theafricareport.com/index.php/news-analysis/ethiopia-injects-us$4-billion-into-sugar-factories-50177916.html.

Agazzi, I. (2010) 'AFRICA: "Everything but Arms deal doesn't benefit enough people"', www.ipsnewsnet/2010/07/africa-everything-but-arms-deal-doesnrsquot-benefit-enough-people/.

Agriculture and Rural Development (2004) 'Growing conflict and unrest in Indonesian forests. A summary paper', Vermont: Agriculture and Rural Development and USAID.

Alden, C. (2005) 'China in Africa', *Survival*, 47(3): 147–64.

— (2007) 'Emerging countries as new ODA players in LDCs: the case of China and Africa', *Gouvernance Mondiale*, 1(2007): 1–14.

Alden, C. and C. Alves (2008) 'History and identity in the construction of China's Africa Policy', *Review of African Political Economy*, 35(115): 43–58.

Alden, C. and C. R. Hughes (2009) 'Harmony and discord in China's Africa strategy: some implications for foreign policy', *China Quarterly*, 199: 563–84.

Alden, C. and D. Large (2011) 'China's exceptionalism and the challenges of delivering difference in Africa', *Journal of Contemporary China*, 20(68): 21–38.

Aledo, A. (2008) 'De la tierra al suelo: la transformación del paisaje y el Nuevo Turismo Residencial', *ARBOR Ciencia, Pensamiento y Cultura*, 729: 99–113.

Alves, A. C. (2006) 'Emerging postcolonial solidarities: China's new economic diplomacy towards Subsaharan Africa', Paper presented to the 16th Biennial Conference of the Asian Studies Association of Australia, Wollongong, 26–29 June.

— (2008) 'Chinese economic diplomacy in Africa: the Lusophone strategy', in C. Alden, D. Large and R. Soares de Oliveira (eds), *China Returns to Africa: A superpower and a continent embrace*, London: C. R. Hurst, pp. 69–81.

ANA (2009) *Política y Estrategia Nacional de Recursos Hídricos del Perú*, Lima: Autoridad Nacional del Agua.

Andersen, K. E., F. Thomberry and S. Sophorn (2007) 'Establishment of indigenous communities as legal entities, Cambodia – the development bylaws', Phnom Penh: Support to Indigenous People Project in Cambodia, ILO.

Andersson, K. (2006) 'Understanding decentralized forest governance: an application of the institutional analysis and development framework', *Sustainability: Science, Practice, and Policy*, 2(1): 20–35.

Anseeuw, W. (2012) Roundtable discussant, 'Roundtable on methodologies: identifying, counting and understanding land grabs', Second Conference on Global Land Grabbing, Cornell University, USA, 17–19 October.

Anseeuw, W., L. Alden Wily, L. Cotula and M. Taylor (2012) *Land Rights and the Rush for Land: Findings of the Global Commercial Pressures on Land Research Project*, Rome: International Land Coalition.

Anseeuw, W., M. Boche, T. Breu, M. Giger, J. Lay, P. Messerli and K. Nolte (2012) *Transnational Land Deals for Agriculture in the Global South. Analytical report based on the land matrix database*, Bern/Montpellier/Hamburg: Land Matrix Partnership (CDE, CIRAD, GIGA, GIZ, ILC).

Aranda, D. (2011) *Argentina originaria. Genocidios, saqueos y resistencia*, Buenos Aires: La Vaca.

Arroyo A. and R. Boelens (eds) (2013) *Aguas Robadas. Despojo Hídrico y Movilización Social*, Alianza Justicia Hídrica and Abyayala, Quito: Abyayala.

Ayonga, J., J. Klopp, R. Musyoka and P. Ngau (2010) 'Challenges in land governance in Nairobi's urban-rural fringes: dynamics and issues', Unpublished manuscript.

Badan Pusat Statistik Propinsi Riau (2011) *Riau dalam angka 2010*.

BAKOSURTANAL (2012a) 'Land reform in Indonesia'.

— (2012b) 'Tugas dan fungsi'.

Banerjee, A. K. (1997) 'Asia-Pacific forestry sector outlook study', Working Paper APFSOS/WP/21, Rome: FAO.

Báo Quân đội Nhân dân (2009) *Mỗi năm diện tích trồng lúa của Việt Nam bị thu hẹp 59.000ha*, www.baomoi.com/Home/DauTu-QuyHoach/www.qdnd.vn/Moi-nam-dien-tich-trong-lua-cua-Viet-Nam-bi-thu-hep-59000ha/3110840.epi.

BAPPENAS (2008) *Rencana Pembangunan Lima Tahun 1969–1974*.

— (2010) *Rencana Aksi Nasional Penurunan Gas Rumah Kaca*.

Barczewski, B. (2013) 'How well do environmental regulations work in Kenya? A case study of Thika Highway', Policy brief, Center for Sustainable Urban Development, Columbia University.

Barr, C., E. Wollenberg, G. Limberg, N. Anau, R. Iwan, I. M. Sudana and T. Djogo (2001) *The Impacts of Decentralization on Forest and Forest-dependent Communities in Kabupaten Malinau, East Kalimantan*, Center for International Forestry Research (CIFOR).

Barr, C., I. A. P. Resosudarmo, A. Dermawan, J. McCarthy, M. Moeliono and B. Setiono (2006) *Decentralization of Forest Administration in Indonesia, Implication for Forest Sustainability, Economic Development and Community Livelihood*, Bogor, Indonesia: Center for International Forestry Research (CIFOR).

Barrantes-Reynolds, M. P. (2010) 'Costa Rica – "no artificial ingredients": the "green" state's challenge in the management of the residential tourism sector in the coastal area', Unpublished MPhil thesis, St Antony's College, University of Oxford.

Barsky, O. and L. Fernández (2008) *Cambio técnico y transformaciones sociales en el agro extrapampeano*, Buenos Aires: Teseo.

Basiron, Y. (2002) 'Palm oil and its global supply and demand prospects', *Oil Palm Industry Economic Journal*, 2(1): 1–10.

Bauer, C. (1997) 'Bringing water markets down to earth. The political economy of water rights in Chile, 1976–95', *World Development*, 25(5): 639–56.

Bebbington, A. (1999) 'Capitals and capabilities. A framework for analyzing peasant viability, rural livelihoods, and poverty', *World Development*, 27(12): 2021–44.

Bebbington, A., D. Humphreys and J. Bury (2010) 'Federating and defending: water, territory and extraction in the

Andes', in R. Boelens, D. Getches and A. Guevara (eds), *Out of the Mainstream: Water Rights, Politics and Identity*, London and Washington DC: Earthscan, pp. 307–27.

Behrman, J., R. Meinzen-Dick and A. Quisumbing (2011) 'The gender implications of large-scale land deals', IFPRI Discussion Paper 01056, Washington, DC: International Food Policy Research Institute.

Benbrook, C. (2005) 'Rust, resistance, run-down soils and rising costs. Problems facing soy bean producers in Argentina', Technical Paper no. 8, Benbrook Consulting Services and Ag BioTech InfoNet, www.greenpeace.de/fileadmin/gpd/user_upload/themen/gentechnik/Benbrook-StudieEngl.pdf/, accessed 30 October 2011.

Benson, M. and K. O'Reilly (2009) 'Migration and the search for a better way of life: a critical exploration of lifestyle migration', *Sociological Review*, 57(4): 608–25.

Berg, M. S. van den, M. S. van Wijk and Pham Van Hoi (2003) 'The transformation of agriculture and rural life downstream of Hanoi', *Environment and Urbanization*, 15(1): 35–52.

Berge, J. van den (2011) 'Acumulación y la expropiación de los derechos de agua potable por parte de las empresas multinacionales', in R. Boelens, L. Cremers and M. Zwarteveen (eds), *Justicia Hídrica: Acumulación, Conflicto y Acción Social*, Lima: IEP, pp. 155–76.

Bergius, M. (2012) 'Large scale agro investments for biofuel production in Tanzania – impact on rural households', Master's thesis, Norway Institute of Development Studies, University of Agder.

Bishaw, B. (2001) 'Deforestation and land degradation in the Ethiopian highlands: a strategy for physical recovery', *Northeast African Studies*, 8(1): 7–25.

Bộ Xây dựng (1999) *Định hướng quy hoạch tổng thể phát triển đô thị Việt Nam đến năm 2020*, Hà Nội: Nhà xuất bản Xây dựng.

Boelens, R. (2009) 'The politics of disciplining water rights', *Development and Change*, 40(2): 307–31.

Boelens, R. and J. Vos (2012) 'The danger of naturalizing water policy concepts. Water productivity and efficiency discourses from field irrigation to virtual water trade', *Journal of Agricultural Water Management*, 108: 16–26.

Boelens, R. and M. Zwarteveen (2005) 'Prices and politics in Andean water reforms', *Development and Change*, 36(4): 735–58.

Boelens, R., R. Bustamante and T. Perreault (2010) 'Networking strategies and struggles for water control: from water wars to mobilization for day-to-day water rights defence', in R. Boelens, D. Getches and A. Guevara (eds), *Out of the Mainstream: Water Rights, Politics and Identity*, London and Washington, DC: Earthscan, pp. 281–306.

Boesen, J., B. Storgaard Madsen and T. Moody (1977) *Ujamaa: Socialism from above*, Uppsala: Scandinavian Insitute of African Studies.

Boreak, S. and Cambodia Development Resource Institute (2000) 'Land ownership, sales and concentration in Cambodia: a preliminary review of secondary data and primary data from four recent surveys', Working Paper 16, www.cdri.org.kh/webdata/download/wp/wp16e.pdf.

Borras, S., Jr, and J. Franco (2010a) 'From threat to opportunity? Problems with the idea of a "code of conduct" for land-grabbing', *Yale Human Rights and Development Law Journal*, 13: 507–23.

— (2010b) 'Towards a broader view of the politics of global land grab: rethinking land issues, reframing resistance', ICAS Working Paper Series No. 1.

— (2012) 'Global land grabbing and trajectories of agrarian change: a preliminary analysis', *Journal of Agrarian Change*, 12(1): 34–59.

Borras, S., Jr, R. Hall, I. Scoones, B. White and W. Wolford (2011) 'Towards a better understanding of global land grabbing: an editorial introduction', *Journal of Peasant Studies*, 38(2): 209–16.

Borras, S., Jr, J. Franco, S. Gomez, C. Kay and M. Spoor (2012) 'Land grabbing in Latin America and the Caribbean', *Journal of Peasant Studies*, 39(3/4): 845–72.

Brady, B. (2010) *The Cambodian Army: Open for Corporate Sponsors*, www.time.com/time/world/article/0,8599,1995298,00.html.

Brailovsky, A. E. and D. Fogelman (2004) *Memoria verde: historia ecológica de la Argentina*, Buenos Aires: Deva's.

Bräutigam, D. A. (1998) *Chinese Aid and African Development: Exporting Green Revolution*, New York: St Martin's Press.

Bräutigam, D. A. and X. Tang (2009) 'China's engagement in African agriculture: "down to the countryside"', *China Quarterly*, 199: 686–706.

Breslin, S. (2009) 'Understanding China's regional rise: interpretations, identities and implications', *International Affairs*, 85(4): 817–35.

Brockhaus, M., K. Obidzinski, A. Dermawan, Y. Laumonier and C. Luttrel (2012) 'An overview of forest and land allocation policies in Indonesia: is the current framework sufficient to meet the needs of REDD+?', *Forest Policy and Economics*, 18: 30–7.

Bryceson, D. F. and J. B. Jönsson (2010) 'Gold digging careers in rural East Africa: small-scale miners' livelihood choices', *World Development*, 38(3): 379–92.

Buckley, L. (2011) 'Eating bitter to taste sweet: an ethnographic sketch of a Chinese agriculture project in Senegal', Paper presented at the International Conference on Global Land Grabbing, Institute of Development Studies (IDS), Brighton, 6–8 April.

Budds, J. and L. Hinojosa (2012) 'Las industrias extractivas y los paisajes hídricos en transición en los países andinos: análisis de la gobernanza de recursos y formación de territorios en Perú', in E. Isch, R. Boelens and F. Peña (eds), *Agua, Injusticia y Conflictos*, Cuzco: CBC, pp. 45–61.

Budidarsono, S., A. Susanti and A. Zoomers (2013) 'Oil palm plantation in Indonesia: the implication for migration, settlement/resettlement, and local economics development', in Z. Fang (ed.), *Biofuels – Economy, Environment, and Sustainability*, Rijeka: InTech, pp. 173–92.

Bueno de Mesquita, M. (2011) 'Agua, concentración de recursos naturales y los conflictos en el Perú', in R. Boelens, L. Cremers and M. Zwarteveen (eds), *Justicia Hídrica: Acumulación, Conflicto y Acción Social*, Lima: IEP, pp. 179–94.

Bui Ngoc Thanh (2009) 'Việc làm cho hộ nông dân thiếu đất sản xuất – vấn đề và giải pháp', *Tạp chí cộng sản* [Communist Review], www.tapchicongsan.org.vn/Home/nong-nghiep-nong-thon/2009/1040/Viec-lam-cho-ho-nong-dan-thieu-dat-san-xuat-van.aspx.

Bui Van Hung (2004) 'Rural diversification: an essential path to sustainable development for Viet Nam', in M. Beresford and Tran Ngoc Angie (eds), *Reaching for the Dream: Challenges for Sustainable Development in Viet Nam*, Singapore: Institute of Southeast Asian Studies Press, pp. 183–215.

Burgers, P. and A. Susanti (2011) 'A new equation for oil palm', *International Institute for Asian Studies Newsletter*, 58: 22–3.

Burneo, Z. (2011) *El proceso de concentración de la tierra en el Perú*, Coalición Internacional para el Acceso a la Tierra/CIRAD/CEPES.

Bush, R., J. Bujra and G. Littlejohn (2011) 'The accumulation of dispossession', *Review of African Political Economy*, 38(128): 187–92.

Butler, R. A., L. P. Koh and J. Ghazoul (2009) 'REDD in the red: palm oil could undermine carbon payment schemes', *Conservation Letters*, 2: 67–73.

Butt, S. (2011) 'Foreign investment in Indonesia. The problem of legal uncertainty', in V. Bath and L. Nottage (eds), *Foreign Investment and Dispute Resolution Law and Practice in Asia*, London and New York: Routledge, pp. 112–34.

CAAI News Media (2009) 'KhonKaen plant set to go online in January', khmernz. blogspot.nl/2009/12/khon-kaen-plant-set-to-go-online-in.html.

Cabrera, J. and S. Sánchez (2009) *Marco legal y estructura institucional del desarrollo turístico e inmobiliario en la costa Pacífica de Costa Rica* [The impact of tourism-related development along Costa Rica's Pacific coast], Report for the Center for Responsible Travel, Washington, DC, and Stanford, CA: Center for Responsible Travel.

Callick, R. (2008) 'Chinese firms eye Aussie farmland', *The Australian*, 12 May.

Calvo-Alvarado, J., B. McLennan, A. Sánchez-Azofeifa and T. Garvin (2009) 'Deforestation and forest restoration in Guanacaste, Costa Rica: putting conservation policies in context', *Forest Ecology and Management*, 258: 931–40.

CAMAREN (2010) 'Análisis de las concesiones de riego', Report by CAMAREN, Quito.

Campbell, S. (2011) 'Revealed: the bitter taste of Cambodia's sugar boom', *The Ecologist*, www.theecologist.org/News/news_analysis/847972/revealed_the_bitter_taste_of_ cambodias_sugar_boom.html.

Cañada, E. (2010) *Turismo en Centroamérica: nuevo escenario de conflicto social*, Report for Informes en Contraste – Programa Turismo Responsable 1, April, Barcelona: Alba Sud.

— (2011) 'Costa Rica: comunidades costeras en lucha. Entrevista a Wilmar Matarrita', *Alba Sud – Opiniones en Desarrollo*, 12, June.

Cárdenas, A. (2012) 'La carrera hacia el fondo. Acumulación de agua subterránea por empresas agro-exportadoras en el Valle de Ica, Perú', Research report, Justicia Hídrica and Wageningen University, www.justiciahidrica.org.

Center for Advanced Study, Ministry of Land Management, Urban Planning and Construction – National Cadastral Commission Secretariat, World Bank and German Development Cooperation (2006) *Towards Institutional Justice? A Review of the Work of Cambodia's Cadastral Commission in Relation to Land Dispute Resolution*, siteresources.worldbank.org/INTJUSFORPOOR/Resources/TowardsInstitutionalJustice.pdf.

CEPAL (Comisión Económica para América Latina y el Caribe – UN) (2007) *Turismo y condiciones sociales en Centroamérica: las experiencias en Costa Rica y Nicaragua*, Santiago: CEPAL.

CGR (Contraloría General de la República de Costa Rica) (2007) *Memoria Anual 2007*, San José: CGR.

Chambers, R., A. Pacy and L. A. Thrupp (1989) *Farmer First: Farmer innovation and agricultural research*, London: Intermediate Technology Publications.

Chao, S. (2012) *Masyarakat Hutan: jumlahnya di seluruh dunia*.

Cheung, Y.-W. and X. Q. Suny (2009) 'Empirics of China's outward direct investment', *Pacific Economic Review*, 14(3): 312–41.

CHRAC (2009) *Losing Ground. Forced Evictions and Intimidation in Cambodia*, www.hrpcambodia.info/Video/Losing Ground.pdf.

Chu, J. (2011) 'Gender and "land grabbing" in sub-Saharan Africa: women's land rights and customary land tenure', *Development*, 54(1): 35–9.

Clough, M. (1998) *Mau Mau Memoirs*, Boulder, CO: Lynne Rienner.

CODE, Center for Development Consultation (2010) 'Study of the situation and effects of Thuong Kon Tum on socio-economic and environmental factors – the proposal of displacement and resettlement consultation for the Thuong Kon Tum hydropower dam', Hanoi: CODE.

Colchester, M., N. Jiwan, M. Sirait, A. Y. Firdaus, A. Surambo and H. Pane (2006) *Lahan yang dijanjikan: Minyak Sawit dan Pembebasan Tanah di Indonesia – Implikasi terhadap Masyarakat Lokal dan Masyarakat Adat*, Forest Peoples Programme, Perkumpulan Sawit Watch, HuMA and the World Agroforestry Centre.

Consultation Company on Electricity I

(2007) 'Result of livelihood surveys in the reservoirs of hydropower dam and resettlement planning for Lai Chau hydropower dam', Hanoi: Vietnam Electricity Cooperative.

Contreras-Hermosilla, A. and C. Fay (2005) *Strengthening Forest Management in Indonesia through Land Tenure Reform: Issues and framework for action*, Bogor, Indonesia: Forest Trends.

Coordinating Ministry for Economic Affairs of the Republic of Indonesia (2011) *Masterplan for Acceleration and Expansion of Indonesia Economic Development*, Jakarta: Coordinating Ministry for Economic Affairs, Republic of Indonesia.

Cotula, L. (2012) 'The international political economy of the global land rush. A critical appraisal of trends, scale, geography and drivers', *Journal of Peasant Studies*, 39(3/4): 649–80.

— (2013) *The Great African Land Grab? Agricultural Investments and the Global Food System*, London: Zed Books.

Cotula, L., S. Vermeulen, R. Leonard and J. Keeley (2009) *Land Grab or Development Opportunity? Agricultural investment and international land deals in Africa*, London/Rome: IIED/FAO/IFAD.

Coulson, A. (1982) *Tanzania: A political economy*, Oxford: Clarendon Press.

— (2013) *Tanzania: A political economy* (new and extended edn), Oxford: OUP.

Coulthart, A., Q. Nguyen and H. Sharpe (2006) *Urban Development in Vietnam: An Assessment and Recommendations for Improvement*, Washington, DC: World Bank.

Crewett, W. and B. Korf (2008) 'Ethiopia: reforming land tenure', *Review of African Political Economy*, 35(116): 203–20.

Cribb, R. (2000) *Historical Atlas of Indonesia*, London: NIAS/Turton Press.

— (2010) 'Administrative division in Dutch Sumatra 1873–1906. Map no.4.26', *Digital Atlas of Indonesian History*, Nordic Institute of Asian Studies (NIAS) of Copenhagen University, Copenhagen.

Cypher, J. and J. Dietz (2009) *The Process of Economic Development*, London and New York: Routledge.

d'Hooghe, I. (2010) 'The expansion of China's public diplomacy system', in J. Wang (ed.), *Soft Power in China: Public diplomacy through communication*, New York: Palgrave Macmillan, pp. 19–35.

Daniel, S. and A. Mittal (2009) *The Great Land Grab. Rush for World's Farmland Threatens Food Security for the Poor*, Oakland, CA: Oakland Institute.

Dararath, Y., N. Top and L. Vuthy (2011) *Rubber Plantation Development in Cambodia: At What Cost?*, Singapore: EEPSEA.

De Janvry, A. and E. Sadoulet (2002) 'Land reforms in Latin America: ten lessons toward a contemporary agenda'. World Bank's Latin American Land Policy Workshop, Pachuca, Mexico, 14 June.

De Schutter, O. (2011) 'How not to think of land-grabbing: three critiques of large-scale investments in farmland', *Journal of Peasant Studies*, 38(2): 249–79.

De Soto, H. (2000) *The Mystery of Capital: Why Capitalism Triumphs in the West and Fails Everywhere Else*, New York: Basic Books.

Deininger, K. (2003) *Land Policies for Growth and Poverty Reduction. A World Bank research report*, Oxford and Washington, DC: Oxford University Press and World Bank.

— (2011) 'Challenges posed by the new wave of farmland investment', *Journal of Peasant Studies*, 38(2): 217–48.

Deininger, K. and D. Byerlee (2011a) *Rising Global Interest in Farmland: Can it yield sustainable and equitable benefits?*, Washington, DC: World Bank.

— (2011b) *The Rise of Large Farms in Land Abundant Countries: Do They Have a Future?*, Washington, DC: World Bank.

Deloitte-Exeltur (Alianza para la Excelencia Turística) (2005) *Impactos sobre el entorno, la economía y el empleo de los distintos modelos de desarrollo turístico del litoral Mediterráneo Español, Baleares y Canarias – Resumen Ejecutivo*, Madrid: Exeltur.

Department of Co-operatives and Rural

Development (2007) 'Displacement and resettlement policies for national programs in the mountainous areas and ethnic minority groups – problems and needs to be addressed', Hanoi: Ministry of Agriculture and Rural Development.

Di Gregorio, M. (2011) 'Into the land rush: facing the urban transition in Hanoi's western suburbs', *International Development Planning Review*, 33(3): 294–319.

Diana, A. (2008) 'Navigating the way through the market: a first assessment of contract farming in Luang Namtha', Paper prepared for GTZ/RDMA (Germany), Vientiane.

Diaz-Chavez, R., S. Mutimba, H. Watson, S. Rodriguez-Sanchez and M. Nguer (2010) 'Mapping food and bioenergy in Africa', Report prepared on behalf of FARA (Forum for Agricultural Research in Africa).

Dietz, T., K. Havnevik, M. Kaag and T. Oestigaard (2011) *African Engagements. Africa Negotiating an Emerging Multipolar World*, Leiden: Brill.

Dinas Perkebunan Provinsi Riau (2011) *Statistik perkebunan provinsi Riau tahun 2010*, Pekanbaru: Pemerintah Provinsi Riau.

Dixon, R. (2013) 'Biofuel project in Kenya ignites land, environmental disputes', *Los Angeles Times*, 22 June, www.latimes.com/news/nation world/world/la-fg-kenya-biofuel-20130622,0,7594341,print.story.

Djatmiko, B. (2008) *Tanah dan hukum tanah. Tanah negara dan wewenang pemberian haknya*, Yogyakarta, Indonesia.

Domínguez, D. I. and P. Sabatino (2010) *Los señores de la soja. La agricultura transgénica en América Latina*, Buenos Aires: CLACSO, CICCUS.

Duy Huu (2008) 'Deal with the jobs for land losers', www.baomoi.com/Giai-quyet-viec-lam-cho-nong-dan-bi-thu-hoi-dat/147/3220550.epi.

Edelman, M. (1998) *La lógica del latifundio. Las grandes propiedades del noroeste de Costa Rica desde fines del siglo XIX* [The logic of the latifundio: the large estates of north-western Costa Rica since the late nineteenth century], San José: Editorial de la Universidad de Costa Rica.

— (2005) *Campesinos contra la globalización. Movimientos sociales rurales en Costa Rica* [Peasants against globalization: rural social movements in Costa Rica], San José: Editorial de la Universidad de Costa Rica.

— (2013) 'Messy hectares: questions about the epistemology of land grabbing data', *Journal of Peasant Studies*, 40(3): 485–501.

Edwards, R., D. Mulligan and L. Marelli (2010) 'Indirect land use change from increased biofuels demand, comparison of models and results for marginal biofuels production from different feedstock', EUR 24485 EN, Luxembourg: Publications Office of the European Union, Joint Research Centre of the European Commission and Institute for Energy.

Ellis, F. (1983) 'Agricultural marketing and peasant–state transfers in Tanzania', *Journal of Peasant Studies*, 10(4): 214–42.

Elson, D. (2011) *An Economic Case for Tenure Reform in Indonesia's Forests*, Washington, DC: Right and Resources Initiative.

European Commission (2006) *The European Sugar Sector. A Long Term Competitive Future*, aoatools.aua.gr/pilotec/files/bibliography/The%20European%20sugar%20sector- 025660 4928/The%20European%20sugar%20sector.pdf.

— (2012) *Trade, Generalised System of Preferences, Everything but Arms, the Origins*, ec.europa.eu/trade/wider-agenda/development/generalised-system-of-preferences/everything-but-arms/

European Commission Delegation of the EU to Cambodia (2011) 'The EU holds seminar on new rules for Cambodian exports', 1 August, eeas.europa.eu/delegations/cambodia/press_corner/all_news/news/2011/20110801_01_en.htm.

Fairhead, J., M. Leach and I. Scoones (2012) 'Green grabbing. A new appropriation of nature?', *Journal of Peasant Studies*, 39(2): 237–61.

Falkenmark, M. and C. Widstrand (1992) 'Population and water resources: a delicate balance', *Population Bulletin*, 47(3): 1–36.

FAO (2009a) 'How to feed the world in 2050', *World Summit of Food Security*, 2050: 1–3, www.fao.org/fileadmin/templates/wsfs/docs/expert_paper/How_to_Feed_the_World_in_2050.pdf.

— (2009b) 'Small-scale bioenergy initiatives: brief description and preliminary lessons on livelihood impacts from case studies in Asia, Latin America and Africa', Prepared for PISCES and FAO by Practical Action Consulting, Rome.

— (2009c) *State of the World's Forests 2009*, Rome: Food and Agriculture Organization of the United Nations.

— (2010a) *FAO at Work 2009–2010. Growing food for nine billion*, Rome: Food and Agriculture Organization of the United Nations.

— (2010b) *FAOSTAT*, Rome: Food and Agriculture Organization of the United Nations.

— (2011a) *FAO at Work 2010–2011. Women – key to food security*, Rome: Food and Agriculture Organization of the United Nations.

— (2011b) *Foreign Land Investments in Developing Countries: Contribution or Threat to Sustainable Development?*, Ministry for Rural Affairs and Swedish FAO Committee.

FDRE (Federal Democratic Republic of Ethiopia), and Ministry of Agriculture and Rural Development (2010a) *Ethiopia's Agriculture Sector Policy and Investment Framework: Ten Year Road Map (2010–2020)*, tinyurl.com/7bgzful.

— (2010b) *Agricultural Investment and Land Lease Implementation Directive*, Addis Ababa: Ministry of Agriculture and Rural Development.

— (2011a) *Ethiopia: A land of unique opportunity for agricultural investment*, Addis Ababa: Agricultural Investment Support Directorate.

— (2011b) *Agricultural Investment Areas*, Addis Ababa: Agricultural Investment Support Directorate.

— (2011c) *Social and Environmental Codes of Conduct*, Addis Ababa: Agricultural Investment Support Directorate.

FDRE (Federal Democratic Republic of Ethiopia), and Ministry of Mines and Energy (2007a) *The Biofuel Development and Utilization Strategy*, Addis Ababa: Ministry of Mines and Energy.

FDRE (Federal Democratic Republic of Ethiopia), and Ministry of Water Resources (2007b) *Arjo-Didessa Irrigation Project: Feasibility Study Report*, Addis Ababa: Ministry of Water Resources.

Fenn, J. and M. Raskino (2008) *Mastering the Hype Cycle: How to choose the right innovation at the right time*, Cambridge, MA: Harvard Business School Press.

Fernández Morillo, M. T. (2002) 'Dinámica de uso y tenencia de la tierra en la zona marítimo terrestre de dos áreas del Pacífico de Costa Rica', in E. Fürst and W. Hein (eds), *Turismo de larga distancia y desarrollo regional en Costa Rica*, San José: Asociación Departamento Ecuménico de Investigaciones, pp. 347–74.

FIAN (2010) *Land Grabbing in Kenya and Mozambique*, Heidelberg: FIAN.

Firman, T. (1997) 'Land conversion and urban development in the Northern Region of West Java, Indonesia', *Urban Studies*, 34(7): 1027–46.

Fischer, N. (2010) 'Strategic Asia: food versus fuel? Biofuel boom requires the govt to get policies right', *Jakarta Globe*, 9 January.

Fitzherbert, E. B., M. Struebig, A. Morel, F. Danielsen, C. A. Bruhl, P. F. Donald and B. Phalan (2008) 'How will oil palm expansion affect biodiversity?', *Trends in Ecology and Evolution*, 23(10): 538–45.

FOEI (2008) 'Los agrocombustibles en el banco interamericano de desarrollo: soluciones falsas para el cambio climático y la pobreza rural', www.foei.

org/es/resources/publicaciones/pdfs-por-ano/2008/los-agrocombustibles-en-el-banco-interamericano-de/view, accessed July 2012.

Fofack, H. (2009) 'Africa and Arab Gulf states divergent development paths and prospects for convergence', Report 5025, Washington, DC: World Bank.

Forest Climate Center (2009) Intervention by HE Dr Susilo Bambang Yudhoyono, President of the Republic of Indonesia, on climate change at the G020 leaders' summit, 25 September, Pittsburg, PA.

Freeman, D. (2008) 'China's outward investment: challenges and opportunities for the EU', BICCS Policy Paper, Brussels Institute of Contemporary China Studies.

Freeman, D., J. Holslag and S. Weil (2008) 'China's foreign farming policy: can land provide security?', BICCS Asia Paper 3(9), Brussels Institute of Contemporary China Studies.

Friis, C. and A. Reenberg (2010) 'Land grab in Africa: emerging land system drivers in a teleconnected world', GLP Report no. 1, Copenhagen: GLP-IPO.

Frost, S. (2004) 'Chinese outward direct investment in Southeast Asia: how big are the flows and what does it mean for the region?', Pacific Review, 17(3): 323–40.

Frost, S. and M. Ho (2005) '"Going out": the growth of Chinese foreign direct investment in Southeast Asia and its implications for corporate social responsibility', Corporate Social Responsibility and Environmental Management, 12: 157–67.

Furnivall, J. S. (1948) Colonial Policy and Practice: A comparative study of Burma and Netherlands India, Cambridge: Cambridge University Press.

Fürst, E. and K. Ruiz (2002) 'Turismo y empleo en Costa Rica: características nacionales y tendencias de desarrollo reciente', in E. Fürst and W. Hein (eds), Turismo de larga distancia y desarrollo regional en Costa Rica, San José: Asociación Departamento Ecuménico de Investigaciones, pp. 115–44.

GAIA Foundation, Biofuelwatch, African Biodiversity Network, Salva La Selva, Watch Indonesia and EconNexus (2008) Agrofuel and the Myth of Marginal Land, www.cbd.int/doc/biofuel/Econexus%20Briefing%20AgrofuelsMarginalMyth.pdf.

Gallup (2011) 'In U.S., 53% worry about having enough money in retirement', 25 April.

Gaybor, A. (2008) El despojo del agua y la necesidad de una transformación urgente, Quito: Foro de los Recursos Hídricos.

— (2011) 'Acumulación en el campo y despojo del agua en el Ecuador', in R. Boelens, L. Cremers and M. Zwarteveen (eds), Justicia Hídrica: Acumulación, Conflicto y Acción Social, Lima: IEP, pp. 195–208.

German, L., G. Schoneveld and E. Mwangi (2011) 'Contemporary processes of large-scale global governance: critical perspectives', Globalizations, 10(1): 1–23.

Global Witness (2012) Dealing with Disclosure. Improving transparency in decision-making over large-scale land acquisitions, allocations and investments, London: Global Witness/Oakland Institute/International Land Coalition.

Goldfarb, L. and A. Zoomers (2013) 'The drivers behind the rapid expansion of genetically modified soy production into the Chaco region of Argentina', INTECH, dx.doi.org/10.5772/53447.

González, M. C. and M. Román (2009) 'Expansión agrícola en áreas extrapampeanas de la Argentina. Una mirada desde los actores sociales', Cuadernos Desesarrollo Rural, 6(62): 99–120.

GRAIN (2008) SEIZED! The 2008 land grab for food and financial security, Briefing, October, www.grain.org/article/entries/93-seized-the-2008-landgrab-for food-and-financial-security.

— (2009) 'Twelve years of GM soy in Argentina – a disaster for people and the environment', Seedling, January, pp. 16–19.

— (2012) GRAIN/Land Grab Deals/Jan 2012/1, www.grain.org.

— (2013) 'Secando el continente africano: detrás de la acumulación de tierras está la acumulación del agua', in A. Arroyo and R. Boelens (eds), *Aguas Robadas*, Alianza Justicia Hídrica and Abyayala, Quito: Abyayala, pp. 27–42.

Grammaticas, D. (2011) 'Why China won't save the world', *BBC News Asia*, 2 November, www.bbc.co.uk/news/15550691.

Gray, D. D. (2009) 'China appropriates foreign and domestic land to build its rubber empire', *Agweek*, 12 January, www.farmlandgrab.org/post/view/2676.

Grevi, G. (2009) 'The interpolar world: a new scenario', EUISS Occasional Paper 79, Paris: EU Institute for Security Studies.

GSO (1996, 2001, 2010, 2011) *Statistical Yearbook of Vietnam*, Hanoi: Statistical Publishing House.

GTZ (2009) *Foreign Direct Investment (FDI) in Land in Cambodia*, www2.gtz.de/wbf/4tDx9kw63gma/gtz2010-0061en-foreign-direct-investment-cambodia.pdf.

Gu, J. (2009) 'China's private enterprises in Africa and the implications for African development', *European Journal of Development Research*, 21: 570–87.

— (2011) 'The last golden land? Chinese private companies go to Africa', IDS Working Paper 365, Brighton: Institute of Development Studies.

Guardian (2008) 'Biggest deals', 22 November, www.guardian.co.uk/environment/2008/nov/22/food-biofuels1?intcmp=239.

Guerrero, P. (2006) 'La importancia del Programa de Formalización de Derechos de Uso de Agua – PROFODUA – en la gestión integrada de los recursos hídricos', Paper presented to the Eighth National Congress of Users' Boards, Cajamarca, Peru.

Gustafson, P. (2008) 'Transnationalism in retirement migration. The case of North European retirees in Spain', *Ethnic and Racial Studies*, 31(3): 451–75.

Guzman, R. (2010) 'Global land grabbing – eroding food sovereignty', PANAP Pesticide Action Network Asia & The Pacific.

Hall, R. (2011) 'Land grabbing in Southern Africa: the many faces of the investor rush', *Review of African Political Economy*, 38(128): 193–214.

Hammond, L. (2008) 'Strategies of invisibilization: how Ethiopia's resettlement programme hides the poorest of the poor', *Journal of Refugee Studies*, 21(4): 517–36.

Han, S. S. and K. T. Vu (2008) 'Land acquisition in transitional Hanoi, Vietnam', *Urban Studies*, 45: 1097–117.

Harbeson, J. (1971) 'Land reform and politics in Kenya, 1954–70', *Journal of Modern African Studies*, 9(2): 231–51.

Harrison, P. (1987) *The Greening of Africa: Breaking through the battle for land and food*, London: Paladin.

Harvey, D. (2003) *The New Imperialism*, Oxford: Oxford University Press.

Havnevik, K. (1993) *Tanzania: The limits to development from above*, Uppsala: Nordic Africa Institute.

— (1995) 'Pressing land tenure issues in Tanzania in light of experiences from other sub-Saharan countries', *Forum for Development Studies*, 2: 267–85.

Havnevik, K. and H. Haaland (2011) 'Biofuel, land and environmental issues: the case of SEKAB's agrofuel plans in Tanzania', in P. B. Matondi, K. Havnevik and A. Beyene (eds), *Biofuels, Land Grabbing and Food Security in Africa*, London and New York: Zed Books, pp. 106–34.

Havnevik, K. and A. C. Isinika (eds) (2010) *Tanzania in Transition: From Nyerere to Mkapa*, Tanzania: Mkuki na Nyota Publishers Ltd in association with the Nordic Africa Institute and Sokoine University of Agriculture.

Hepworth, N., J. Postigo, B. Güemes and P. Kjell (2010) *Drop by Drop. Understanding the impacts of the UK's water footprint through a case study of Peruvian asparagus*, London: PROGRESSIO, CEPES and Water Witness International.

Hilhorst, T., J. Nelen and N. Traoré (2011) 'Agrarian change below the radar screen: rising farmland acquisitions by domestic investors in West Africa. Results from a survey in Benin, Burkina Faso and Niger', LANDac short-term research paper.

Ho, P. (2005) *Institutions in Transition: Land ownership, property rights and social conflict in China*, Oxford: Oxford University Press.

— (2009) 'Beyond development orthodoxy: Chinese lessons in pragmatism and institutional change', in P. van Lieshout (ed.), *Doing Good or Doing Better*, Wetenschappelijke Raad voor het Regeringsbeleid (WRR, Dutch Scientific Council for Government Policy), University of Amsterdam Press.

Ho Moong Commune People's Committee (2009) 'The situation of displacement and resettlement in the Pleikrong hydropower dam in Ho Moong Commune, Kon Tum Province', Ho Moong Commune People's Committee.

Hofman, I. (2013) 'Understanding forms of contention in the post-Soviet setting: rural responses to Chinese land investments in Tajikistan', LDPI Working Paper 35.

Holland, M. (2003) '20/20 vision? The EU's Cotonou Partnership Agreement', *Brown Journal of World Affairs*, 9(2), www.watsoninstitute.org/bjwa/archive/9.2/EU/Holland.pdf.

Hồng Minh (2005) 'Hà Nội giải quyết việc làm cho lao động khu vực chuyển đổi mục đích sử' dụng đâ't', *Lao động và Xã hội*, số 270.

Hoogendoorn, G. and G. Visser (2010) 'The role of second homes in local economic development in five small South African towns', *Development Southern Africa*, 27(4): 547–62.

Horta, L. (2008) 'The Zambezi valley: China's first agricultural colony?', Washington, DC: Center for Strategic & International Studies, csis.org/publication/zambezi-valley-chinas-first-agricultural-colony.

HRW (Human Rights Watch) (2012) *'Waiting for death': Forced Displacement and 'Villagization' in Ethiopia's Gambella Region*, New York: Human Rights Watch.

Hultman, N. E., E. B. Sulle, C. W. Ramig and S. Sykora-Bodie (2012) 'Biofuels investments in Tanzania: policy options for sustainable business models', *Journal of Environment and Development*, 21(3): 339–61.

Humphrey, J. and H. Schmitz (2007) 'China: its impact on the developing Asian economies', IDS Working Paper 295, Brighton: Institute of Development Studies.

Hunt, D. (1984) *The Impending Crisis in Kenya*, Hampshire: Gower.

IEA (2006) *World Energy Outlook 2006*, Paris: OECD/IEA.

IFC and World Bank (2012) *Doing Business in a More Transparent World*, Washington, DC: International Bank for Reconstruction and Development/World Bank.

Iliffe, J. (1967) 'The organization of the Maji Maji rebellion', *Journal of African History*, 8(3): 495–512.

— (1979) *A Modern History of Tanganyika*, Cambridge: Cambridge University Press.

INEC (Instituto Nacional de Estadísticas y Censos Costa Rica) (1997–2011) *Household Surveys*.

— (2000) *Census 2000*.

— (2002) *III Censo Nacional Agropecuario*, Quito.

— (2011) *Census 2011*.

INEI (Instituto Nacional de Estadística e Informática) (2012) Resultados Definitivos IV Censo Nacional Agropecuario 2012, Lima, Perú.

Institute of Architecture and Planning (2011) 'Economic zones in Vietnam', www.tinkinhte.com/cong-nghiep/khu-cong-nghiep-khu-kinh-te/toan-quoc-co-276-khu-cong-nghiep-va-khu-kinh-te.nd5-dt.135923.136147.html.

Institute of Development (2010) 'Displacement, resettlement, living stability and environmental and resources protection in hydropower dam projects', Research report, Hanoi: Institute of Development/CODE, Vietnam.

Institute of Strategy and Policy on Resources and Environment (2009) 'The status of resettlement programmes in the hydropower dams in Vietnam', Hanoi: Ministry of Natural Resources and Environment.

Isch, E., F. Peña and R. Boelens (eds) (2012) *Agua, Injusticia y Conflictos*, Cuzco: CBC.

Jamal, V. and K. Jansen (2000) 'Agrarian transition in Vietnam', *International Labour Organization Report*, 1: 1–34.

James, R. W. (1971) *Land Tenure and Policy in Tanzania*, Toronto: University of Toronto Press.

Janoschka, M. (2009) 'The contested spaces of lifestyle mobilities. Regime analysis as a tool to study political claims in Latin American retirement destinations', *Die Erde*, 14: 251–74.

Jelsma, I., K. Giller and T. Fairhurst (2009) *Smallholder Oil Palm Production System in Indonesia: Lessons from the NESP Ophir project*, Wageningen: Wageningen University.

Jiang, W. (2009) 'Fuelling the dragon: China's rise and its energy and resources extraction in Africa', *China Quarterly*, 199: 585–609.

Kaag, M., Y. Gaye and M. Kruis (2011) 'Land conflicts in Senegal revisited: continuities and emergent dynamics', in J. Abbink and M. de Bruijn, *Land, Law and Politics in Africa. Mediating Conflict and Reshaping the State*, Leiden: Brill Publishers, pp. 141–61.

— (2012) 'Accountability in land governance. A study into the stakes in Senegal', LANDac Research Report, Utrecht: IS Academy on Land Governance for Equitable and Sustainable Development.

Kaarhus, R., R. Haug, J. P. Hella and J. R. Makindara (2010) 'Agro-investment in Africa: impact on land and livelihoods in Mozambique and Tanzania', Noragric report no. 53, Department of International Environment and Development Studies, Norwegian University of Life Sciences, Oslo.

Kaimowitz, D., C. Vallejos, P. Pacheco, P. P. Balanza and R. Lopez (1998) 'Municipal governments and forest management in lowland Bolivia', *Journal of Environment and Development*, 7(1): 45–59.

Kamanga, K. C. (2008) *The Agrofuel Industry in Tanzania: A Critical Enquiry into Challenges and Opportunities*, Dar es Salaam: Land Rights Research and Resources Institute, Joint Oxfam Livelihood Initiative for Tanzania.

Kanogo, T. (1987) *Squatters and the Roots of Mau Mau*, London/Kenya/Ohio: James Currey/Heinemann, Kenya/Ohio University Press.

Kanyinga, K., O. Lumumba and K. S. Amanor (2008) 'The struggle for sustainable land management and democratic development in Kenya: a history of greed and grievance', in K. J. Amanor and S. Moyo (eds), *Land and Sustainable Development in Africa*, London: Zed Books, pp. 100–23.

Kaplinsky, R. and M. Morris (2009) 'Chinese FDI in sub-Saharan Africa: engaging with large dragons', *European Journal of Development Research*, 21(4): 551–69.

KARA (Kenya Alliance of Residents Associations) (2011) 'Research report on the involvement of the public in public procurement in Kenya's local authorities'.

Kay, S. and J. Franco (2012) *The Global Water Grab. A primer*, Amsterdam: TNI.

Kebede, B. (2011) 'Land deals in Ethiopia bring food self-sufficiency, and prosperity', *Guardian*, 4 April, www.guardian.co.uk/global-development/poverty-matters/2011/apr/04/ethiopia-land-deals-food-self-sufficiency.

Kerkvliet, B. J. T. (1995) 'Village–state relations in Vietnam: the effect of everyday politics on decollectivization', *Journal of Asian Studies*, 54(2): 396–418.

— (2006) 'Agricultural land in Vietnam: markets tempered by family, community and socialist practices', *Journal of Agrarian Change*, 6(3): 285–305.

Kingdom of Cambodia (2001) *Law on Land*, www.gocambodia.com/laws/data%20pdf/Law%20on%20Land/Law%20on%20Land,%202001%28EN%29.pdf.

— (2005) *Sub-Decree on Economic Land Concession*, www.opendevelopment cambodia.net/law/en/ANK-146-05-Concession-Land-E.pdf.

— (2009) *National Strategic Development Plan Update 2009–2013*, www.gafspfund. org/gafsp/sites/gafspfund.org/files/ Documents/Cambodia_6_of_16_ STRATEGY_National_Strategic_%20 Development_Plan. NSDP0.pdf.

Kituo cha Katiba (2002) 'Report of a fact-finding mission of the Kituo cha Katiba on the progress of the constitutional review exercise in Kenya', www.kituochakatiba.org/index2.php? option=com_docman&task=doc_ view&gid=29&Itemid=36.

Klopp, J. M. (2000) 'Pilfering the public: the problem of land grabbing in contemporary Kenya', *Africa Today*, 47(1): 7–26.

— (2001) '"Ethnic clashes" and winning elections: the case of Kenya's electoral despotism', *Canadian Journal of African Studies*, 35(2): 473–517.

— (2008) 'Remembering the Muoroto Uprising: slum demolitions, land and democratization in Kenya', *African Studies*, 67(3): 295–314.

KNCHR (2012) *29 Days of Terror in the Delta*, Nairobi: Kenya National Commission on Human Rights.

KNCHR and KLA (2006) *Unjust Enrichment: The Making of Land Grabbing Millionaires*, Nairobi: Kenya National Commission on Human Rights and the Kenya Land Alliance.

Koh, L. P. and J. Ghazoul (2010) 'Spatially explicit scenario analysis for reconciling agricultural expansion, forest protection, and carbon conservation in Indonesia', *Proceedings of the National Academy of Sciences*, 107(24): 11140–4.

Krishnan, J. and A. George (2012) 'Las tribus y los bosques, la gente pescadora y el río: un repensar de la justicia hídrica en Kerala, India', in E. Isch, R. Boelens and F. Peña (eds), *Agua, Injusticia y Conflictos*, Cuzco: CBC.

KSL Group (2003) *About Us*, www.kslgroup. com/aboutus.html.

— (2009) *About KSL*, www.kslsugar.com/ en/profile.

Kugelman, M. and S. L. Levenstein (2009) *Land Grab? The Race for the World's Farmland*, Washington, DC: Woodrow Wilson Center for Scholars Asia Program.

Kurlantzick, J. (2007) *Charm Offensive: How China's soft power is transforming the world*, New Haven, CT, and London: Yale University Press.

Kuroiwa, J. (2012) 'Recursos hídricos en el Perú: una visión estratégica', in *Diagnóstico del Agua en las Américas*, Mexico City: Red Interamericana de Academias de Ciencias/Foro Consultivo Científico y Tecnológico.

Labbé, D. and J. A. Boudreau (2011) 'Understanding the causes of urban fragmentation in Hanoi: the case of new urban areas', *International Development Planning Review*, 33(3): 273–91.

Labour News (2012) 'The job training for rural labors is not adequate and low efficiency', laodong.com.vn/Xa-hoi/ Dao-tao-nghe-cho-lao-dong-nong-thon-ket-qua-rat-thap/82650.bld.

Land and Housing Working Group (2009) *Land and Housing Rights in Cambodia Parallel Report 2009*, www2.ohchr. org/english/bodies/cescr/docs/ngos/ CHRE_Cambodia_CESCR42.pdf.

Land Law (1993) *Luật Đất Đai*, Hanoi: Nhà xuất bản Chính trị Quốc gia.

— (2003) *Luật Đất Đai*, Hanoi: Nhà xuất bản Chính trị Quốc gia.

Laruelle, M. and S. Peyrouse (2012) *The Chinese Question in Central Asia: Domestic order, social change and the Chinese factor*, New York: Columbia University Press.

Lavers, T. (2012) '"Land grab" as development strategy? The political economy of agricultural investment in Ethiopia', *Journal of Peasant Studies*, 39(1): 105–32.

Lê Du Phong (2007) *Thu nhập, đời sống, việc làm của người có đất bị thu hồi để xây dựng khu công nghiệp, khu đô thị, kết cấu hạ tầng kinh tế-xã hội và các công trình công cộng phục vụ lợi ích quốc* gia, Hanoi: Nhà xuất bản Chính trị Quốc gia.

Lee, C. K. (2009) 'Raw encounters: Chinese managers, African workers and the politics of casualization in Africa's Chinese enclaves', *China Quarterly*, 199: 647–66.

Leo, C. (1984) *Land and Class in Kenya*, Toronto: University of Toronto Press.

Leys, C. (1975) *Underdevelopment in Kenya*, Berkeley: University of California Press.

LHWG (Land and Housing Working Group) (2009) *Land and Housing Rights in Cambodia Parallel Report 2009*, www2.ohchr.org/english/bodies/cescr/ docs/ngos/CHRE_ Cambodia _CESCR 42.pdf.

Lippman, T. W. (2010) 'Saudi Arabia's quest for "food security"', *Middle East Policy*, 17(1): 90–8.

Locher, M. and E. Sulle (2013) 'Foreign land deals in Tanzania. An update and a critical view on the challenges of data (re)production', LDPI Working Paper 31, May.

Loehr, D. (2010) 'External costs as driving forces of land use changes', *Sustainability*, 2: 1035–54.

Lohmar, B., F. Gale, F. Tuan and J. Hansen (2009) 'China's ongoing agricultural modernization: challenges remain after 30 years of reform', Economic Information Bulletin no. 51, Economic Research Service, US Department of Agriculture.

Luttrell, C. (2001) 'Institutional change and natural resource use in coastal Vietnam', *GeoJournal*, 54: 529–40.

LYP Group Co. Ltd (n.d.) *Company Profile*, lypgroup.com/download/lyp-group-brochure.pdf.

Mabikke, S. (2011) 'Escalating land grabbing in post-conflict regions of northern Uganda: a need for strengthening good land governance in Acholi region', Unpublished paper.

MAGAP (2012) *Plan Nacional de Riego*, Quito.

Mahmoud, A. H. A. and M. A. El Sayed (2011) 'Development of sustainable urban green areas in Egyptian new cities: the case of El Sadat City',

Landscape and Urban Planning, 101(2): 157–70.

Mai Thành (2009) 'Về chuyển dịch cơ cấu lao động nông thôn sau thu hồi đất', *Tạp chí Cộng Sản*, 15(183).

Makutsa, P. (2010) *Land Grab in Kenya: Implications for Small-holder Farmers*, East African Farmers Federation.

Maliyamkono, T. L. and M. S. D. Bagachwa (1990) *The Second Economy in Tanzania*, London: James Currey.

Management Board of the Projects 747 and 472 (2009) 'The summary report of the living stability assistance for displaced people in the Hoa Binh hydropower dam', Hoa Binh: Management Board of the Projects 747 and 472.

Manji, A. (2012) 'The grabbed state: lawyers, politics and public land in Kenya', *Journal of Modern African Studies*, 50(3): 467–92.

— (forthcoming) 'The politics of land law reform in Kenya', *African Studies Review*.

Margulis, M. E., N. McKeon and S. M. Borras, Jr (2013) 'Land grabbing and global governance: critical perspectives', *Globalizations*, 10(1): 1–23.

Massay, G. E. and H. George (2013) *Biofuels in Tanzania: Small Scale Producers and Sustainable Environmental Management*, Dar es Salaam: Haki Ardhi (manuscript).

Matarrita, W. (2009) 'Comunicado del Frente Nacional de Comunidades Amenazadas por Políticas de Extinción', *El Pregón*, 8 May.

Matondi, P. B., K. Havnevik and A. Beyene (2011) *Biofuels, Land Grabbing and Food Security in Africa*, London and New York: Zed Books.

Mawdsley, E. (2012) *From Recipients to Donors. Emerging powers and the changing development landscape*, London and New York: Zed Books.

Mbelle, A., G. D. Mjema and A. A. L. Kilindo (eds) (2002) *The Nyerere Legacy and Economic Policy Making in Tanzania*, Dar es Salaam: Dar es Salaam University Press.

McAndrew, J. P. and O. Il (2009) 'Access

to natural resources: case studies of Cambodia hill tribes', in J. Perera (ed.), *Land and Cultural Survival: The Communal Land Rights of Indigenous Peoples in Asia*, Mandaluyong: ADB.

McCartan, B. (2008) 'China farms abroad', *Asia Sentinel*, 1 August, www.blcu.edu.cn/ielts/reading/Asia%20Sentinel%20-%20China%20Farms%20Abroad.htm.

McCarthy, J. F., J. A. C. Vel and S. Afiff (2012) 'Trajectories of land acquisition and enclosure: development schemes, virtual land grabs, and green acquisitions in Indonesia's outer islands', *Journal of Peasant Studies*, 39(2): 521–49.

McIntyre, N. (2009) 'Rethinking amenity migration. Integrating mobility, lifestyle and social-ecological systems', *Die Erde*, 140(3): 229–50.

McLinden Nuijen, M. (2012) '(In) the way of development. Industrial sugar production and dispossession in Sre Ambel District, SW Cambodia', Unpublished thesis, Utrecht University.

McVey, R. (1992) *South East Asian Capitalists*, Ithaca, NY: Cornell Southeast Asia Program.

McWatters, M. R. (2009) *Residential Tourism. (De)constructing paradise*, Bristol: Channel View.

Meek, C. K. (1949) *Land Law and Custom in the Colonies*, London: Oxford University Press.

Mehta, L., G. J. Veldwisch and J. Franco (2012) 'Introduction to the Special Issue: Water Grabbing? Focus on the (re)appropriation of finite water sources', *Water Alternatives*, 5(2): 193–207.

Meinzen-Dick, R. and H. Markelova (2009) 'Necessary nuance: towards a code of conduct in foreign land deals', in M. Kugelman and S. L. Levenstein (eds), *Land Grab? The race for the world's farmland*, Washington, DC: Woodrow Wilson International Center for Scholars, pp. 69–81.

MEM (2012) *First Draft National Liquid Biofuels Policy*, Dar es Salaam: Ministry of Energy and Minerals.

Men, P. (2011) 'Land acquisition by non-local actors and consequences for local development: impacts of economic land concessions on livelihoods of indigenous communities in northeastern provinces of Cambodia', Utrecht/Phnom Penh: LANDac/Royal University of Phnom Penh.

Ministry of Agriculture of the Republic of Indonesia (2012) *Agricultural Statistics Database*, Jakarta: Ministry of Agriculture of the Republic of Indonesia.

Ministry of Forestry of the Republic of Indonesia (2002) *Forestry Statistics of Indonesia 2001*, Jakarta: Ministry of Forestry of the Republic of Indonesia.

— (2007) *Informasi umum kehutanan 2002*, Jakarta: Ministry of Forestry of the Republic of Indonesia.

— (2008a) *Forestry Statistics of Indonesia 2007*, Jakarta: Ministry of Forestry of the Republic of Indonesia.

— (2008b) *IFCA 2007 Consolidation Report: Reducing Emissions from Deforestation and Forest Degradation in Indonesia*, Indonesia: FORDA Indonesia.

— (2008c) *Statistik Kehutanan Indonesia*, Jakarta: Ministry of Forestry of the Republic of Indonesia.

— (2009) *Rencana Kehutanan Tingkat Nasional 2010–2029*, Jakarta: Ministry of Forestry of the Republic of Indonesia.

— (2011) *Forestry Statistics of Indonesia 2010*, Jakarta: Ministry of Forestry of the Republic of Indonesia.

Ministry of Industry and Trade (2007) *The National Power Development Plan in the Period 2006–2015, Perspective up to 2025*, Hanoi: Ministry of Industry and Trade.

Mitchell, D. (2003) *Sugar Policies: Opportunities for Change*, Washington, DC: World Bank.

Mkenda, A. M., J. K. Mduma and W. W. Ngasamiaka (2011) *Fuel Taxation and Income Distribution in Tanzania, Dar es Salaam*, Department of Economics, University of Dar es Salaam.

Montemayor, R. (2011) *Overseas Farmland Investments in Selected Asian Countries*, Quezon City, Philippines.

Morales, L. and L. Pratt (2010) 'Analysis of the Daniel Oduber Quirós International Airport, Liberia, Guanacaste', Report for Center for Responsible Travel, in *The Impact of Tourism Related Development along Costa Rica's Pacific Coast*, Washington, DC and Stanford, CA: Center for Responsible Travel.

Mousseau, F. and A. Mittal (2011) *Understanding Land Investment Deals in Africa. Country report: Tanzania*, Oakland, CA: Oakland Institute.

MPI (Migration Policy Institute) (2006) *America's Emigrants. US retirement migration to Mexico and Panama*, Washington, DC: MPI.

Muhtadi, B. (2012) *Dilema PKS. Suara dan Syariah*, Jakarta: KPG (Kepustakaan Populer Gramedia).

Mundia, C. N. and M. Aniya (2006) 'Dynamics of landuse/cover changes and degradation of Nairobi City, Kenya', *Land Degradation and Development*, 17: 97–108.

Murray Li, T. (2011) 'Centering labor in the land grab debate', *Journal of Peasant Studies*, 38(2): 281–98.

Musyoka, R. (2004) 'Informal land delivery processes in Eldoret, Kenya', Policy Brief 3, International Development Department, University of Birmingham.

Nelson, F., E. Sulle and E. Lekaita (2012) 'Land grabbing and political transformation in Tanzania', Global Land Grabbing II Conference, Cornell University, Ithaca, NY.

Neraca.co.id. (2012) *Investasi asing di kebun sawit kebablasan*, Jakarta: Harian Ekonomi Neraca, 23 April.

Nghị Định số 69/2009/NĐ-CP (của Thủ Tướng Chính phủ) *về bổ sung quy hoạch sử dụng đất, giá đất, thu hồi đất, bồi thường, hỗ trợ và tái định cư*, Ngày 13 tháng 8 năm 2009.

Ngo, S. and S. Chan (2010) 'Does large-scale agricultural investment benefit the poor?', Research Report 2, Phnom Penh: CEA.

NGO Forum (2010a) *The Rights of Indigenous People in Cambodia*, UN Committee on the Elimination of Racial Discrimination, 76th Session, Phnom Penh: Indigenous People NGO Network.

— (2010b) *Statistical Analysis on Land Dispute Occurring in Cambodia 2009*, Phnom Penh: Land Information Centre, NGO Forum.

Ngo Tho Hung (2010) *Urban Air Quality Modeling and Management in Hanoi, Vietnam*, Aarhus: Aarhus University.

Ngo Viet Hung (2007) 'The changes of land use plan and impacts to the poor in Vietnam rural areas', Paper submitted to the international conference on Sustainable Architectural Design and Urban Planning, Hanoi Architectural University, Vietnam.

Ngotho, A. (2012) 'Researchers break the Jatropha myth', *The Star*, www.the-star.co.ke/news/article-97630/researchers-break-jatropha-myth.

Nguyen Cong Quan (2011) 'Lessons learnt for addressing the problems of resettlement in the Hoa Binh hydropower dam construction', Conference proceedings of *Resettlement in the Hydopower Dam Construction: do people have a better life?*, Hanoi, pp. 72–85.

Nguyen Van Suu (2009) 'Agricultural land conversion and its effects on farmers in contemporary Vietnam', *Focaal – European Journal of Anthropology*, 54: 106–13.

NIAAP (Institute of Agriculture Planning and Design) (2008) *The Master Planning of Resettlement in Ban Chat Hydropower Dam*, Hanoi: Vietnam Electricity Co-operation.

Nkrumah, K. (1965) *Neo-Colonialism: The Last Stage of Imperialism*, London: Thomas Nelson Ltd.

Nooteboom, G. and M. Rutten (2012) 'Magic bullets in development. Assumptions, teleology and popularity of three solutions to end poverty', in L. Botes, R. Jongeneel and S. Strijbos, *Small Entrepreneurial Development, Technology, Economy and Ethics*, Rotterdam and Bloemfontein: IIDE, pp. 103–20.

North Energy (2011) 'Lifecycle assessment

of refined vegetable oil and biodiesel from jatropha grown in Dakatcha woodlands of Kenya', www.rspb.org.uk.

NTS (2010) *NTS Alert 1: 'Land Grabbing': The Global Search for Food Security in Southeast Asia*, vol. 1, Singapore: Consortium of Non-Traditional Security Studies in Asia.

Nunow, A. A. (2013) 'Land deals and the changing political economy of livelihoods in the Tana River Delta, Kenya', in A. Catley, J. Lind and I. Scoones, *Pastoralism and Development in Africa: Dynamic Change at the Margins*, London: Earthscan/Routledge, pp. 154–63.

Nurjana, I. N. (2007) 'Sejarah hukum pengelolaan hutan di Indonesia', *Jurisprudence*, 2(1): 35–55.

Nuy, B. (2010) *Reviews on the Process and Activity Plan for Collective Land Titling of Indigenous Communities in RatanakKiri and MondulKiri Province*, Phnom Penh: MRD.

Nyberg, J. (n.d.) 'Sugar. International market profile', Background paper for the Competitive Commercial Agriculture in Sub-Saharan Africa (CCAA) Study, site resources.worldbank.org/INTAFRICA/Resources/257994-1215457178567/Sugar-Profile.pdf.

Nyerere, J. (1962) *Ujamaa: The Basis for African Socialism*, TANU pamphlet, Dar es Salaam.

— (1966) 'Socialism and rural development', in J. Nyerere, *Ujamaa: Essays on Socialism*, Dar es Salaam, pp. 106–44.

Oakland Institute (2011) *Understanding Land Investment Deals in Africa*, media. oaklandinstitute.org/understanding-land-investment-deals-africa-ethiopia.

Obidzinski, K. and C. Barr (2003) *The Effect of Decentralization on Forest and Forest Industries in Berau District, East Kalimantan*, Center for International Forestry Research (CIFOR).

OECD (Organisation for Economic Co-operation and Development) (2007) *Sugar Policy Reform in the European Union and in World Sugar Markets*, www.keepeek.com/ Digital-Asset-Management/oecd/agriculture-and-food/sugar-policy-reform-in-the-european-union-and-in-world-sugar-markets_9789264040212-en.

OECD and FAO (2011) *OECD-FAO Agricultural Outlook 2011–2020*, www.agri-outlook.org/dataoecd/2/37/48184295.pdf.

Okoth-Ogendo, H. W. O. (1991) *Tenants of the Crown: The evolution of agrarian law and institutions in Kenya*, Nairobi: ACTS Press.

Onoma, A. (2008) 'The use of land to generate political support', *Africa Development*, 33(3): 147–55.

Onyango, P. (2012) 'Revealed: mad rush to grab public land in city', *County Weekly*, 19–25 November, pp. 14–15.

Oré, M. T. (2011) 'Las luchas por el agua en el desierto Iqueño: el agua subterránea y la reconcentración de tierras y agua', in R. Boelens, L. Cremers and M. Zwarteveen (eds), *Justicia Hídrica: Acumulación, Conflicto y Acción Social*, Lima: IEP, pp. 423–34

ORGUT Consulting AB (2008) *Preliminary Environmental and Social Impact Analysis (ESIA) of BioEthanol Production from Sugar Cane Production on the former Razaba Ranch, Bagamoyo District*, Stockholm: ORGUT Consulting.

Oxfam (2011) 'Land and power: the growing scandal around the new wave of investments in land', Oxfam Briefing Paper 151, www.oxfam.org/sites/www.oxfam.org/files/bp151-land-power-rights-acquisitions-220911-en.pdf.

Oxfam International (2011) *Growing a Better Future. Food justice in a resource-constrained world*, www.oxfam.org/grow.

Oya, C. (2012) Roundtable discussant, 'Roundtable on methodologies: identifying, counting and understanding land grabs', Second Conference on Global Land Grabbing, Cornell University, 17–19 October.

Pantuliano, S. and M. Wekesa (2008) *Improving Drought Response in Pastoral Areas of Ethiopia, Somali and Afar Regions and Borena Zone of Oromiya Region*, London: Overseas Development Institute.

Pearce, F. (2012) *The Land Grabbers: The New Fight over Who Owns the Earth*, Boston, MA: Beacon Press.

Pedersen, R. H. (2012) 'Decoupled implementation of new wave land reforms: decentralisation and local governance of land in Tanzania', *Journal of Development Studies*, 48(2): 268–81.

Peluso, N. and C. Lund (2011) 'New frontiers of land control: introduction', *Journal of Peasant Studies*, 38(4): 667–81.

Peña, F. (2011) 'Acumulación de derechos de agua en México: el poder de las élites', in R. Boelens, L. Cremers and M. Zwarteveen (eds), *Justicia Hídrica: Acumulación, Conflicto y Acción Social*, Lima: IEP, pp. 209–24.

Pengue, W. A. (2009) 'Bioinvasiones, agricultura industrial y transformaciones ambientales', *Fronteras*, Año 8, pp. 1–6.

Perreault, T., S. Wraight and M. Perreault (2011) *The Social Life of Water. Histories and geographies of environmental injustice in the Onondaga Lake watershed*, Justicia Hídrica Research Document, Onondaga Environmental Institute and Syracuse University, NY, www.justiciahidrica.org.

Phan Xuan Nam et al. (1997) 'Rural development in Viet Nam: the search for sustainable livelihoods', *Vietnam's Socio-economic Development: A social science review*, pp. 17–40.

— (2000) 'Rural development in Viet Nam: the search for sustainable livelihoods', www.idrc.ca/en/ev-33170-201-1-.

Pike, A. and J. Pollard (2010) 'Economic geographies of financialization', *Economic Geography*, 86(1): 29–51.

Ping, L. (2008) 'Hopes and strains in China's oversea farming plan', *Economic Observer Online*, 3 July, www.eeo.com.cn/ens/Industry/2008/07/03/105213.html.

Ploeg, J. D. van der (2008) *The New Peasantries. Struggles for autonomy and sustainability in an era of empire and globalisation*, London: Earthscan.

Polack, E., L. Cotula and M. Côte (2013) *Accountability in Africa's Land Rush. What Role for Legal Empowerment?*, London: IIED.

Potter, L. and S. Badcock (2001) 'The effects of Indonesia's decentralization on forest and estate crops in Riau Province: case studies of the original district of Kampar and Indragiri Hulu', CIFOR reports on decentralization and forest in Indonesia, Bogor, Indonesia: Center for International Forestry Research.

Power, M. and G. Mohan (2010) 'Towards a critical geopolitics of China's engagement with African development', *Geopolitics*, 15(3): 462–95.

Powers, D. (2012) 'Notes on hype', *International Journal of Communication*, 6: 857–73.

Programa Estado de la Nación (2000) 'Capítulo 6. Los desafíos de la Región Chorotega', in Programa Estado de la Nación, *Informe Estado de la Nación en desarrollo humano sostenible 6*, San José: Programa Estado de la Nación, pp. 307–60.

— (2007) 'Aporte especial: Diversidad de destinos y desafíos del turismo en Costa Rica: los casos de Tamarindo y La Fortuna', in Programa Estado de la Nación, *Informe Estado de la Nación en desarrollo humano sostenible 13*, San José: Programa Estado de la Nación, pp. 193–224.

— (2010) *Informe Estado de la Nación en desarrollo humano sostenible 16*, San José: Programa Estado de la Nación.

Ramírez Cover, A. (2008) 'Conflictos socioambientales y recursos hídricos en Guanacaste; una descripción desde el cambio en el estilo de desarrollo (1997–2006)', *Anuario de Estudios Centroamericanos*, 33(3): 359–85.

Regt, M. de and A. Moors (2008) 'Migrant domestic workers in the Middle East', in M. Schrover, J. van der Leun, L. Lucassen and C. Quispel (eds), *Illegal Migration and Gender in a Global and Historical Perspective*, Amsterdam: IMISCOE.

Reilly, D. (2010) 'Challenges ahead for the GCC', *Arabian Business*, 2 July, m.arabianbusiness.com/challenges-ahead-for-gcc-303911.html.

Rendón, E. (2009) 'Exportaciones agrarias y gestión sostenible del agua en la Costa Peruana: el caso del valle de Ica', *Cuadernos de Investigación de la Escuela de Postgrado de la UPC*, 3(8), Lima.

Republic of Kenya (2002) *Report of the Commission of Inquiry into the Land Law System of Kenya (Njonjo Commission)*, Nairobi: Government Printer.

— (2004) *Report of the Commission of Inquiry into the Illegal/Irregular Allocation of Public Land (Ndung'u Commission)*, Nairobi: Government Printer.

— (2009) *Sessional Paper No. 3 of 2009 on National Land Policy*, Nairobi: Ministry of Lands.

— (2010) *The Constitution of Kenya*, Nairobi: Kenya Law Reports.

Resosudarmo, I. A. P. (2004) 'Closer to people and trees. Will decentralization work for the people and the forest of Indonesia?', *European Journal of Development Research*, 16(1): 104–24.

RevealEstate (2009) *The 2009 Annual Central America International Real Estate PriceRank*, Blog post, 16 October.

Revista Agraria (2011) 'La multiplicación del minifundio', *Revista Agraria*, 126, February, Lima: CEPES.

— (2011b) 'Fernando Eguren: Límites a la propiedad: importante cambio de política', *Revista Agraria*, 133, September, Lima: CEPES.

— (2012a) 'Fernando Eguren: El debate sobre los límites a la propiedad', *Revista Agraria*, 136, January, Lima: CEPES.

— (2012b) '¿Por qué el Estado subsidia a los latifundios?', *Revista Agraria*, 137, February, Lima: CEPES.

— (2012c) 'Beatriz Salazar: El secreto del boom del espárrago: la sobre-explotación del agua', *Revista Agraria*, 139, April, Lima: CEPES.

Roa, A. T. and B. Duarte (2013) 'Desarrollo hidroeléctrico, despojo y transformación territorial. El caso de Hidrosogamoso, Santander, Colombia', in A. Arroyo and R. Boelens (eds), *Aguas Robadas*, Quito: Alianza Justicia Hídrica and Abyayala, pp. 313–33.

Robin, M. M. (2010) *The World According to Monsanto. Pollution, corruption and the control of the world's food supply*, New York: New Press.

Román, M. (2009) *Dinámica del mercado inmobiliario en la costa pacífica de Costa Rica* [The impact of tourism-related development along Costa Rica's Pacific coast], Washington, DC, and Stanford, CA: Center for Responsible Travel.

Rubinstein, C. (2009) 'China's eye on African agriculture', *Asia Times Online*, 2 October, www.atimes.com/atimes/China_Business/KJ02Cb01.html.

Rugasira, A. (2103) *A Good African Story: How a Small Company Built a Global Coffee Brand*, London: Random House.

Salas Roiz, A. (2010) 'Polo Turístico Golfo de Papagayo, Guanacaste, Costa Rica. Análisis del Polo Turístico Golfo de Papagayo como un modelo único gubernamental de concesión turistica', Report for Center for Responsible Travel, in *The Impact of Tourism Related Development along Costa Rica's Pacific Coast*, Washington, DC and Stanford, CA: Center for Responsible Travel.

Salazar, C. (2010) 'Fiscalía Ambiental ordenó paralizar obras en proyecto turístico de Guanacaste', *El País*, 30 October.

Salerno, T. (2010) 'Land deals, joint investments and peasants in Mindanao, Philippines', Research paper, Institute of Social Studies, The Hague.

Sàn giao dịch bất động sản An Biên (2011) *Việt Nam có bao nhiêu khu đô thị đạt tiêu chuẩn kiểu mẫu?*, www.nhadatanbien.com/default.aspx?id=2803andpageid=newsdt.

Sánchez, G. (2006) *Patagonia vendida*, Buenos Aires: Marea.

Sassen, S. (2005) 'When national territory is home to the global. Old borders to new borderings', *New Political Economy*, 10(4): 523–36.

Sastrosumarto, S., A. Setyarso, T. Suhartati and A. Sulistyowati (2007) *Sinkronisasi perencanaan pembangunan kehutanan untuk kehidupan yang lebih baik dan lestari*, Jakarta: Ministry of Forestry of the Republic of Indonesia.

Saudi Economic Survey (2010) 'Indonesia seeks Saudi Arabian investments in agricultural projects', 23 June.

Savitri, L. A. (2010) 'Merauke Integrated Food and Energy Estate (MIFEE): a neoliberal development scenario with a pro-poor language', Workshop on Agro-Investments in Land and Food Production in Indonesia and the Philippines, Davao, Mindanao: Sayogyo Institute Bogor, Indonesia.

Schoneveld, G. C. (2011) 'Anatomy of large-scale farmland acquisition in sub-Saharan Africa', Working Paper 85, Bogor: Center for International Forestry Research.

— (2013) *The Governance of Large-scale Farmland Investments in Sub-Saharan Africa. A Comparative Analysis of the Challenges for Sustainability*, PhD thesis, International Development Studies, Utrecht University, Delft: Eburon.

Schönweger, O. et al. (2012) *Concessions and Leases in the Lao PDR: Taking stock of land investments*, Bern: Geographica Bernensia, www.cde.unibe.ch/v1/CDE/pdf/Concessions-Leases-LaoPDR_2012.pdf.

Scissors, D. (2011) 'China's investment overseas in 2010', Webmemo no. 3133, The Heritage Foundation, 3 February, www.heritage.org/Research/Reports/2011/02/Chinas- Investment-Overseas-in-2010.

Scoones, I., R. Hall, S. M. Borras, Jr, B. White and W. Wolford (2013) 'The politics of evidence: methodologies for understanding the global land rush', *Journal of Peasant Studies*, 40(3): 469–83.

Seghezzo, L. (2009) 'The five dimensions of sustainability', *Environmental Politics*, 18(4): 539–56.

Sen, A. (1997) 'Editorial: human capital and human capability', *World Development*, 25(12): 1959–61.

SENAGUA (2010) Database on national water allocations, Quito.

Shepherd, B. (2010) 'Above carrying capacity: Saudi Arabia's external policies for security food supplies', World Congress of Middle Eastern Studies, Barcelona: Centre for International Security Studies.

Shete, M. and G. C. Schoneveld (forthcoming) 'Stakeholder perspectives of large-scale land transfers in Ethiopia', *Journal of Rural Studies*.

Shi, W. (2008) 'Rubber boom in Luang Namtha: a transnational perspective', Paper prepared for GTZ/RDMA (Germany), Vientiane.

Shun, C. (2008) 'La Chine contribue à l'autosuffisance alimentaire du Sénégal', *Casafree/Xinhua*, 22 December, www.casafree.com/modules/news/article.php?storyid=26204.

Sida Helpdesk (2009) *General Environmental Assessment Comments*, Uppsala: Swedish University of Agricultural Sciences.

— (2012) 'Review of project documentation for the "Bagamoyo Sugar Project" of Agro EcoEnergy in Tanzania', Uppsala: Gothenburg University and the Swedish University of Agricultural Sciences.

Skarstein, R. and S. M. Wangwe (1986) *Industrial Development in Tanzania: Some critical issues*, Uppsala: Nordic Africa Institute and Tanzania Publishing House.

Slutzky, D. (2010) 'Los cambios recientes en la tenencia de la tierra en el país con especial referencia a la región pampeana: nuevos y viejos actores sociales', IADE/*Realidad Económica*, www.iade.org.ar/modules/noticias/article.php?storyid=3203/, accessed July 2011.

Smaller, C. and H. Mann (2009) *A Thirst for Distant Lands: Foreign Investment in Agricultural Land and Water*, Winnipeg: International Institute for Sustainable Development.

Smalley, R. and E. Corbera (2012) 'Large-scale land deals from the inside out: findings from Kenya's Tana River Delta', *Journal of Peasant Studies*, 39(3/4): 1039–75.

Sosa, M. (2012) 'La influencia minera en los Andes peruanos: acumulación por despojo y conflictos por el agua', in

E. Isch, R. Boelens and F. Peña (eds), *Agua, Injusticia y Conflictos*, Cuzco: CBC, pp. 63–79.

Stockholm Environment Institute (2007) 'Strategic environmental assessment of hydropower in Vietnam, 1993–2004, in the context of Power Development Plan VI', Hanoi: National Political Publisher.

Strauss, J. C. (2009) 'The past in the present: historical and rhetorical lineages in China's relations with Africa', *China Quarterly*, 199: 777–95.

Sudan Tribune (2010) 'Chinese firm given land deal in Sudan', *Sudan Tribune*, 16 March, www.sudantribune.com/Chinese-firm-given-land-deal-in,34444.

Sulle, E. and F. Nelson (2009) *Biofuels, Land Access and Rural Livelihoods in Tanzania*, London: IIED.

Sumardjan, S. (1962) 'Land reform in Indonesia', *Asian Survey*, 1(12): 23–30.

Sumardjani, L. (2005) 'Sejarah kehutanan, konflik sosial kehutanan', *Sejarah Kehutanan*, APHI, pp. 99–123.

Sumargo, W., S. G. Nanggara, F. A. Nainggolan and S. Apriani (2010) *Potret keadaaan hutan Indonesia periode tahun 2000–2009*, Bogor: Forest Watch Indonesia.

Sundet, G. (1997) 'The politics of land in Tanzania', Unpublished PhD dissertation, University of Oxford.

Susanti, A. and P. Burgers (2011) 'Oil palm expansion: competing claim of lands for food, biofuels and conservation', Unpublished paper for the ICCAFFE Conference, 19–21 May, Morocco.

— (2012) 'Oil palm expansion in Riau Province, Indonesia: serving people, planet, profit?', Background paper for the European Report on Development, *Confronting Scarcity: managing water, energy and land for inclusive and sustainable growth*, Brussels: European Union.

— (forthcoming) 'Oil palm expansion: competing claim of lands for food, biofuels, and conservation', in M. Behnassi, O. Pollmann and G. Kissinger (eds), *Sustainable Food Security in the Era of Local and Global Environmental Change*, Dordrecht: Springer.

Sussangkarn, C., Y. C. Park and S. J. Kang (2011) 'Overview', in Chalongphob Sussangkarn, Yung Chul Park and Sung Jin Kang (eds), *Foreign Direct Investments in Asia*, London and New York: Routledge, pp. 1–17.

Swyngedouw, E. (2005) 'Dispossessing H_2O: the contested terrain of water privatization', *Capitalism, Nature, Socialism*, 16(1): 81–98.

Swynnerton, R. J. M. (1954) *A Plan to Intensify the Development of Agriculture in Kenya*, Nairobi: Ministry of Agriculture and Water Resources.

Syagga, P. and A. Mwenda (2010) 'Political economy and governance issues surrounding policy interventions in the land sector in Kenya', Unpublished paper prepared for the World Bank.

Szent-Ivanyi, T. (2011) 'Das ist auch menschengemacht', *Frankfurter Rundschau*, 28 July, www.fr-online.de/politik/hungersnot-in-afrika--das-ist-auch-menschengemacht-,1472596,8719210.html.

Tambunan, T. (2011) 'Do multinational companies transfer technology to local small and medium-sized enterprises? The case of the Tegal metalworking industry cluster in Indonesia', in E. Rugraf and M. Hansen (eds), *Multinational Corporations and Local Firms in Emerging Economies*, Amsterdam: Amsterdam University Press, pp. 75–92.

Tan, R., V. Beckmann, L. Berg and F. Qu (2009) 'Governing farmland conversion: Comparing China with the Netherlands and Germany', *Land Use Policy*, 26: 961–74.

Tang, L. and H. Li (2010) 'Chinese corporate diplomacy: Huawei's CSR discourse in Africa', in J. Wang (ed.), *Soft Power in China: Public diplomacy through communication*, New York: Palgrave Macmillan, pp. 95–116.

Tan-Mullins, M., G. Mohan and M. Power (2010) 'Redefining "aid" in the China–Africa context', *Development and Change*, 41(5): 857–81.

Tạp Chí Cộng Sản (2011) *Các khu công nghiệp ở Việt Nam: Hướng*

tới sự phát triển bền vững, www.
tapchicongsan.org.vn/Home/kinh-
te-thi-truong-XHCN/2011/12504/
Cac-khu-cong-nghiep-o-Viet-Nam-
Huong-toi-su-phat-trien.aspx.

Teklemariam, S. (2012) 'Reply from the
Government of Ethiopia to Human
Rights Watch regarding Gambella',
in Human Rights Watch, *'Waiting for
death': Forced Displacement and 'Villagization' in Ethiopia's Gambella Region*,
New York: Human Rights Watch.

Thorburn, C. C. (2004) 'The plot thickens:
land administration and policy in
post-New Order Indonesia', *Asia Pacific
Viewpoint*, 45(1): 33–49.

Tin Moi Newspaper (2012) 'Hàng loạt khu
đô thị mới, khu dân cư bị bỏ hoang'.

TNI, Carbon Trade Watch and Econexus
(2007) 'Paving the way for agrofuels.
EU policy, sustainability criteria, and
climate calculations', Amsterdam:
Transnational Institute.

TNRF (2008) Biofuels workshop presentation on 'Status of biofuels industry in
Tanzania'.

Tolera, A. and A. Abebe (2007) 'Livestock production in pastoral and
agro-pastoral production systems of
southern Ethiopia', *Livestock Research
for Rural Development*, 19(177), www.
lrrd.org/lrrd19/12/tole19177.htm.

Tomei, J. and P. Upham (2011) 'Argentine
clustering of soy biodiesel production:
the role of international networks and
the global soy oil and meal markets',
Open Geography Journal, 4: 45–54.

Torres, R. M. and J. D. Momsen (2005)
'Gringolandia: the construction of a
new tourist space in Mexico', *Annals of
the Association of American Geographers*,
95: 314–35.

Tran Thi Van (2008) 'Research on the
effect of urban expansion on agricultural land in Ho Chi Minh City by
using remote sensing method', *VNU
Journal of Science, Earth Sciences*, 24:
104–11.

Transnational Institute (2013) *Land Concentration, Land Grabbing and People's
Struggles in Europe*, Amsterdam:

Transnational Institute for European
Coordination, Via Campesina and
Hands off the Land network.

Tsing, A. L. (2005) *Friction: An Ethnography
of Global Connection*, Princeton, NJ:
Princeton University Press.

UNCOHCHR (2007) *Economic Land Conces-
sions in Cambodia. A Human Rights
Perspective*, cambodia.ohchr.org/Web
DOCs/DocReports/2-Thematic-Reports/
Thematic_CMB12062007E.pdf.

UNCTAD (United Nations Commission on
Trade and Development) (2009) *World
Investment Report 2009: Transnational
corporations, agricultural production and
development*, New York: UNCTAD.

UNDESA (2010) *World Population Prospects:
The 2010 Revision*, New York: Popula-
tion Division of the Department of
Economic and Social Affairs of the
United Nations Secretariat.

UNECE (1996) *Land Administration Guidelines with Special Reference to Countries
in Transition*, New York and Geneva:
United Nations Economic Commission
for Europe.

UNEP Regional Resource Center for Asia
and the Pacific (2009) *National Sustainable Development Strategy for Cambodia*,
www.rrcap.unep.org/nsds/uploaded
files/file/Publication%202-NSDS%20
Cambodia.pdf.

United Nations Conference on Trade
and Development (2013) *UNCTADStat*,
unctadstat.unctad.org/ReportFolders/
reportFolders.aspx?sCS_referer=&sCS_
ChosenLang=en.

United Nations Office of the High
Commissioner for Human Rights
in Cambodia (2007) 'Economic land
concessions in Cambodia: a human
rights perspective', Phnom Penh:
United Nations Cambodia Office of
the High Commissioner for Human
Rights, cambodia.ohchr.org/WebDOCs/
DocReports/2-Thematic-Reports/
Thematic_CMB12062007E.pdf.

United Republic of Tanzania (1994a)
*Report of the Presidential Commission of
Inquiry into Land Matters*, vol. I: *Main
Report*, Uppsala: Ministry of Lands,

Housing and Urban Development in cooperation with the Scandinavian Institute of African Studies.

— (1994b) *Report of the Presidential Commission of Inquiry into Land Matters*, vol. II: *Selected Land Disputes and Recommendations*, Printed and prepared for publication by the Scandinavian Institute of African Studies, Uppsala, but withheld from distribution by the United Republic of Tanzania.

UNOHCHR (2010) 'Mandate of the special rapporteur on the right to food. Mission to the People's Republic of China from 15 to 23 December 2010: Preliminary observations and conclusions', Beijing: United Nations Office of the High Commissioner for Human Rights.

Urteaga, P. (2010) 'Ingenieria legal, acumulación por desposesión y derechos colectivos en la gestion del agua', in R. Bustamante (ed.), *Lo Colectivo y el Agua: Entre los Derechos y las Prácticas*, Lima: IEP, pp. 51–74.

USAID (2009) *Kenya Land Policy: Analysis and Recommendations*, Washington, DC: USAID.

USDA Economic Research Service (2006) *European Union-25 Sugar Policy*, www.ers.usda.gov/media/584297/eu25sugarpolicysss245_1_.pdf.

USDA Foreign Agricultural Service (2010) 'Northern Argentina production potential continues to grow', Foreign Agricultural Services, www.pecad.fas.usda.gov/highlights/2010/06/Argentina/2010jun24publictravelmcwill.pdf/, accessed April 2012.

— (2011) *Global Agriculture Information Network Report, Argentina, Biofuels Annual 2011*, gain.fas.usda.gov/Recent%20GAIN% 20Publications/Biofuels% 20Annual_Buenos% 20Aires_Argentina_7-8-2011.pdf/.

— (2013) 'Indonesia oilseeds and products update', GAIN Report ID1307, Jakarta: USDA Foreign Agricultural Service.

Van Eeghen, S. (2011) 'Water conflicts in Costa Rica? Sardinal: a case study on the emergence of a water conflict in the context of high speed growth in real estate and tourism', MSc thesis, Utrecht University.

Van Noordwijk, M., A. D. Suyamto, B. Lusiana, A. Ekadinata and K. Hairiah (2008) 'Facilitating agroforestation of landscapes for sustainable benefits. Tradeoffs between carbon stocks and local development benefits in Indonesia according to the FALLOW model', *Agriculture, Ecosystems and Environment*, 126(1/2): 98–112.

Van Noorloos, F. (2011a) 'A transnational networked space: tracing residential tourism and its multi-local implications in Costa Rica', *International Development Planning Review*, 33(4): 429–44.

— (2011b) 'Residential tourism causing land privatization and alienation: new pressures on Costa Rica's coasts', *Development*, 54(1): 85–90.

— (2012) 'Whose place in the sun? Residential tourism and its implications for equitable and sustainable development in Guanacaste, Costa Rica', PhD thesis, University of Utrecht, Delft: Eburon.

— (2013) 'Residential tourism and multiple mobilities: local citizenship and community fragmentation in Costa Rica', *Sustainability*, 5(2): 570–89.

Van Westen, A. C. M. (2011) 'Land in China: struggle and reform', *Development*, 54(1): 55–8.

Vann, P. and B. Chantrea (2010) *ILO Project to Support Indigenous Peoples in Cambodia: Final Evaluation Report*, Phnom Penh: ILO.

Ve Wong Corporation (n.d.) *Company Profile*, www.asian-food-supplier.com/company-profile.htm.

Verbitsky, H. (2009) 'Verano del '96', *Diario Página*, 12, 22 February, www.minutouneuquen.com/notas/2009/2/22/editoriales-8771.asp, accessed November 2011.

Visser, O. and M. Spoor (2011) 'Land grabbing in post-Soviet Eurasia: the world's largest agricultural land reserves at stake', *Journal of Peasant Studies*, 38(2): 299–323.

Von Braun, J. and R. Meinzen-Dick (2009) *Land Grabbing by Foreign Investors in Developing Countries: Risks and Opportunities*, International Food Policy Research Institute.

Waibel M. (2006) 'The production of urban space in Vietnam's metropolis in the course of transition: internationalization, polarization and newly emerging lifestyles in Vietnamese society', *Trialog*, 89(2): 37–42.

Wang, J. (2010) 'Introduction: China's search of soft power', in J. Wang (ed.), *Soft Power in China: Public diplomacy through communication*, New York: Palgrave Macmillan, pp. 1–18.

Wang, J.-Y. (2007) 'What drives China's growing role in Africa?', IMF Working Paper WP/07/211, Washington, DC: IMF.

Wester, P. and J. Hoogesteger (2011) 'Uso intensivo y despojo del agua subterránea: hacia una conceptualización de los conflictos y la concentración del acceso al agua subterránea', in R. Boelens, L. Cremers and M. Zwarteveen (eds), *Justicia Hídrica: Acumulación, Conflicto y Acción Social*, Lima: IEP, pp. 111–34.

White, B., S. M. Borras, Jr, R. Hall, I. Scoones and W. Wolford (2012) 'The new enclosures: critical perspectives on corporate land deals', *Journal of Peasant Studies*, 39(3/4): 619–47.

Williams, A. M. and C. M. Hall (2000) 'Tourism and migration: new relationships between production and consumption', *Tourism Geographies*, 2(1): 5–27.

Wily, L. A. (2011) 'The law is to blame. The vulnerable status of common property rights in sub-Saharan Africa', *Development and Change*, 42(3): 733–57.

— (2012) 'Looking back to see forward: the legal niceties of land theft in land rushes', *Journal of Peasant Studies*, 39(3/4): 751–75.

Woertz, E. (2007) *Gulf Geo-economics*, Dubai: Gulf Research Centre.

— (2011) 'Arab food, water, and the big landgrab that wasn't', *Brown Journal of World Affairs*, XVIII (1): 119–32.

— (2013) 'The governance of Gulf agro-investments', *Globalizations*, 10(1): 87–104.

Woertz, E., S. Pradhan, N. Biberovic and C. Jingzhon (2008a) *Potential for GCC Agri-Investments in Africa and Central-Asia*, Dubai: Gulf Research Centre.

Woertz, E., S. Pradhan, N. Biberovic and C. Koch (2008b) *Food Inflation in the GCC Countries: GRC Report*, Dubai: Gulf Research Centre.

Woodhouse, P. (2012) 'New investment, old challenges. Land deals and the water constraint in African agriculture', *Journal of Peasant Studies*, 39(3/4): 777–94.

Woolcock, S. and B. Bayne (eds) (2007) *The New Economic Diplomacy*, London: Ashgate.

World Bank (1961) *The Economic Development of Tanganyika*, Baltimore, MD: Johns Hopkins Press.

— (1981) *Accelerated Development in Sub-Saharan Africa: An Agenda for Action*, Washington, DC: World Bank.

— (1989) *Sub-Saharan Africa: From Crises to Sustainable Development*, Washington, DC: World Bank.

— (2004) *Four Ethiopias: A Regional Characterization: Assessing Ethiopia's Growth Potential and Development Obstacles*, Washington, DC: World Bank.

— (2005) *World Development Report 2006: Equity and Development*, Washington, DC: World Bank.

— (2008) *Poverty Reduction and Economic Management Unit Africa Region, Report No. 44190-KE: Kenya Poverty and Inequality Assessment Vol. 1: Synthesis Report*, Washington, DC: World Bank.

— (2010) *Rising Global Interest in Farmland: Can It Yield Sustainable and Equitable Benefits?*, Washington, DC: World Bank.

— (2011) *World Development Indicators*, data.worldbank.org/data-catalog/world-development-indicators.

World Bank, Poverty Reduction and Economic Management Unit Africa Region (2008) Report no. 44190-KE: *Kenya Poverty and Inequality Assessment*, vol. 1: *Synthesis Report*, Washington, DC: World Bank.

World Growth (2011) *The Economic Benefit of Palm Oil to Indonesia*, Arlington, VA.

WRM (World Rainforest Movement) (2010) 'The plunder of Africa continues', *WRM's Bulletin*, no. 158, September.

WWF Indonesia (2010) 'Illegal oil palm plantation in Tesso Nilo National Park destroyed', Pekanbaru, Indonesia.

Yan, H. and B. Sautman (2010) 'Chinese farms in Zambia: from socialist to "agro-imperialist" engagement?', *African and Asian Studies*, 9(3): 307–33.

Yourdon, E. (2004) *Outsource: Competing in the global productivity race*, New Jersey: Prentice Hall.

Zeleke, G. (2003) *State of Natural Resources Base in Ethiopia: Challenges and opportunities*, www.fao.org/docrep/006/y5359e/y5359e06.htm.

Zoomers, A. (2010) 'Globalization and the foreignization of space: the seven processes driving the current global land grab', *Journal of Peasant Studies*, 37(2): 429–47.

— (2013) 'A critical review of the policy debate on large scale land acquisition: fighting the symptoms or killing the heart?', in S. J. T. M. Evers, C. Seagle and F. Krijtenburg (eds), *Africa for Sale? Positioning the state, land and society in foreign large-scale land acquisitions in Africa*, Leiden: Brill, pp. 55–78.

Zoomers, A. and G. van Westen (2011) 'Introduction: Translocal development, development corridors and development chains', *International Development Planning Review*, 33(4): 377–88.

Zwarteveen, M. and R. Boelens (2011) 'La investigación transdisciplinaria referente a la temática de "justicia hídrica": unas aproximaciones conceptuales', in R. Boelens, L. Cremers and M. Zwarteveen (eds), *Justicia Hídrica: Acumulación, Conflicto y Acción Social*, Lima: IEP, pp. 29–58.

Index